W9-CRT-334

The Prevention of Depression

The Johns Hopkins Series in Psychiatry and Neuroscience

PAUL R. McHUGH, M.D., AND RICHARD T. JOHNSON, M.D.
CONSULTING EDITORS

The Prevention of Depression

RESEARCH AND PRACTICE

RICARDO F. MUÑOZ
San Francisco General Hospital
Department of Psychiatry, School of Medicine
University of California, San Francisco

— AND —

YU-WEN YING
School of Social Welfare
University of California, Berkeley

— WITH —

ELISEO J. PÉREZ-STABLE

— AND —

JEANNE MIRANDA

THE JOHNS HOPKINS UNIVERSITY PRESS
BALTIMORE AND LONDON

Printed in the United States of America
on acid-free paper

The Johns Hopkins University Press
2715 North Charles Street
Baltimore, Maryland 21218-4139
The Johns Hopkins Press Ltd., London

Library of Congress Cataloging-in-Publication Data

Muñoz, Ricardo F.
The prevention of depression : research and practice /
Ricardo F. Muñoz and Yu-Wen Ying with Eliseo J. Pérez-Stable
and Jeanne Miranda.
p. cm.—(The Johns Hopkins series in psychiatry
and neuroscience)
Includes bibliographical references and index.
ISBN 0-8018-4496-7 (hc : alk. paper)
1. Depression, Mental—Prevention. 2. Depression, Mental—
Prevention—Research. I. Ying, Yu-Wen. II. Title. III. Series.
[DNLM: 1. Depression—prevention &
control. WM 171 M967p]
RC537.M864 1993
616.85'27—dc20
DNLM/DLC
for Library of Congress 92-49536

A catalog record for this book is available
from the British Library.

To Albert Bandura, James G. Kelly, and Peter M. Lewinsohn
RFM

To my Mother, my first and foremost teacher, Yi-Chih Lee
YWY

And to the research team and the participants in the San Francisco Depression Prevention Research Project

Contents

Contents

Preface

The notion that scientific and professional advances occur (or ought to occur) based on dispassionate reviews of the literature and completely logical decision-making is far from accurate. Devoting major amounts of energy, time, and emotional commitment to mental health research often stems from personal values and life influences. Before launching into the substance of the book, we would like to share the confluence of ideas that contributed to our work on the prevention of depression.

The authors of this book were the Principal Investigator (Muñoz) and the Project Coordinator (Ying) for the Depression Prevention Research Project (DPRP), a randomized controlled trial on the prevention of depression funded by the National Institute of Mental Health starting in 1983. In the course of planning and conducting the study, we learned many lessons, and in Part III of the book we share those lessons with our readers, not as an example of a flawless prevention intervention research project but as the first attempt in what we hope will be a series of depression prevention trials. Eventually, we hope these trials will lead to effective methods to reduce new cases of depression. Here we present the personal experiences that helped provide the conceptual background for the project.

The earliest identifiable sources of ideas in Muñoz's professional development about the possibility of intervening preventively were Albert Bandura's (1969) social learning concepts. Muñoz became acquainted with them as an undergraduate at Stanford University in the early 1970s. The most salient elements of these concepts were reciprocal determinism and symbolic control of behavior. These concepts helped complement some of the unsatisfying elements of the psychodynamic and behavioral approaches that dominated the field of psychology in the 1960s.

> Psychodynamic theories of personality typically depict the deviant actions of individuals as being impelled by powerful internal forces that they not only are unable to control, but whose existence they do not even recognize. On the other hand, behavioral formulations often characterize response patterns as depending on environmental contingencies. The environment is presented as a more or less fixed property that impinges upon individuals and to which their behavior eventually adapts. Neither

> view of man is particularly heartening nor entirely accurate.
>
> Psychological functioning, in fact, involves a continuous reciprocal interaction between behavior and its controlling conditions. (Bandura, 1969, pp. 45–46)

Social learning approaches suggested that individuals had the ability to mold their environment and, by doing so, to mold themselves. And they provided clear foci for the process of human change: thoughts and behavior.

> Social learning theory approaches the explanation of human behavior in terms of a continuous reciprocal interaction between cognitive, behavioral, and environmental determinants. Within the process of reciprocal determinism lies the opportunity for people to influence their destiny as well as the limits of self-direction. This conception of human functioning then neither casts people into the role of powerless objects controlled by environmental forces nor free agents who can become whatever they choose. Both people and their environments are reciprocal determinants of each other. (Bandura, 1977, p. vii)

Freedom, that philosophical conundrum, was addressed in a relatively straightforward manner:

> Within the social learning framework, freedom is defined in terms of the number of options available to people and the right to exercise them. The more behavioral alternatives and prerogatives people have, the greater is their freedom of action. (Bandura, 1977, p. 201)

Aspects of social learning theory relating to self-regulatory mechanisms were highlighted in what became known as the self-control literature. For example, Carl Thoresen and Michael Mahoney, who were also at Stanford at this time, offered a seminar in this area, which resulted in two books (Mahoney & Thoresen, 1974; Thoresen & Mahoney, 1974). The idea of reciprocal determinism clearly served as a cornerstone for this line of work: "the old Greek maxim 'know thyself' can be paraphrased to 'know thy controlling variables.' To exercise self-control the individual must understand what factors influence his actions and how he can alter those factors to bring about the changes he desires" (Thoresen & Mahoney, 1974, p. 9).

The symbolic aspects of human functioning were also central to this perspective: "the term 'behavior' is defined very broadly—thoughts, feelings, and images are just as 'behavioral' as push-ups and conversation" (Thoresen & Mahoney, 1974, p. 10). Thus, some of our "controlling variables" were the stimuli that we presented to ourselves, in the forms of self-talk, attitudes, beliefs, expectations, self-labeling, and so on.

Although most of the examples given and the studies performed within this school of thought were focused on the individual (indeed, Mahoney and Thoresen's (1974) book was titled *Self-control: Power to the Person*), the broader implications of the concepts were explicit: "Behavioral problems of vast proportions can never be adequately eliminated on an individual basis but require treatment and prevention at the social systems level" (Bandura, 1969, p. 112).

Social learning theory presented a paradigm that lent itself readily to preventive thinking: it recognized the impact of personal history on development but presented methods by which one could reassess and change one's patterns of thinking, behaving, and feeling. It emphasized the continuum view of normal and abnormal behavior, avoiding the labeling of individuals as having particular types of "personality" or "disease," and highlighting the influence of situations on both behavior and the definition of the behavior as pathological; and it specified a number of methods for self-change. However, it presented itself as principally a conceptual and methodological tool, which could be used for any purpose: "Social-learning theory is not a system of ethics; it is a system of scientific principles that can be successfully applied to the attainment of any moral outcome" (Bandura, 1969, p. 112). A source of values, of purpose, which could guide the use of social learning and other psychological principles, would be required to set a direction that was still missing at the time. It would come from the newly formed field of community psychology.

The branch of psychology called *community psychology* is generally traced to a national conference on the "Education of Psychologists for Community Mental Health" held in the spring of 1965 in Swampscott, Massachusetts (Iscoe & Spielberger, 1977). One of the major elements of community psychology involved a move beyond the traditional professional therapist mode, in which a mental health provider would serve only those persons who chose to accept the roles prescribed by the professional's training. Specifically, such roles generally involved a person's self-identification as having some kind of emotional problem or mental illness, placing oneself in the care of an expert, and agreeing to come for therapy sessions at the expert's office for what were usually talk therapies with the somewhat nebulous goal of achieving insight. Community psychologists strongly criticized this arrangement as perpetuating private practice models of treatment; as catering primarily to white, middle class groups; as ignoring the needs of populations of low socioeconomic status that did not subscribe to such practices; and as implicitly attributing the causes of psychological problems to the individual, without evaluating environmental factors.

The community psychology movement was strongly influenced by the social forces of the 1960s. In 1961, the Joint Commission on Mental Health and Illness, which had been established by the Mental Health Study Act passed by the U.S. Congress in 1955, published its final report, *Action for Mental Health*. The report led to the Community Mental Health Centers Act, which was signed by President Kennedy on October 31, 1963—less than a month before his death (Bloom, 1977, p. 29). "The basic principles of such centers was to be early detection and treatment of acute mental illness, by means of a delivery system that would provide services locally and avoid the necessity of removing those with problems from their home community. The aim is to avoid the buildup of chronic patients residing in large state institutions" (Rappaport, 1977, p. 13).

The centers were to provide five essential services: inpatient care, outpatient care, emergency services, partial hospitalization, and consultation and education. Five additional services were also envisioned: diagnostic services, rehabilitation services, precare and aftercare services, training, and research and evaluation (Bloom, 1977). Prevention interventions were intended to be included as part of consultation and education services, and were mentioned explicitly in Kennedy's 1963 message to Congress: "Prevention is far more desirable for all concerned. It is far more economical and it is far more likely to be successful. Prevention will require both selected specific programs directed especially at known causes, and the strengthening of our fundamental community, social welfare, and vocational programs which can do much to eliminate or correct the harsh environmental conditions which often are associated with mental retardation and mental illness" (Kennedy, 1963, as reprinted in Bloom, 1977, p. 264).

In the eyes of many mental health professionals, the values inherent in these words appeared not to have been fully implemented as the community mental health centers became a reality. Community psychologists criticized the centers for doing business as usual, rather than taking on the challenge of assessing the effect of environmental factors on psychological dysfunction. Issues related to community control over their centers, increasing the utilization of traditionally unrepresented cultural and ethnic groups, and providing community-based preventive interventions became central to the community psychology movement.

Moves toward the definition of community psychology as an independent approach to psychology are recounted by Rappaport (1977). They include the establishment of a Division of Community Psychology (now called the Society for Community Research and Action) within the American Psychological Association, the creation of journals devoted to the new field, and the inclusion of chapters on social and community interventions in the *Annual Review of Psychology.*

A national conference on Training in Community Psychology was held in Austin, Texas, in April 1975. Muñoz attended as a graduate student under the sponsorship of James G. Kelly. Seven "models" for community psychology were discussed, from "clinical-community," which was an extension of the clinical model, through "activities directed toward achieving social change designed to promote human well-being" (Iscoe, 1977, p. 69). There was general agreement about focusing on populations formerly ignored by mental health services and providing services formerly not available. However, there was considerable disagreement over the level of analysis and the level of intervention. Some of the poles of the continuum involved individually based versus community-wide interventions, and prevention (of at least implied pathology) versus enhancement of strengths and competencies. Interestingly, the preventive intervention model was placed in the middle of this continuum, representing an approximate balance between individual and group focuses (Dorr, 1977).

Personal involvement in community psychology-inspired prevention efforts at both applied and academic levels helped to hone the type of intervention that finally became implemented in the DPRP. Between 1972 and 1974, Muñoz chaired the Primary Prevention and Education Committee of the Lane County Community Mental Health Center, in Eugene, Oregon. The planning, implementation of, and participation in projects intended to be preventive continually left a feeling of ambiguity regarding the effect of these interventions. These feelings were heightened by the concurrent training in the scientific method Muñoz was receiving as a graduate student in clinical psychology at the University of Oregon. Issues of evaluation of outcome were being discussed in a community psychology practicum led by Edward Lichtenstein. It was clear that the gap between textbook approaches to testing the effect of interventions and what was occurring in the field was major.

Collaboration with James G. Kelly on several publications also had a major influence on Muñoz's views of prevention interventions. In 1975, they published *Prevention of Mental Disorders* (Muñoz & Kelly, 1975). This monograph included sections on "reclaiming and changing social structures" (for example, in terms of racial and sexual discrimination, pp. 23–37) as well as on specific psychological dysfunctions. Among the latter was a section on depression, in which the use of cognitive, behavioral, and social skills training is mentioned as having potential in prevention interventions (pp. 10–12). In completing the 1977 *Annual Review of Psychology* on "Social and Community Interventions," Kelly, Snowden and Muñoz (1977) systematically reviewed several areas, including the prevention intervention literature. The three studies, considered "exemplary" in that review (because of their use of control groups and a longitudinal design), focused on child behavior problems, mental retardation, and heart disease risk. The authors concluded: "What is needed now is a major effort to conduct competency training and concurrent longitudinal evaluation. We need to determine empirically which skills, if learned, will lead to healthier lives" (Kelly, Snowden & Muñoz, 1977, p. 333).

A review of the primary prevention of psychological problems prepared around the same time led to the following comments:

> What we have *not* seen in these model studies is also worth nothing. They do not include efforts at major social or organizational change. The most comprehensive environmental intervention . . . provided an alternative environment for the experimental children, but did not attempt to intervene in changing the existing neighborhood. None of the other examples attempted to change the external quality of life of its target population.
>
> Limited, specifiable goals are easier to evaluate than more global, though perhaps ultimately more important ones. The desire to effect essential primary prevention changes in our society must be weighed against the need to show that we can produce preventive effects at all. (Muñoz, 1976, p. 7)

The continuing tension between attempting to meet the broad goals and values of community-oriented investigators and issues of research rigor and feasibility remains unresolved. It is well described in an interview with Nathan Maccoby, of the Stanford Heart Disease Prevention Project:

> We've had some problems getting published. . . . It's not just the writing or the publication problem—that's only part of it. There is a problem in getting peer review of both the research process and the research product. . . . On the other hand, some people feel that the research is not precise enough; for example, we should be sticking to one risk factor at a time. We should be working on smoking and nothing else, or we should be working on certain aspects of nutrition and nothing else, and so on. And we feel that, because the problem is so urgent and because of the synergistic nature of risk factors and the environmental influences on lifestyle, a multiple-intervention method applied in a field setting was necessary. It also turns out that, once you get people into the role of changing, it's easier for them to change in a number of ways. It's like learning how to learn; the skills involved apply to all risk factors. So, there's a very important rationale for *not* doing a piece at a time as a controlled experiment or clinical trial. . . .
>
> I like to put it this way: You can either work on only the most important problems that you can handle *with precision*, or you can work on the *most*

important problems with the best of inadequate research methods. (Maccoby & Alexander, 1979, pp. 99–100)

The cognitive-behavioral methods used in the DPRP were learned under the mentorship of Peter M. Lewinsohn. Muñoz was part of a team that implemented a randomized controlled trial evaluating the comparative effect of three behaviorally oriented treatment approaches on nonbipolar, nonpsychotic, clinical depression (Zeiss, Lewinsohn & Muñoz, 1979). In the process of putting together this project, he became acquainted with the cognitive-behavioral techniques that would later be used in the DPRP (Lewinsohn et al., 1986). These methods were the practical extrapolations of the earlier social learning principles, and they were so easily adapted to an educational format that their fusion with prevention seemed most natural.

The focus on medical settings and primary care populations was influenced in part by Muñoz's position on the faculty of the School of Medicine of the University of California, San Francisco, at one of its teaching hospitals, San Francisco General Hospital Medical Center (SFGH). The psychiatry department there is a tertiary care center, and Muñoz's role for the first few years at SFGH was as a psychologist on the inpatient units. Here he learned about severe psychopathology, including acute suicidal states, and manic and psychotic conditions. Here, too, he learned a new language: that of disorder-focused treatment, the uses of pharmacotherapy, and the ways of medical institutions.

His interest in the prevention of depression continued unabated, however, leading to the evaluation of a television intervention (Muñoz et al., 1982) and the pilot work for the DPRP. At the same time, the literature was beginning to show that most persons with emotional problems sought help not in mental health clinics but in primary care settings. It all started to jell: as a member of the hospital staff, he had the potential to gain entry into the SFGH primary care clinics. The focus of SFGH, as the county hospital, was to serve the most in need. In San Francisco, as in many other urban areas, this included large numbers of ethnic minority individuals. This public service and minority focus (Muñoz, 1991a) fit well with the community psychology ideals of culturally appropriate service to the underserved. Depression was common among the primary care patients. Methods to try to prevent it were welcome by the medical staff. The idea of conducting a prevention project and evaluating its efficacy made sense. In 1983, a grant from the National Institute of Mental Health brought this idea to fruition.

Yu-Wen Ying served as Project Coordinator for the Depression Prevention Research Project (DPRP). She joined the DPRP team upon completing her postdoctoral clinical training, recognizing the inadequacies of the existing mental health services in meeting the needs of ethnic minority members and the potential role to be played by prevention interventions. She had received extensive pre- and postdoctoral clinical training, particularly in working with Asian American populations. She was trained in outpatient psychotherapy at various community-based clinics, including San Francisco's Richmond Maxi Center, the site of the National Asian American Psychology Training center; crisis intervention at the two major hospitals providing psychiatric emergency service in San Francisco at the time (San Francisco General Hospital and Mount Zion Hospital), and inpatient treatment at San Francisco General Hospital's Asian-focused inpatient unit.

Although these settings varied in the extent to which they attended to the needs of ethnic minority clients and modified their services to better fit them, Ying was impressed with the fact that Asians, by and large, were quite hesitant to seek and remain in psychotherapy. This reluctance has been attributed to a lack of understanding of the curative value of psychotherapy and a sense of stigma and shame associated with mental illness and its treatment. Due to these factors, Asian clients appeared more disturbed and more difficult to treat by the time they came to the attention of the mental health service provider.

The philosophy behind depression prevention addressed the shortcomings of the current treatment model by utilizing an educational approach, generally highly regarded and valued by the Asian community. The connotations of being a student and learning something about oneself and how to live life well are quite different from those of being a patient and in need of being "fixed." The former is encouraged, valued, and likely to be supported by one's family and friends, while the latter may be discouraged. One person's mental illness involves a loss of face for the entire family, and thus the patient may be shunned (as Ying observed on numerous occasions on the inpatient unit at San Francisco General Hospital). Thus, with hopes of learning about and testing a method holding great promise in its application to currently underserved ethnic minorities, Ying decided to participate in the DPRP. Under her direction, a Chinese-language (Cantonese and Mandarin) pilot study of the project took place, resulting in Chinese versions of the measures and the intervention.

It is interesting that both of us are immigrants, and have personally experienced the value of learning and choosing among alternative ways of thinking and behaving in order to get along and thrive in novel situations. Thus, it is perhaps not coincidental that the preventive intervention we tested focused on changing thoughts and behaviors to engender improved coping ability in life situations that might otherwise lead to depression and dysfunction.

Acknowledgments

The professional experiences that contributed to the conceptual and practical aspects of this book span more than twenty years. During this time, people too numerous to mention have supported our efforts to develop and implement this research program. In this section, we will focus on those who specifically contributed to the Depression Prevention Research Project (DPRP), its extensions and subsequent applications, and the completion of this book.

Part III of the book describes the DPRP. This randomized controlled prevention trial was implemented by a team of investigators that included, in addition to the coauthors, Guillermo Bernal, William A. Hargreaves, Eliseo J. Pérez-Stable, James L. Sorensen, and Herbert Wong. Manuel Barrera, Jr., contributed to the project during this sabbatical at the University of California, San Francisco. Steve Batki, James Dilley, Roberto Gurza, Hector Rivera, and Michael Sam-Vargas participated in the pilot study that was the basis for the proposal that resulted in National Institute of Mental Health Grant MH 37992 (Muñoz, P.I.). We particularly thank NIMH staff from the Office of Prevention (Steve Goldston) and from the Prevention Research Branch (Morton Silverman, Tom Owan, Jane Steinberg, and Joyce Lazar), who supported our efforts and facilitated the process of funding.

Several other sources of funding were crucial before funding became available from NIMH and after it ended, most importantly, Faculty Research Grants and Biomedical Research Support Grants from our universities (the University of California, San Francisco and the Langley Porter Psychiatric Institute BRSG program for Muñoz, and the University of California, Berkeley, for Ying). Thanks are also due to funding that has supported the application of depression prevention methods developed in the DPRP to maintaining nonsmoking (National Institute of Drug Abuse Grant DA02538; Sharon Hall, P.I.), smoking cessation interventions with Latinos (National Cancer Institute Grant CA39260; Eliseo J. Pérez-Stable, P.I.), the reduction of behaviors that place individuals at risk for AIDS in intravenous drug users (NIDA Grant DA06097; James L. Sorensen, P.I.), and computerized approaches to screening for depression using speech input and output and diagnostic expert systems (University of California MEXUS program; Muñoz, P.I.).

The study would not have been possible without the support and assistance of many colleagues and students. We are grateful to them for their interest, dedication, and humor when times got rough. We want to thank the administrators and staff of the medical clinics from which patients were recruited, including Joyce Brady, Robert Drickey, Richard Fine, and Albert Martin, for allowing us entry and assisting us in the recruitment of the participants. Regina Armas was responsible for the training and quality control of the interviewers who administered the Diagnostic Interview Schedule, as well as for overseeing the scoring of the instruments. Catherine Bany, Silvia Bajarano, Joan Canty, Yotvat Elberbaum, Krishna Evans, Raymond Hsu, David Huang, Larry Lee, Paige Lee, Jane Lo, Steven Long, Selina Mok, Eileen Moy, Sergio Stern, Rebecca Tissue, Kim Troxel, Catherine Tse, Dina Quan, Lucy Vargas, Dominic Wang, and Kelly Wong recruited and interviewed the participants and assisted in the class intervention. Alicia Carranza, Pauline Lee, and Lorretta Morales provided secretarial assistance. Eliseo J. Pérez-Stable coordinated the medical chart review, which was conducted by Erin Heath, Sue Katz, Steven Long, Susan Stringari, and Sylvia Correro. Guillermo Bernal coordinated the Spanish-speaking component of the study, including the translation and adaptation of the measures, which were completed by Regina Armas, Alicia Carranza, Roberto Gurza, Graciela Koch, Martha Martinez, Eileen Moy, Eliseo J. Pérez-Stable, and Lucy Vargas. The classes were taught by the coauthors, Florentius Chan, and Ana I. Alvarez.

Several people contributed to the data management and statistical analysis for the DPRP. Florentius Chan, Martha Shumway, and Cheri Araki were invaluable at early and middle stages of the process. Xiulan Zhang is responsible for conducting the major analyses and for compiling the tables as they appear in the book. She has been untiring and devoted to the project, being available all hours of the day and weekends. We owe her a very special Xie-Xie. We also thank Leonard S. Miller, a valued friend and colleague, whose devotion "to doing the right analysis" we admire and who continued to challenge and advise us in striving to succeed in this endeavor.

We are most grateful to the study participants, who allowed us to be a part of their lives for more than a year. We learned much from them about maintaining dignity in facing the adversity of illness, poverty, or both. From our work with them, it became clear to us that these methods *can* be of use to people with "real problems."

Some sections of this book were developed as paper presentations. Parts of Chapter 23 were prepared for a conference organized by Bernard Bloom and Kurt Schlesinger, entitled the "Boulder Symposium on Clinical Psychology: Depression," Boulder, Colorado, April, 1989. Parts of Chapter 19 were presented at the National Institute of Mental Health (NIMH) Workshop on "Mental Disorders in the Hispanic Population," Washington, D.C., April, 1990. Parts of Chapters 3 and 22 were prepared for the NIMH "National Conference on Prevention Research," Washington, D.C., June, 1990. It was at this conference that we first heard the term "prevention science" used to refer to prevention studies in the field of mental health. We thank the sponsors and organizers of these conferences for having contributed to the development of the ideas presented in this book.

Wendy Harris, our editor at the Johns Hopkins University Press, deserves special thanks for having suggested to us that our ideas and experiences could well benefit the field if presented in the form of a book, and for having encouraged us in a gently persistent and supportive manner to undertake this task.

We also gratefully acknowledge the support of our departments, with a special thanks to John T. Hopkin, former Chief of Service, and Robert L. Okin, current Chief of Service, at the University of California Department of Psychiatry at San Francisco General Hospital, and Harry Specht, Dean of the School of Social Welfare at the University of California, Berkeley.

Finally, we would like to thank our families.

I, Ricardo, want to thank Pat, Rodrigo, and Aubrey for their understanding when I had to work extra hours to complete this book, but even more importantly, for helping me to manage my reality within a healthy range: they keep the time I spend working on projects such as this book from getting out of hand by making the time we spend together so rewarding.

I, Yu-Wen, would like to thank my mother, who fed me and stood by me when I felt frustrated and overwhelmed at various points in the writing.

Introduction

The premise behind this book is that much human suffering is unnecessary and may be reduced substantially if we systematically identify and change those factors that increase suffering for ourselves and others. Moreover, rather than wait until suffering has begun, a preferable strategy is to forestall avoidable suffering whenever possible. This strategy is what we mean by *prevention.*

This book is intended to address one source of human suffering: depression. This human condition can be pervasively debilitating: it can take away a sense of hope, promote a sense of helplessness against the challenges of life, and even erode the sense of meaning and worth in one's existence. In its severe forms, it is felt as one of the most devastating and painful experiences: it is the human condition that most often leads to suicide.

The range of conditions denoted by the term *depression* is quite extensive. In this book, we will focus on the types of depression which have been studied by mental health professionals, primarily depressions that meet professionally defined criteria as disorders, and depressions that are defined by scores on psychometric instruments reflecting a certain level of depressive symptoms.

Assuming that one agrees with our premise that suffering can be reduced, ideally through prevention, and that one of the sources of human suffering is depression, the next two logical questions are: How would one prevent depression, and how would one test the claim that depression has been prevented? The main goal of this book is to address the second of these questions, that is, how to evaluate systematically the effects of interventions intended to prevent depression. In doing so, we will offer our ideas on how depression can be prevented (see Chapters 7 and 9). But one might take many possible theoretical and practical directions to prevent depression. The one we chose to study is only one of many alternatives. No matter what approach we choose, however, methods to test its efficacy need to be developed and agreed upon to facilitate progress. Otherwise, we will be limited to espousing approaches merely on the basis of personal preference.

Scientific methods can serve humanistic goals well, if properly used. In this case, the goal of reducing human suffering related to depression can be well served by bringing together knowledge about depression accumulated in the professional literature and the methods of hypothesis testing developed to evaluate medical and psychological interventions. This book attempts to do both, and thereby to contribute to the human quest of pushing back the boundaries of what is currently considered inevitable suffering.

This book has one focus, the prevention of depression, but it has many facets. It discusses the concepts of prevention, depression, and research on depression prevention (Part I); describes the elements involved in developing and evaluating an intervention to prevent depression (Part II); reports one randomized controlled trial in depression prevention to illustrate the process and the problems involved when one undertakes such a study (Part III); discusses the implications of our findings and of the goals of the prevention field (Part IV); and gives personal reflections on the philosophical issues involved in this endeavor as well as recommendations to individuals involved in mental health research and services and other interested readers (Part V).

The purpose behind these aspects of the book is fivefold:

1. to argue for the importance of developing preventive interventions in the field of mental health.
2. to suggest strategies by which progress in prevention could be made and evaluated.
3. to specify how such strategies could be applied by focusing on one disorder, major depression.
4. to illustrate what one might find once such methods are implemented (through the experiences of the San Francisco Depression Prevention Research Project).
5. to suggest potentially productive next steps.

We suggest varied approaches to the book. For example, the reader interested in our perspectives on depression may want to focus on Chapters 2 and 5. The reader interested in the prevention intervention itself is directed to Chapter 7 and Appendix A. The prevention researcher would profit most from Parts II and III. The health policymaker may find Part I (especially Chapter I) and Parts IV and V particularly relevant. Those interested in the philosophical and ethical implications of this type of work will find our struggles with these issues in Chapters 21 and 24.

We gladly welcome the reader who will stay with us throughout the entire book. We hope the quest for the prevention of depression or, more generally, the prevention of psychological problems, will find a place in your endeavors. This quest has a long history. Philosophical, religious, and psychological writings for centuries have addressed aspects of the quest. The systematic evaluation of the effects of specific interventions using scientific methods has barely begun, however. Until this stage in the quest reaches maturity, choices regarding preventive interventions can be made only on the basis of anecdotal evidence or personal preference. Though these methods are not without merit, concerted societal efforts on behalf of prevention would be on a sturdier footing if they have been subjected to careful, more generalizable evaluation. We hope this book will contribute to such efforts and, by doing so, will serve as a guidepost in this segment of the quest.

Part I

Key Concepts in the Prevention of Depression

1. The Prevention of Mental Disorders

In this chapter, we describe the concept of prevention, placing it in context in the mental health field and recounting some of the arguments for and against its implementation. We try to address many of the connotations of the word *prevention* in the minds of mental health professionals, both advocates and critics, and we highlight differences between prevention and treatment services.

As we near the end of the twentieth century, we can note with some satisfaction that the psychological and emotional aspects of human existence are receiving increasing attention. Behavioral and mental disorders are now accepted as "real" entities, not just moral weakness or instances of possession by a supernatural force. They are considered reasonable targets of study, and the development of therapies for these problems is a priority in the scientific community. A number of health professionals specialize in the treatment of these disorders. The disruption of human lives, the emotional suffering that accompanies many of these disorders, and the effect on those close to the victims of mental disorders have galvanized support for concerted efforts to treat them. However, very few resources have been dedicated to the *prevention* of these disorders.

Whether all mental disorders will turn out to be preventable (or treatable, for that matter) is an open question. Rather than take on such a broad question, we focus on only one disorder in this book: depression. We feel strongly that the prevention of depression is feasible at present, as we argue in Chapter 2. We also feel that, to benefit humanity with tools to accomplish this goal, interventions need to be developed and rigorously tested. Knowledge gained in search of the prevention of depression is likely to be of use in the prevention of other disorders.

The progress made in the study and treatment of behavioral and mental disorders has come about primarily in the more economically well-off countries. Indeed, the concerns about the health of minority communities which prompted our involvement with prevention also raise issues about whether resources should be allocated for emotional and psychological well-being when such basic elements of health as enough food, clean running water, and even physical safety are not yet available to large segments of the world population.

Progress tends to be uneven across the world. When a particular society has the resources to venture beyond the status quo, such use of resources can often benefit those societies that do not have the resources at present. This has been true in technological areas, such as the development of the printing press and other means of mass communication, as well as in such areas as the development of representative forms of government. Often, it is through societies that can afford more than the basics that humanity has a chance to surge ahead.

It is important that such opportunities be used wisely. In the United States and other Western countries, where the mental health professions have gained the most acceptance and support, it is imperative that attention be paid to both prevention and treatment. If prevention turns out to be feasible, as we argue, then its impact on the population as a whole may someday be greater than that of treatment. Similarly, it is possible that certain psychological patterns and conditions, including psychopathological levels of fear, anger, suspicion, and demoralization, act as obstacles to a more materially healthy world. The payoff of focusing on such conditions is potentially great.

The historical trend from interventions (often barbaric ones) for only the most floridly insane people to the current focus on mental disorders at all levels of severity may someday culminate in preventive psychological practices as widespread as current public health practices. Such "preventive interventions" as sewage facilities, the fluoridation of water, and immunization programs are now mandatory and are applied to communities as a whole, at least in the developed world. Educational campaigns (which require individual choice and behavioral acquiescence) similar to those encouraging proper hygiene, exercise, and adequate nutrition may someday become routine parts of our cultural environment. The big questions, of course, are: What kind of preventive program would be analogous to water fluoridation? What ought educational campaigns for psychological well-being to teach the public? Prescriptive advice in the area of thinking and behavior can smack of "brainwashing," "propagandizing," and constraints on individual liberty. Balancing public health policies and public freedom will need to be a major focus of societal decision making in this area, as in many others.

Placing Preventive Efforts in Context

For most mental health professionals, *prevention* is a relatively straightforward term, and one of minor importance. As such, its meaning is both nebulous and limited. For those who specialize in prevention, the concept has many facets and many levels, and each of these has nuances and implications that take on importance when preventive efforts are to be implemented and evaluated. In this section, we will describe several bands within the continuum of prevention efforts, to "unfold" the concept and assist the reader in making more precise distinctions within it.

The Prevention of Disorder versus the Promotion of Health

The literature on prevention often intermingles efforts to prevent specific disorders with efforts to promote good health. Efforts at health promotion, intended to provide resistance to disorders by "strengthening the host," are intended to prevent a wide array of disorder and dysfunction in individuals (the "hosts" to the "agent" of pathology). We find it helpful to think of these efforts as follows:

Pure prevention efforts. Efforts designed specifically to prevent certain disorders are of two kinds:

— keeping something negative from happening (for example, not using alcohol at all to prevent alcohol abuse or dependence. Substance abuse is one of the few examples of a psychiatric disorder that is 100 percent preventable merely by not ingesting the substance involved);
— reducing the probability that something negative will happen (for example, giving persons with phenylketonuria a special diet to reduce the likelihood of mental retardation).

Promotion efforts with preventive goals. These efforts are intended to produce "healthy behaviors," to reduce the chances of either developing certain disorders or becoming seriously dysfunctional should these disorders develop:

— increasing the probability that something positive will happen, to reduce the probability that something negative will occur (for example, increasing pleasant activities to prevent episodes of depression);
— increasing the probability that something positive will happen, to diminish the dysfunctional effects of something negative (for ex-

ample, increasing social supports to buffer the possible effects of episodes of depression).

Pure promotion efforts. Campaigns designed to bring about healthy behavior without necessarily intending to reduce negative conditions:

— increasing the probability that something positive will happen, even if this has no necessary relation to a specific disorder (for example, increasing literacy in a population).

Prevention, Treatment, and Maintenance: A Continuum of Care

Alexander Leighton (1990) suggested a way of conceptualizing the activities of the mental health field as a spectrum of efforts designed to reduce prevalence. He identified five "bundles" of effort:

1. *curing:* removal of the pathological process.
2. *alleviating:* improvement of functioning by reducing disability, shortening the duration of episodes, and diminishing symptoms.
3. *averting relapse:* averting a return to disability in a patient who has improved.
4. *preventing the first occurrence:* averting the occurrence of an episode of the disorder in persons who might otherwise become ill (that is, a high-risk group).
5. *health promotion:* enhancing well-being to reduce the rates and severity of illness.

Muñoz (1990) proposed that these five types of effort be subsumed into three chronologically ordered stages of intervention: prevention, treatment, and maintenance.

Prevention. Preventive activities include:

— health promotion, which could be delivered to communities at large, not just to high-risk groups, and which, by strengthening the host, would be expected to have a large range of impact on the incidence of several disorders;
— preventing the first occurrence, which would focus on groups at high risk for a specific disorder;
— preventing new occurrences in persons who have had episodes in the past but have been functioning normally for significant periods of time.

Treatment. Treatment activities are in order when clinical episodes develop because preventive approaches were not made available to affected individuals or because they did not have the desired effect. Treatment includes:

— curing the pathological condition, if possible;
— alleviating conditions that we cannot cure at present. (This is what we currently do with most cases of severe mental disorder.)
— early case finding (that is, identifying persons who meet diagnostic criteria for a mental disorder) in the community. Efficient treatment systems do not limit themselves to the treatment of cases that present themselves to caregivers. Early case finding does *not* prevent clinical episodes. Ideally, it provides treatment to someone in the midst of a clinical episode who would not otherwise have sought treatment or who would have sought treatment only when the clinical episode reached a more severe stage.

The treatment phase lasts as long as the person continues to meet the criteria for the disorder, remains in an acute episode or exacerbation, or remains unable to function as a result of the disorder.

Maintenance. Maintenance activities follow upon treatment in cases of recurrent or chronic disorder. In Leighton's terminology, this would be

— averting relapse. This focus has become the standard of practice in several mental disorders, such as manic depressive disorder, major depression, and schizophrenia. There is some lack of clarity in terms of whether such disorders are considered chronic disorders with acute exacerbations (such as schizophrenia), cyclical disorders (such as many types of manic depressive disorder and some types of major depression), or merely disorders that can recur after periods of normal functioning (most cases of major depression). In chronic or cyclical disorders, *maintenance* is clearly the appropriate term. In disorders that may or may not recur in one's lifetime, persons who have had the disorder and returned to normal functioning might be key candidates for preventive interventions. They would become "new cases" again if a clinical episode would recur in the future.

There is still much room for improvement in the areas of treatment and maintenance. Nevertheless, these services are generally available within mental health systems. Preventive services, on the other hand, are rarely included in such systems. In fact, most so-called preventive services merely provide consultation to community agencies (such as schools) on how to deal with pathological behavior in their settings. Although this is an important endeavor, it is not prevention.

Those familiar with the prevention field may have noted our avoidance of the traditional terminology *primary, secondary,* and *tertiary* prevention. Primary prevention is defined as efforts designed to prevent the disease from occurring at all. Secondary prevention involves early case finding, so that early treatment can stop the disease from progressing. Tertiary prevention consists of clinical interventions to limit deterioration, complications, or disability once the disease has reached full-blown proportions. Proponents of prevention in the area of mental health and mental disorders have strongly advocated that these terms not be used because, strictly speaking, only the first level (primary prevention) is designed to prevent a disorder. Secondary prevention refers to treatment (albeit early treatment), and tertiary prevention refers to rehabilitation. Treatment and rehabilitation are important health services. However, given the minimal level of support for prevention, it is important to ensure that when resources are allocated for prevention, treatment and rehabilitation projects not compete for such funds under the guise of secondary or tertiary "prevention." We will abide by these warnings, and generally refrain from using the traditional terms. In this book, prevention refers to interventions intended for persons who do not currently meet criteria for depressive disorders. The goal is to reduce the probability that they will suffer from clinical episodes of depression in the future.

Conceptual Obstacles to Prevention

Is Current Etiological Knowledge Sufficient to Justify Prevention Research and Practice?

A common argument for not practicing prevention is that we have insufficient knowledge about etiology. Yet, a lack of knowledge in other areas is used as a justification for further research. For example, research on biological approaches to depression and pharmacotherapy of depression is considered justifiable even though "no definitive biologic marker for depression has yet been identified" (Gold et al., 1988, p. 348). Here are some comments from other researchers: "Although the major classes of antidepressant drugs have been available for over 30 years, clinicians are still unable to predict accurately the response of their depressed patients to medication" (Joyce & Paykel, 1989, p. 89); "the short answer to the difficult question of how antidepressants work is that no one knows" (Baldessarini, 1983, p. 90); and "there is, as yet, no compelling general theory of the mechanism of antidepressant action, in part due to the lack of a compelling neurobiological or metabolic theory of depression itself" (Baldessarini, 1983, p. 131). Clearly, a lack of knowledge is not the main reason for a lack of funding for either research or practice.

As the example of pharmacotherapy illustrates, it is possible to show reliable therapeutic effects without knowing the exact mechanisms for such effects. Effective preventive interventions could be developed even before disorders such as depression are better understood. In fact, effective preventive interventions may give us further clues to understand depression.

A classic piece of epidemiological detective work serves as an example of what can be done with hard work, creativity, and some good fortune. In 1854, London was undergoing a massive epidemic of cholera. John Snow, an anesthesiologist, noted a correspondence between deaths and persons who frequented a drinking well in the Soho district of London. By carefully mapping out fatalities, he was able to incriminate the common pump in Broad Street as the source of the epidemic that had killed more than five hundred people in the neighborhood of the well (Fox, Hall & Elveback, 1970). Snow did not know the exact cause of the cholera, but he was able to pinpoint a concrete contributor to its spread. Later work identified the specific bacterium responsible for cholera. Preventive work can begin without a knowledge of the exact causes of a disorder, and it can contribute to its eventual understanding.

Acute Treatment versus Prevention

By definition, treatment of an acute disorder *is* more pressing, of course. It is also quite clear that clinical treatment is grossly underfunded. Only 20 percent of those with mental disorders are seen in mental health facilities (Shapiro et al., 1984). Thus, it is understandable that some mental health professionals advocate adequate funding for treatment services before preventive programs are given financial support. We must deal with current pain and suffering, they reason, before we attempt to forestall potential pain.

Advocates of prevention respond that, given the prevalence and growth of mental disorders, we will not be able to treat all who are afflicted. There aren't enough trained professionals to do so, nor are there likely to be in the future. Precisely because the state of affairs is so dismal, we must try other approaches, such as prevention. Although, theoretically, a reduction in the total number of cases, that is, in the prevalence of a disorder, could be achieved by successfully treating them, Albee (1985) argued that, in practice, such strategies have not been successful.

> John Gordon, a professor of epidemiology at Harvard . . . in the late fifties sat me down and said: "No mass disorder afflicting humankind has ever been brought under control or eliminated by attempts at treating the afflicted individual nor by training large numbers of therapists." I never forgot his words, and I make my classes memorize them because this is the essence, the whole spirit of public health. One does not get rid of mass plagues afflicting humankind, including the plague of mental and emotional disorders, by attempts at treating the individual. (P. 213)

Albee's message is that we must also reduce the number of new cases, that is, the incidence of the disorder.

Several metaphors are used to denote the urgency and the logic behind preventive approaches. Laycock (1966) conveyed a commonly used one: "In Cornwall, England, there is an old tradition that the way to tell whether or not a person is mentally ill is to put him in a room where an open tap is running and tell them to mop up. If he turns off the tap before starting to mop up, he is considered sane; if he lets it continue to run and still tries to mop up, he is considered unbalanced." Finding the "tap" in the case of mental disorders is, of course, a challenging quest because in all probability, most disorders will have multiple contributing factors.

Another metaphor is that of a river, on the banks of which are arrayed groups of lifeguards. As people pass by, drowning in the powerful current, lifeguards jump in and attempt to bring them to shore and provide first aid. Prevention advocates suggest that some of the lifeguards ought to be sent upriver, to determine why so many people are falling in and to intervene by fixing loose planks on bridges, building fences and handrails along the treacherous banks, putting up danger signs, and teaching people how to swim so that, should all other safety measures fail, they can reach shore before being dragged downriver.

A similar cautionary tale is that of the people at the bottom of a certain cliff clamoring for more ambulances because of all the cars that periodically plunge over the cliff. They point to the mangled bodies and demand more and more emergency personnel. They criticize those who want to send people up to the top of the cliff to see what can be done to prevent further accidents, calling them insensitive to the immediate needs of the wounded.

These tales illustrate some of the frustration among prevention advocates over a mental health system that has never responded adequately to their suggestions. Even those who say they support preventive efforts often raise objections to their implementation.

Should Preventive Programs be Tested in Outcome Trials Before Receiving Funding?

Lamb (1985) stated this view quite clearly: "Sound, well-conceived research and prevention based on controlled studies is sorely needed. But this research ought to be funded separately from direct treatment programs. The prevention of mental illness is a vitally important goal and we fully support generous funding of research to reach it. We do advocate however, that applied programs, except on a pilot basis, await the outcome of further research" (p. 224). This viewpoint appears quite reasonable at first glance. There is no question that research on prevention is needed. In fact, the bulk of this book is dedicated to furthering scientific approaches to the prevention of depression. However, the argument ignores several factors.

First, most interventions that society funds have not been tested for effectiveness before implementation. There surely have not been controlled trials for all medical procedures currently considered standard, nor for most mental health treatments. Why should prevention be asked to meet a higher criterion of evidence before it is given support? Furthermore, much of what we have learned from clinical research has come from hypotheses derived from well-documented clinical experience. Preventive programs have the same potential to teach the field what the issues are in the delivery of preventive interventions. Researchers will be better able to plan useful projects based on the experiences gained by practitioners in the field. The alternative is to build research programs based on armchair planning. Such programs are likely to be wasteful because they may ignore key factors that can be learned only in practice settings. Generalizing these programs is particularly problematic, since preventive programs ideally should reach large segments of the public, and research projects often sample selected segments of a population. For example, in the treatment field, controlled trials with well-selected populations often produce effects that are not as striking when administered to public-sector patients (Organista, Muñoz & González, 1991).

Are Some Preventive Interventions Outside the Mental Health Field?

Many proponents of preventive approaches argue that societal conditions can increase stress and place populations at risk for mental disorder. Thus, they argue, preventive programs ought to include community-wide strategies, some of which would deal with such issues as poverty, racism, sexism, and other social ills. Critics of such approaches hold that, as far as diagnosable psychiatric disorders are concerned, the evidence does not point to differences among social classes for most major disorders, and, even if it did, social change goes beyond the area of expertise of mental health professionals. Lamb (1985) made the point crisply: "Even if it could be demonstrated that poverty is a causative agent of mental illness, this would not make it a condition to be dealt with by mental health professionals. To quote the eminent sociologist Elaine Cumming, 'There is a certain arrogance in someone trained to heal the sick, imagining that he therefore, has a certain expertise beyond that of any other thoughtful citizen in patching up the cracks in society' " (p. 220).

This statement is helpful in that it identifies a basic issue in arguments about prevention: the definition of the mental health field and its scope. Many of those who emphasize "the limits of mental health" are really referring to the limits of certain mental health specialties, such as psychoanalysis, biological psychiatry, or neuropsychology. Individuals who have limited their training to specialization in such areas may have an overly narrow perspective on the scope of mental health activities. For example, some of the proponents of a strict biological psychiatry are critical of such areas as social and community psychiatry because they believe that these areas do not focus on "real" disorders or, if they do, attempt to address them with strategies outside the realm of medicine. What such critics ignore, however, is that biological psychiatry is only one of many disciplines in the mental health field. Other disciplines have expertise in such areas as normal development, learning, social psychology, community research, community organization, epidemiology, self-control approaches, and countless other areas that are applicable to broad-based prevention and that are not necessarily clinical in nature.

To return to Lamb's example, if poverty were demonstrated to be a causative agent of psychological problems, and if mental health professionals could demonstrate an effective method to increase family incomes, which, if successful, decreases the incidence of psychological problems, it would be logical to use public funds for such an intervention as a mental health primary prevention program. Okin (1977), a psychiatrist who at the time was Commissioner of Mental Health for the State of Vermont, said it well:

> Some have viewed social, economic, and environmental concerns as "not mental health," as if the latter had been somehow immutably defined. Some might say that in involving ourselves in social, economic, and political issues we have trespassed upon territories staked out by other groups. But I would urge that the very complexity of modern society has made it impossible to define simplistically precise boundaries between traditional

> territories of responsibility. . . . We must recognize that we own parts of this problem and begin to involve ourselves systematically in the broader issues of social policy in very pragmatic ways. (P. 296)

The etiology of a problem does not always determine the realm from which effective intervention can stem. Depression is a good example, in that both biological and psychological approaches are successful in its treatment, and each treatment seems to affect variables in the other realm (Imber et al., 1990). One could imagine radical proponents of biological approaches suggesting that those types of depression that respond to educational interventions are not true "mental illnesses" and that only those that do not respond to such interventions ought to be considered within "the limits of mental health." The tautological nature of this type of thinking ("if it responds to nonsomatic methods, it must not be a psychiatric disorder") should be guarded against. If mental health problems are presently accepted as true disorders, any method that successfully prevents or treats the problem should be considered within the realm of mental health practice.

This controversy is now more than merely of theoretical importance. An article based on data from the Epidemiological Catchment Area study, conducted under the auspices of the National Institute of Mental Health in the mid-1980s, examined the effect of poverty on psychiatric status. Of those who were healthy at an initial interview, respondents in poverty had a twofold increased risk for having an episode of psychiatric disorder in the following six months. The authors concluded:

> For the aggregate measure of disorder, 6% of all new cases occurring in the 6-month period to the at-risk population were a consequence of poverty in the population. Among the other disorders in which the effect of poverty approached significance, approximately 10% of new episodes of major depression, 10% of alcohol abuse, and 7% of phobia in the respective at-risk populations could be attributed to the effects of poverty. These figures indicate, for example, that during the 6-month interview period, more than 1200 new episodes of major depression in the greater New Haven adult population were a result of poverty. (Bruce, Takeuchi & Leaf, 1991, p. 473)

Using accepted epidemiological methods, this analysis addresses Lamb's earlier comment about demonstrating that poverty is a causative agent of mental illness. Had the analysis shown that a substantial portion of new episodes of major depression were a result of psychological thinking styles, biological factors, or genetic factors, the findings would be readily accepted by the mental health research establishment, and proposals to study how to modify these factors would be forthcoming. It remains to be seen how the demonstrated connection between poverty and specific disorders will be treated by the field.

Practical Obstacles to Prevention

Having described several conceptual obstacles, we cannot overlook some practical stumbling blocks regarding treatment and preventive efforts. These include the need for adequate funding at all levels of the mental health system, and the need for more knowledge to guide our interventions. Yet, treatment services continue to be implemented even with inadequate knowledge and inadequate funding. Why are preventive services lacking?

Freymann (1975) pointed out that even the most primitive societies demand curative services, that is, clinical treatment. When pain is present, entreaties for intervention—any intervention—are always heard. Many practices have been accepted by officials governing medical care at one time but are no longer acceptable. Freymann (1975) argued that public health and preventive efforts are possible only when six societal requirements are satisfied: (a) a future orientation, (b) a positive attitude toward health as a controllable asset, (c) valuing of other individuals' life and health instead of a spirit of "every man for himself," (d) the existence of epidemiologic and demographic data that define the health problems of a society, (e) an effective administrative organization, and (f) personnel qualified for the task. The last two of these items are almost nonexistent at this time. There is no organization whose primary job it is to implement and coordinate mental health prevention programs, and no cadre of professionals trained specifically to develop, carry out, and evaluate preventive interventions. Until these two needs are met, progress in prevention will be in the hands of the few interested clinicians and medical and social scientists who can come up with individual sources of support.

Glidewell (1983) commented on several related reasons why prevention does not receive sufficient public and professional support: individuals rarely perceive preventive actions as urgent; expertise about prevention is less convincing than expertise about, say, surgery; successful prevention is invisible, that is, one never knows who would have become a case had there been no preventive effort; and, as long as this holds true, no one knows whom to thank (or pay): "The most brilliant preventive interventionist simply cannot expect a bequest from a deeply grateful rich family" (Glidewell, 1983, p. 311).

Okin (1977) expanded upon the issue of financial incentives:

> Health insurance plans in general and mental health insurance plans in particular do not provide adequate reimbursement to the professional for time expended in activities of prevention, but only for time spent in the treatment of established pathological conditions. This is a critical problem: as long as preventive activities yield little financial reward, we will

never see large-scale efforts in this direction. Patients are reimbursed upon developing illness and providers for treating it; and no one is reimbursed for preventing it. (P. 294)

Prevention in Mental Health Needs a Success Story

It is said that nothing succeeds like success. Prevention in mental health, though recognized as a good idea, has remained a relatively esoteric subfield and is certainly not being applied extensively. Advocates of prevention envision a time when preventive programs are the accepted standard of practice for mental health systems everywhere. Such is already the case in certain areas within the U.S. health system: insurance now pays for childhood immunizations as well as for adult and child preventive dental care. Ideally, mental health insurance coverage for preventive mental health care will someday be a reality. What is needed now is a way to achieve this goal from our current state.

A clear example of a major reduction in new clinical episodes of a serious disorder would be the best argument for widespread implementation of a preventive intervention. We believe that major depression provides the most likely target for a breakthrough in prevention.

2. Depression: A Key Target for Prevention

Depression ranks as one of the most debilitating and painful human experiences. A recent study (Wells et al., 1989) compared physical, social, and role functioning, number of days in bed, perceived current health, and amount of pain felt for 11,242 medical outpatients with hypertension, diabetes, current advanced coronary artery disease, angina, arthritis, back problems, lung problems, gastrointestinal disorder, depressive disorder, and high symptom levels of depression. In general, patients with either depressive disorder or high levels of depressive symptoms had impaired functioning as bad as or worse than those with the other disorders. The only exceptions were that patients with advanced coronary artery disease had worse physical and role functioning, more days in bed, and poorer perceived health; patients with angina had worse physical functioning and poorer perceived health; and patients with arthritis had more felt pain.

In a separate study, the pain of severe depression was again considered worse than that of physical disorders in a population of depressed psychiatric inpatients with a history of life-threatening medical illness (Osmond, Mullaly & Bisbee, 1984). A third study found that persons with terminal illnesses generally did not wish to die unless they were also clinically depressed (Brown et al., 1986). These findings help to explain why suicide may be such a common occurrence in depressed populations, with a long-term risk of between 10 and 15 percent (Teuting, Koslow & Hirschfield, 1981). The magnitude of this problem is clear when we note that in the United States, suicide is more common than homicide. In 1970, 1980, and 1988, death rates per 100,000 population were, respectively, 11.8, 11.4, and 11.4 from suicide, and 9.1, 10.8, and 9.0 from homicide and legal intervention (U.S. Bureau of the Census, 1991). It is sobering to realize that people in the United States are more likely to die by their own hand than to be murdered by others.

The total impact of depression on our communities is hard to measure. Economists estimate that in 1985, depression cost the United

States $16.3 billion, $2.1 billion of which were in direct treatment costs (Stoudemire, Frank, Kamlet & Hedemark, 1987). But how can one accurately estimate the effects of depression on general productivity, absenteeism, marital harmony, parental care of children, or the effects of prolonged depression on physical health? Clinical speculation attributes some undetermined portion of high-risk behaviors (such as reckless driving, unsafe sex, violent crimes, substance abuse, as well as explicitly self-destructive acts) to depression-engendered desperation. Research evidence is now beginning to support this clinical impression: Zuravin (1989) reported that depression in mothers was related to higher frequencies of aggression toward their children. Interestingly, "moderately depressed, but not severely depressed, mothers are at increased risk for child abuse and physical aggression—the two forms of violence that are most physical in nature and most likely to result in injury to the child. Both moderately and severely depressed mothers are at increased risk for verbal/symbolic aggression" (p. 385).

These studies emphasize that depression, at severe and moderate levels, produces intense emotional suffering and major disruptions in functioning. At the same time, it increases the risk of life-threatening behavior directed against the self and those around one.

In a chapter on training issues for research and practice regarding the prevention of depression, Muñoz (in press) stated:

> I sometimes think that when depressed, human beings are closest to experiencing subjectively the process of entropy, of the degradation of matter and energy, of the dissolution of the organization inherent in life itself:
>
> > . . . as things evolve they seem to become more complex. This happens in spite of the fact that entropy—a measure of disorder—always must increase for a closed physical system (the second law of thermodynamics). Somehow nature is able to create little islands of order and complexity within the great ocean of entropy. The evolution of life seems to violate the spirit of the second law even while it adheres to the letter. (Pagels, 1988, p. 68)
>
> The quest for preventive interventions in depression is an attempt consciously to bring about greater coherence and organization into human lives so that the subjective elements of human intentionality can bring added strength to the objective processes which organize life itself. It is another instance of life appearing to violate the spirit of the second law. Ultimately, the process of creating psychological integrity will involve construing a pattern to our lives, a sense of meaning which can even encompass the eventual end of our lives.

Types of Depression

The word *depression* is used in many ways. It can refer to a normative, usually transient, mood state; to a symptom that may be related to several disorders; to a syndrome (a collection of symptoms that frequently occur together), and to one of several disorders (pathological entities that are hypothesized to have distinctive mechanisms, prognosis, and implications for treatment) (Clayton, 1987).

In the prevention literature, it is important to make a distinction between depressive disorders (clinical depression) and depressive symptoms. A depressive disorder is defined as a condition in which an individual exhibits a specified number of symptoms of enough severity and duration to meet well-delineated and widely accepted criteria. Disorders are conceptualized as being either present or absent in an individual. From a research perspective, depressive disorders are dichotomous variables. Depressive symptoms represent a level within a continuum. Generally, this approach uses self-report scales to determine how depressed a person is. From a research perspective, the level of depressive symptoms is a continuous variable.

The above distinction has led to many disagreements over whether there is evidence that depression can be prevented. Several studies have reported reduction in depressive symptoms in nonclinical populations who were administered interventions designed to be preventive. Advocates of prevention point to these as evidence that depression can be prevented.

Critics of the prevention field state categorically that there is no evidence that depression can be prevented. They contend that no study has yet shown that clinical episodes of depression have been significantly reduced by any intervention in initially nondepressed populations.

Both of these statements are correct: interventions can reduce the level of depressive symptoms reliably in clinical and nonclinical populations. But no study has yet shown conclusively that clinical episodes of depression are significantly fewer in initially nonclinical groups who receive such interventions versus a randomly chosen control group.

Although it appears that reducing depressive symptoms will decrease the chances that an at-risk individual will cross the threshold into a clinical depression, such a hypothesis has not been tested. However, evidence that, after treatment ends, clinically depressed persons who were treated with cognitive-behavioral therapy are less likely to relapse within one year than those who were treated with pharmacotherapy provides a justification for testing explicitly preventive effects (Hollon, Shelton & Loosen, 1991; Rehm, in press).

The current state of the science suggests that studies be conducted to test whether clinical episodes can be prevented. Results showing such a reduction in incidence would be clear-cut evidence that depression can be prevented. In addition, studies showing the effects of reducing depressive symptomatology in initially nonclinically depressed populations should also be conducted. One such effect that ought to be tested is the above-mentioned reduction of clinical episodes, of course. But other effects, such as a reduction in substance abuse, violence, high-risk behavior, and improvement in job productivity, role functioning, and socially beneficial activities would also be worth documenting.

Preventing Depressive Disorder

In pursuing the prevention of depressive disorders, it will be important to specify which of them to focus on. According to the current Diagnostic and Statistical Manual of Mental Disorders (DSM-III-R; American Psychiatric Association, 1987), depression is a major feature in several disorders. These include organic mood syndrome, bipolar disorder, cyclothymia, major depression, dysthymia, and adjustment disorder with depressed mood. In addition, two other conditions are sometimes present with depression as the major complaint: uncomplicated bereavement, which is not considered a disorder; and late luteal phase dysphoric disorder (known popularly as premenstrual syndrome, or PMS), which appears as a "proposed diagnostic category needing further study."

Of these possible disorders, major depression is the most likely candidate for successful prevention for the following reasons:

1. Major depression is a severe enough disorder to be acceptable as an important target for prevention to current critics of the field. Focusing on something like adjustment disorder with depressed mood might be dismissed as merely addressing "problems in living" and not "real" disorders.
2. Major depressive episodes, as defined in DSM-III-R, have relatively well-specified onset and termination. Most last about six months or less; thus, their frequency of occurrence can be measured within reasonable periods of time. Other disorders, such as cyclothymia and dysthymia, are chronic in terms of duration and relatively minor in terms of intensity, and thus harder to count. Moreover, there is still some controversy in the field regarding whether cyclothymia and dysthymia are more similar to personality disor-

ders (that is, long-lasting "characterological" patterns) or to Axis I diagnoses.

3. Major depression is the most prevalent of the depressive disorders. The National Institute of Mental Health (NIMH) Epidemiological Catchment Area (ECA) Project found lifetime prevalence rates of 5.8 percent for major depressive episode, 3.3 percent for dysthymia, and 0.8 percent for manic episode (Regier et al., 1988). Certain subgroups in the population are more at risk for depression. For example, one-month prevalence rates of affective disorders for adult women average 6.6 percent, and for women between the ages of 25 and 44 reach 8.2 percent (rates for major depressive episode alone are 3.9 percent) (Regier et al., 1988).
4. There is reason to believe that interventions that are not physically intrusive might have preventive effects. Several types of treatment for nonpsychotic nonbipolar major depression have been found to be effective in randomized controlled trials. The scientific study of treatments for dysthymia is not as advanced. And treatment for bipolar disorder generally requires pharmacotherapy. Indeed, pharmacotherapy and psychotherapies designed to increase control of mood (such as cognitive behavioral therapy) are effective in the acute phase of major depression (Weissman, Jarrett & Rush, 1987). Also, the latter may be indistinguishable from pharmacotherapy at moderate levels of depression (Elkin et al., 1989). These findings suggest that psychological interventions have a reasonable chance of producing preventive effects by teaching individuals to reduce the intensity, duration, and frequency of depressive mood states.
5. The stigma is lower for depression than for other mental disorders. Because the word *depression* is commonly used to refer to ordinary states of low mood, it is easier for the general population to identify with the experience of clinical depression than with the experience of, say, substance abuse or schizophrenia.

Diagnostic Criteria for a Major Depressive Episode

The essential feature of major depressive disorder is the occurrence of a major depressive episode. Such an episode is defined as the presence of a major depressive syndrome for which organic factors cannot be established, which is not a normal reaction to the death of a loved one, which does not include delusions or hallucinations in the absence of the mood symptoms, and is not superimposed on schizophrenia, schizophreniform disorder, delusional disorder, or psychotic disorder not otherwise specified.

A major depressive syndrome is defined in DSM-III-R as follows:

> At least five of the following symptoms have been present during the same two-week period and represent a change from previous functioning; at least one of the symptoms is either (1) depressed mood, or (2) loss of interest or pleasure. (Does not include symptoms that are clearly due to a physical condition, mood-incongruent delusions or hallucinations, incoherence, or marked loosening of associations.)
>
> 1. depressed mood (or can be irritable mood in children and adolescents) most of the day, nearly every day, as indicated either by subjective account or observation by others
> 2. markedly diminished interest or pleasure in all, or almost all, activities most of the day, nearly every day (as indicated either by subjective account or observation by others of apathy most of the time)
> 3. significant weight loss or weight gain when not dieting (e.g., more than 5% of body weight in a month), or decrease or increase in appetite nearly every day (in children, consider failure to make expected weight gains)
> 4. insomnia or hypersomnia nearly every day
> 5. psychomotor agitation or retardation nearly every day (observable by others, not merely subjective feelings of restlessness or being slowed down)
> 6. fatigue or loss of energy nearly every day
> 7. feelings of worthlessness or excessive or inappropriate guilt (which may be delusional) nearly every day (not merely self-reproach or guilt about being sick)
> 8. diminished ability to think or concentrate, or indecisiveness, nearly every day (either by subjective account or as observed by others)
> 9. recurrent thoughts of death (not just fear of dying), recurrent suicidal ideation without a specific plan, or a suicide attempt or a specific plan for committing suicide. (P. 222)

A major depressive episode can be further defined as mild, moderate, or severe, with or without psychotic features, which can be mood-congruent or mood-incongruent.

This clinical entity has been the focus of several treatment outcome trials, demonstrating that the majority of patients afflicted with it respond to either pharmacotherapy or psychotherapy (Rehm, in press). We believe that the likelihood of documenting the prevention of clinical episodes of major depression is high.

Preventing High Levels of Depressive Symptoms

There are several reasons why the prevention of high levels of depressive symptoms is a worthwhile goal, even if clinical episodes of major depression are not reduced. As recounted above, moderate and high levels of depressive symptoms are associated with emotional pain, lower functioning, and higher risk for aggression toward one's children (Wells et al., 1989; Zuravin, 1989).

Projects devoted to reducing depression symptoms in nonclinical populations have been derided as services for the worried well or as therapy for subclinical levels of depression. A helpful discussion of the possible relationship between high symptom levels and depressive disorders can be found in Lewinsohn, Hoberman, and Rosenbaum (1988). These authors asked themselves whether depressive disorder and high symptom levels measure the same latent construct or involve qualitative differences. In reviewing the available information, they noted that there truly is a correlation between the two, but that more than half of those with elevated symptom scores do not meet the criteria for depression and that almost no one with very low symptom scores does. It appears that high symptom scores are necessary but not sufficient for depressive disorders.

Lewinsohn and colleagues then suggested that high depressive symptom scores may reflect a nonspecific negative affect (perhaps akin to the concept of "demoralization" (Frank, 1973; Frank & Frank, 1991)) that can be triggered by, among other factors, stressful events and that can in turn increase the likelihood of a variety of medical and psychiatric disorders, including depressive disorders. However, the specific progression from negative affect to depressive disorder depends on other characteristics of the person (e.g., sex, age, history of depression) which elicit the range of systemic disturbances that constitute a depressive episode. Acute negative affect, then, could serve as a trigger in persons who are predisposed to depressive disorder. Chronic negative affect could be a relatively permanent marker of high risk. Using this line of reasoning, interventions that teach persons to manage negative mood so that its intensity, duration, and frequency are reduced, may help prevent depressive disorders as well as a range of other maladaptive behaviors.

Toward the Prevention of Demoralization

Jerome Frank (Frank, 1973; Frank & Frank, 1991) suggested that there is a state that is common to all persons who seek therapy and that is always alleviated when treatment is effective: the state alluded to above, called "demoralization." The concept is hard to operationalize, but it connotes confusion, isolation, helplessness, and hopelessness.

Muñoz (1976) pointed out that diagnosable disorders and demoralization may be related but distinct dimensions: One may or may not meet criteria for a disorder and one may or may not be demoralized. Thus, there are people who are not demoralized and have no diagnosable disorder. There are people with disorders who are not demoralized and feel no need for assistance. There are people with no diagnosable disorder who are nevertheless demoralized and in subjective need of help. And there are those with diagnosable disorders and demoralization, who leave therapy satisfied when their demoralization is alleviated, whether or not the diagnosable disorder is "cured." With this perspective in mind, we might consider the possibility of a universally relevant goal for our efforts, namely, the primary prevention of demoralization—the promotion of assumptive worlds (Frank, 1973) in which even clearly pathological conditions and dire external situations would be faced and dealt with without despair.

The flavor of this notion was captured by Viktor Frankl:

> life has a meaning to the last breath. . . . The possibility of realizing values by the very attitude with which we face our destined suffering . . . exists to the very last moment. I call such values *attitudinal values*. The right kind of suffering . . . is the highest achievement that has been granted to man. . . . It goes without saying that the realization of attitudinal values, the achievement of meaning through suffering, can take place only when the suffering is unavoidable and inescapable. (Frankl, 1955, pp. xii–xiii)

The goal of prevention is to push back the boundaries of the unavoidable and the inescapable. The prevention of demoralization may be the ultimate level of prevention. By striving to change those phenomena that now seem unavoidable, such as major depressive episodes, into experiences that can be greatly diminished in frequency, intensity, and duration, we will learn to escape from their painful grasp.

3. Research on Preventive Interventions

Any knowledge regarding a disorder can have potential relevance to its prevention. Thus, one could state that all research into mental disorders is prevention research. Obviously, such a broad definition would not be very useful. Advocates of prevention have made the point that the term *prevention* should be reserved for projects that are specifically aimed at "reducing the *incidence* of new cases of mental disorder and disability in a population" (Caplan & Grunebaum, 1972, p. 128). Just as *treatment research* evaluates the effect of specific interventions on an existing clinical episode, so also does *prevention research* evaluate the effect of an intervention on averting the onset of a clinical episode. Nevertheless, to make the point even more clearly, the term *prevention intervention research* has been used to emphasize the testing of specific interventions to determine their effect on the incidence of clinical episodes or on the avoidance of disability related to depressive symptoms. In its simplest form, the question being asked by prevention intervention research is whether fewer cases of the target condition will occur if something is done before the onset of the condition.

The kinds of activity that might be part of prevention intervention programs have been described by Goldston (1977):

> Primary prevention encompasses activities directed toward specifically identified vulnerable high-risk groups within the community who have not been labeled psychiatrically ill and for whom measures can be undertaken to avoid the onset of emotional disturbance and/or to enhance their level of positive mental health. Programs for the promotion of mental health are primarily educational rather than clinical in conception and operation, their ultimate goal being to increase people's capacities for dealing with crises and for taking steps to improve their own lives. (P. 20)

Goldston's emphasis on going beyond clinical conceptualizations of mental health interventions, at least in the area of prevention, underscores the value of letting the problems determine the methods needed to solve them, rather than predetermining the methods we will use and then choosing to work only on problems amenable to such methods. In fact, many prevention professionals would go beyond both clinical and educational approaches, suggesting that social change is required to address the unrelenting, chronic stresses (such as poverty, racism, and sexism) within which large segments of the population live (Albee, 1982).

In choosing preventive interventions, the following elements need to be considered: evidence that the factors addressed are causally related to the disorder, that intervening with the chosen factors is practical and efficient, and, in terms of research, that the intervention is amenable to scientific study. (These issues will be discussed in some detail in Chapter 7.) For example, one must consider whether biological, educational, and/or social factors are involved in causing or triggering the target disorder, whether these factors are modifiable, and whether one can exert sufficient control over interventions, focusing on each factor to determine whether the intervention has been successful.

Potential Contributions of Research on Preventive Intervention

In addition to the central goal of preventing mental disorders, research on preventive intervention can also add to the understanding of psychological dysfunction by providing an additional perspective to existing scientific efforts.

Theoretical Contributions

In the area of depression, theories regarding the role of neurotransmitters on depression were greatly influenced by the accidental discovery that tricyclic chemical agents alleviated depressive symptoms. The common action of these pharmacologic agents was to increase the presence of biogenic amines in the synaptic cleft. At around the same time, clinical evidence was showing that reserpine, an antihypertensive agent, was found to produce depressive symptoms in about 15 percent of individuals who took it in doses exceeding .50 mg per day, and studies showed that its mode of action was the depletion of available biogenic amines. The combination of these two lines of work led to several biological models for depression: "While collectively these hypotheses may be recognized as a gross oversimplification, they have been an important stimulus to the development of active research programs in the biology of the mood disorders during the last two decades" (Whybrow, Akiskal & McKinney, 1984, p. 39). Empirical evidence that specific interventions have a preventive effect on clinical episodes of depression is likely to markedly influence future theories of depression. It is hoped that, even if the hypotheses generated in response to findings of early preventive studies eventually turn out to be similarly "gross oversimplifications," they would also stimulate productive and ultimately fruitful research programs for decades to come.

Contributions to Generalizability

Advances made in the area of depression have not reached most of the people who could benefit from them. This might be due, in part, to the limited generalizability of research findings. Consider, for example, the nature of the samples that take part in treatment outcome studies. In the general population, of those who meet criteria for major depression, only about 20 percent seek mental health services (Shapiro et al., 1984). It is probably safe to assume that, in any community, an even smaller percentage would be aware of and participate in treatment outcome studies. Of those who do inquire about such studies, about 10 percent are scheduled for evaluation interviews (Bellack, Hersen & Himmelhoch, 1981). Of those fully evaluated, approximately 36 percent are accepted into the randomized trial (Murphy et al., 1984; Rush et al., 1977). Further bias is introduced by attrition, which ranges between 20 percent and 52 percent in comparative studies of the outcome of treatment for depression (DiMascio et al., 1979; Simons et al., 1984). Clearly, our experimental knowledge about the effects of treatment for depression are based on a minuscule (and, more importantly, very biased) proportion of those affected by the disorder.

Often, greater bias is introduced by research requirements that limit the population to be studied. Even large-scale collaborative studies, such as the NIMH Collaborative Program on the Psychobiology of Depression (Katz et al., 1979), have restricted their samples to English-speaking populations and, more surprisingly, to white people (see, for example, Andreasen et al., 1986).

Given that certain subsegments of the population are much more likely to underutilize treatment services than white people, a possible question to be addressed by prevention studies is how to reach such populations. For example, in the UCLA Epidemiological Catchment Area sample, only 11 percent of Mexican Americans meeting diagnostic criteria for DSM-III disorders had sought mental health services, compared with 22 percent of similarly diagnosed non-Hispanic whites at the same site (Hough et al., 1987). Because research on preventive intervention is, by its very nature, focused on population rates rather than merely on individual responses, prevention trials will have to engage in outreach and will have to report rates of acceptance of the programs as well as comparative incidence rates in those who use the program. This will make future knowledge about depression much more universal.

Prevention research on depression will also allow us greater access to the natural history of the disorder. By sampling from a community at large, we will be able to document characteristics of persons before the disorder begins. Akiskal (1987) explained why this is important:

> Ideally the study of personality in a given patient should begin prior to the first onset of affective episodes; assessing personality during an episode of illness is unsatisfactory because affective states may bias or even mask the patient's personality profile. Even when the affectively ill are examined during a euthymic period, the illness episodes, or the treatments provided for them could have altered significantly personality structure. For these reasons, very few studies have succeeded in prospectively assessing the contribution of personality to affective illness. (P. 267)

Methodological and Theoretical Contributions to Prevention from Other Domains of Research

In this section, we will examine several research areas showing promise for prevention at this time, in the short term, and in the long term, as well as their limitations and potential drawbacks.

Research on the Outcome of Treatment

Advances in treatment outcome methodology can be readily adapted to prevention outcome research. These advances include the use of protocols to increase intervenor's compliance with the techniques being evaluated, and allowing replications of studies by other teams; clear exclusion and inclusion criteria for defining the sample on which the intervention is tested (including structured diagnostic interviews); inclusion of measures of the mediating variables that are expected to produce the final effect; measures of immediate, short-term, and long-term outcomes; and measures of process (see Williams & Spitzer, 1984).

Intervention protocols, especially those that focus on psychosocial interventions, have already been adapted to prevention studies. The more didactic approaches, such as cognitive-behavioral interventions, have been the most researched to date.

Methods to predict the type of individual most likely to respond to specific approaches will be especially useful in tailoring interventions. As of 1993, such methods are not available. In fact, structured approaches teaching skills that can be used to cope with common life situations appear to work about as well whether focused on thoughts, behavior, or interpersonal interactions (Zeiss et al., 1979; Rehm, Kaslow & Rabin, 1987). However, there is some evidence that methods that are congruent with individual coping styles may be most effective (see Rehm, in press).

Our understanding of the longitudinal process of depression would be advanced greatly by consolidating three lines of work: the theoretical assumptions on which treatments are based, the methods designed to change the theorized mechanisms, and approaches to concurrent assessment of these mediating mechanisms and depression levels. We need to know whether our interventions affect depression levels through the hypothesized routes. For example, even though cognitive approaches to the treatment of depression have generally been found to be very effective (Rehm, in press; Weissman, Jarrett & Rush, 1987), there is great controversy over whether certain types of cognitions have a causal relationship to depression, or are even chronologically prior to depressive episodes (Coyne & Gotlib, 1983; Lewinsohn et al., 1981). The attributional reformulation of the learned helplessness model (Abramson, Seligman & Teasdale, 1978) has generated a most impressive collection of support for the hypothesis that explanatory style is a risk factor for depression and other health problems (Peterson, Seligman & Vaillant, 1988). According to this theory, causal explanations of negative events that are stable, internal, and global, place a person at risk for depression (Peterson & Seligman, 1984), especially when negative events occur (Metalsky et al., 1982).

Work by Miranda and Persons (1988) may help consolidate these apparently contradictory findings. They report that dysfunctional attitudes are endorsed more by persons with a history of depression than by those without such a history, *but only when in a negative mood state.* It may be that the probability of accessing depressogenic cognitions increases when negative affect is present, perhaps because affect and cognitions are paired in memory networks (Bower, 1981). Thus, one finds correlations between cognitions and depression in persons who are currently depressed, but not in persons (even persons at risk) before or after a depressive episode. Seligman's methodology requires that participants vividly imagine themselves in specific situations and write down what they feel is the cause of the situation (Peterson & Seligman, 1984, p. 351). When negative situations are elicited, it is very possible that negative affect may be generated, and thus dysfunctional cognitions become available. This may help explain their ability to predict depressive phenomena relatively successfully.

Miranda and Persons (1988) suggested that therapeutic changes in cognitions are unlikely unless the patient is experiencing negative mood states that facilitate access to the attitudes that need change. Such advice concurs with notions of situational specificity in behavior change and implies that preventive approaches will be more effective if consumers practice alternative behaviors, cognitions, and interpersonal skills while imagining themselves in negative or stressful situations.

Although depression is described as a very treatable disorder, a close look at the treatment outcome literature shows that the proportion of clinically depressed persons who seek treatment and are free of depression a year later is disappointingly small. This is the case even though there are several reasons to believe that published treatment outcome studies may result in positively biased estimates of effect: therapists are carefully selected, systematically trained, continuously supervised, and part of a research team motivated to obtain results that will be widely distributed. Patients are carefully screened: only about 10 percent of those who inquire are scheduled for evaluation (Bellack, Hersen & Himmelhoch, 1981), only about 36 to 45 percent of those evaluated are accepted into the study (Elkin et al., 1989; Murphy et al., 1984; Rush et al., 1977). Such patients are likely to be relatively reliable. Still, dropout rates vary between 20 and 52 percent (DiMascio et al., 1979; Simons et al., 1984), response rates are limited, and relapse is high. The NIMH Collaborative Study had a 35 percent dropout rate, and the proportion of patients who recovered ranged from 36 to 56 percent of all who entered treatment, and 51 to 70 percent for all who completed treatment (15 weeks) (Elkin et al., 1989). In the Murphy and Simons study (Murphy et al., 1984; Simons et al., 1984), out of 95 patients, 25 (26%) dropped out; of the 70 completers, 44 (63%) responded to treatment; and of the 44 who responded, only 28 (64%) did not relapse at one year. Thus, of 95 randomized (after careful screening), only 28 (29%) were remitted at one-year follow-up.

It is clear from these results that even if we were to bring all persons who are depressed into treatment, we would only be able to provide long-term relief to a small number of them. Yet, these studies have shown that a relatively low level of depression is the best predictor of successful treatment. By extrapolation, prevention interventions at preclinical levels of depression may be very successful in bringing depression symptoms back to normal levels.

Another major limitation of the treatment outcome literature is the very low representation of ethnic minorities in general, and low-income, low-education populations. The generalizability of treatment outcome study findings to the public sector is questionable (Organista, Muñoz & González, 1991). Prevention studies must not make the same error of omission.

Treatment approaches that focus on the role of thoughts, behaviors, and interpersonal skills on mood have the potential for being misinterpreted as "blaming the victim." That is, persons prone to self-blame could conclude that they are to blame for their depression, and that if only they thought, behaved, or acted differently with others, they would not be depressed. Care must be taken to warn participants about this maladaptive perspective.

Epidemiological Approaches

Advances in epidemiology have provided baseline data and tools with which to measure preventive effects (Hough et al., 1986; Roberts, 1987). In addition to providing prevalence figures for depression, studies such as the Epidemiological Catchment Area (ECA) Project (Eaton & Kessler, 1985; Robins & Regier, 1991) have contributed incidence data (Eaton et al., 1989), which can guide the identification of the groups at highest risk. Epidemiologists have generally been aware of the need to include minority groups in their samples. Thus, the UCLA ECA study (Hough et al., 1987) has been able to point out that Mexican Americans with a DSM-III diagnosis are half as likely as non-Hispanic whites to seek help for mental health problems. This information can help to mount projects to identify clinical cases. It may also suggest which of the groups that are reluctant to use treatment services might be more likely to take advantage of prevention services that do not require them to be identified as "cases." Studies such as the Hispanic Health and Nutrition Examination Survey (Moscicki et al., 1987) have already used measures developed for the ECA to find differences among subgroups of Hispanics, giving prevention researchers and practitioners information needed to identify those most at risk.

Structured diagnostic interviews that can be administered by trained lay interviewers make the screening for cases more practical. Further development of these interviews so that they are automated (Aguilar-Gaxiola, 1991) may make feasible routine screening for depression in such sites as primary care clinics. At present, routine screening for depression is not officially recommended (U.S. Preventive Services Task Force, 1989). Ideally, primary care patients would be able to self-administer the screening interviews. Methods to allow illiterate or non-English speaking persons to do so are underway (Starkweather & Muñoz, 1989; González, Muñoz & Starkweather, 1991).

Epidemiological approaches to prevention could ultimately make the evaluation of community-wide prevention efforts feasible. Imagine, for example, an epidemiologic study that adds a prevention intervention component for a high-risk subsample and uses a comparable segment of its main sample as the control. The inclusion of ethnic minority groups into epidemiologic research also allows innovative methods to assign experimental and control groups: in neighborhoods at high risk for depression in which non-English-speaking persons compose a sizable proportion, interventions administered exclusively in the non-English language could be implemented. This would permit pre-post measurement of depressive symptoms and incidence of disorders in the same location, where all inhabitants would be influenced by the same environmental factors, except for the intervention being evaluated.

Some clinicians question the clinical validity of cases found in door-to-door surveys, or diagnoses made by nonprofessionals. Further examination of these concerns is indicated. A possible approach to help evaluate the utility of these methods would be testing the predictive value of epidemiological versus clinical diagnoses in terms of health and functioning.

Problems with the validity of instruments in specific populations may produce misleading results. For example, high rates of cognitive impairment were found in the UCLA Mexican-American population, which the investigators believe are invalid, and which they attribute to the effect of the significantly lower level of schooling in this group.

Social and Community Approaches

Social and community researchers and practitioners have been the most committed advocates of prevention programs (Kessler & Goldston, 1986). They have served as a balance for the strictly disorder-focused perspective of the clinically minded establishment. Practitioners and researchers newly interested in engaging in prevention activities do not have to reinvent the wheel: they have available to them a plethora of sources on methods to evaluate prevention programs (for example, Price & Smith, 1985), annotated bibliographies on prevention in mental health (Buckner, Trickett & Corse, 1985), suggestions regarding how to conduct prevention research in the community (Kelly et al., 1988), examples of successful prevention research projects (Muñoz, Snowden & Kelly, 1979), and several other sources of information (see Muñoz, 1987, pp. 8–10, for further references).

Conceptual developments, such as the idea of "empowerment" as opposed to "prevention" (Rappaport, 1981) have promise. It remains to be seen exactly what kind of impact perspectives such as these will have.

If community-oriented approaches are able to produce feasible ways to address multiple concerns at once, they might be able to push prevention approaches beyond the single-disorder model. Whether disorder-specific approaches will ultimately be more efficient than broad-based approaches is still debatable. We know that there are connections between depression and such "social problems" as aggression, and that sometimes moderate levels of depressive symptoms may be more predictive of aggression than severe levels (Zuravin, 1989). The likelihood that depression and substance abuse are related is very high. And the greater incidence of depressive symptoms, aggression, and substance abuse in low-income populations is well known. Community-oriented prevention advocates see these problems as inextricably intertwined, and they see social change as necessary to have a real impact on them (Joffe & Albee, 1981).

The broad scope of community-oriented theory and intervention has often resulted in lack of support from the mental health establishment. Issues of evaluation and measurement have been seen as too vague or ambitious, and thus not amenable to strict research methodology. For example, finding that depression could be prevented by reducing social injustice or economic inequities would entail major social campaigns with uncertain outcomes. Whether this is a limitation of the social and community perspective, or a limitation imposed on the field by an insufficiently forward-thinking leadership is a matter of judgment. It remains to be seen whether innovative work that goes beyond the usual mental health intervention (Caplan, Vinokur, Price & van Ryn, 1989; Vinokur, Price & Caplan, 1991) will gradually bridge the gap between the community and clinical camps.

With regard to the prevention of depression, if focusing on individual factors (be they psychological or biological) is sufficient to prevent the onset of depression, focusing on social issues may not be necessary *for this purpose*. Waiting until social change projects can be undertaken may delay achieving this worthwhile goal. It is important to note, however, that the goal of preventing specific disorders stems from a clinical perspective, and that many community researchers would consider this focus to be much too narrow.

Developmental Approaches

Several investigators have emphasized the importance of a developmental perspective for prevention (Bond & Joffe, 1982). Kellam and Werthamer-Larsson (1986) spoke of integrating community epidemiologic and life span developmental orientations, and specifying the stages of life, the major life events, and the social fields that influence individuals at different times.

Clearly, the logic of prevention points to interventions that occur as early as possible. A recent study found evidence of "depressed" behavior in infants of depressed mothers even when interacting with nondepressed adults as early as three months of age (Field et al., 1988). Whether these and similar findings are the result of genetic factors, other biological factors, or the instrumental or emotional nature of these infants' environments, interventions to avert deterioration are desperately needed.

Interventions focused on children and adolescents at risk have been proposed and developed in areas other than depression (Boulette, 1980; Piug-Antich, 1986; Shaffer, Philips & Enzer, 1989). These suggestions involve general heath promotion strategies, which have been described as "protecting the integrity of the central nervous system," and "enhancing psychosocial development" (Eisenberg, 1986). It is likely that such strategies would have a major impact not only on depression but also on several other areas of functioning. Investigators focused on depression prevention specifically would likely benefit from joint projects that include measures of depression. Of course, another approach is to target developmental dysfunctions that are believed to be related to depression. One promising line of research has focused on reducing "anxious attachment" at 12 months of age (Lieberman, Weston & Pawl, 1991).

Beardslee (1990) is developing a clinician-based cognitive psychoeducational prevention intervention for families with parental affective disorder to increase resiliency in the children. Patients and children are given information regarding the disorder and helped to develop concrete plans to cope in the future. Early results show families rate the intervention favorably and show desired behavior and attitude changes. Preventive effects are yet to be studied.

Studies specifically focusing on depression and risk factors for depression in children are starting to appear (see, for example, Seligman et al., 1984; Rehm, 1987). Epidemiological data on adolescent depression are also scarce. Lifetime prevalence rates for major depression in high school students have been reported to be as low as 4 percent in New Jersey (Whitaker et al., 1990) and as high as 20 percent in Oregon (Lewinsohn et al., 1988).

Developmental psychopathology will gradually illuminate some of the processes leading to debilitating depression. This knowledge will help to target specific stages of development in which physical and psychological maturation of depression-related coping mechanisms take place. In addition to issues of timing of intervention, the focus of the intervention for subgroups of at-risk individuals must also be examined. The work of Hammen (in press) exemplifies the possibility of predicting the type of stressful events (interpersonal versus achievement-oriented) that can trigger depressive episodes in children at risk.

The influence of developmental crises on specific disorders is unclear. It is likely that preventive interventions early in life will have protective functions across a number of possible problem areas. This may make it less likely that specific interventions for depression will be found, unless we focus on populations in which the risk for depression is very high, such as children of depressed mothers. However, even this issue (whether disorders in children tend to be the same as those in parents) is far from clear (see Rutter, 1989). Similarly, although depressed children are at risk for adult depression, most depressed adults have not been depressed as children (Harrington et al., 1990). These authors suggested that the causes and nature of adult depression may differ according to the subject's developmental stage at the time of onset.

In seeking high-risk populations, children of depressed mothers have been the focus of much attention. It is important to guard against the possibility that this high-risk factor is not translated into a popularized concept of the "depressogenic mother" so that we do not repeat the blaming that was involved in the "schizophrenogenic mother" concept.

*Contributions of Biological Approaches**

Akiskal (1987) addressed preventive implications of biological approaches in some detail. Some of his suggestions include the reduction of iatrogenically induced depression or elation. For example, depression is known to be induced in some persons by: steroidal hormones (including oral contraceptives), L-dopa, reserpine, alpha-methyldopa, propranolol, indomethacin, cimetidine, sulphonamides, anticholinesterase insecticides, alcohol, barbiturates, vincristine, vinblastine, mercury, thallium, and cycloserine. Elation can be caused by: steroidal hormones, L-dopa, bromocriptine, cocaine, tricyclic antidepressants, and monoamine oxidase inhibitors.

He also suggested that, for persons with a strong family history for affective disorders, the following interventions be considered: prescribing lithium for cyclothymic women for a few months immediately postpartum; educating cyclothymic and hyperthymic members of bipolar families to avoid sleep deprivation as well as catecholaminergic drugs (e.g., caffeine, other stimulants of the central nervous system,

*The sections on biological and genetic contributions benefited from discussions with Victor Reus, M.D., for which the authors are grateful. Interpretations of the literature or factual errors found in these sections are solely the authors' responsibility, of course.

antidepressants, certain cold and antiasthmatic medications); educating primary care physicians to the risks of prescribing certain depressant drugs (e.g., contraceptives, nondiuretic antihypertensives) to those with positive family history.

For those with a personal history of bipolar disorder, the prevention of recurrences may include education regarding the use of lithium; avoiding the use of stimulant drugs; risk of sleep deprivation; possible disturbances of the sleep cycle when crossing time zones; and care with catecholaminergic heterocylic antidepressants. For those with seasonal affective disorder, lithium and prophylactic use of exposure to bright light (with care regarding inducing hypomania) ought to be considered.

Early treatment has been shown to significantly reduce the duration of recurrent depression (Kupfer, Frank & Perel, 1989). This suggests that once treatment for an episode has ended, patients should either be systematically monitored (or taught to self-monitor) and given treatment as soon as a new episode is discovered. Depending on whether one considers recurrent depression a cyclical disorder or one that may or may not recur, this type of intervention could be considered in either the maintenance or prevention category.

Biological approaches may soon improve the taxonomy of depression by helping to identify specific types of dysfunction that may not fit the current syndromal definition of "major depression" but that may have specific biological (e.g., neurochemical or hormonal) characteristics that can help guide treatment. Biologically oriented researchers are also offering conceptually rich models of depression that could unite biological and environmental perspectives. These include:

1. The role of social "zeitgebers" (Ehlers, Frank & Kupfer, 1988) in bringing together such concepts as "loss" and the practical effects on daily behavior with concomitant effects on circadian rhythms. The loss of a partner, for example, might affect the time at which the remaining partner goes to bed and gets up in the morning, meal times, and types of meals eaten. These changes would then have effects on the sleep cycle, digestive patterns, and other biological cycles, in addition to the psychological sense of loss.
2. Depressive syndromes as disorders of neuroendocrine regulation rather than as disease derived from a primary pathogenic locus (Reus, 1987). This highlights the adaptive biological aspects of hypercortisolemia and loss of feedback inhibition in the short term, and suggests the need to consider modifiable methods of coping with stress.
3. Detailing nongenetic sources of biological pathology (e.g., the re-

cent study of identical twins showing differences in ventricle size related to schizophrenic versus nonschizophrenic members of a pair). "Environment" does not need to be psychological.

According to Halbreich (1987), biological approaches may one day help specify levels at which psychopathology might be produced, such as: intraneuronal (e.g., the regulation of cAMP); synaptic (e.g., between neurotransmitter and postsynaptic receptors); between various neurotransmitters (e.g., the balance between DA and Ach); between putative "neuromodulators" (e.g., the interrelationship between trace amines and endorphins); between neuromodulators and neurotransmitters (e.g., prostaglandins and NA); between hormones and hormones or hormones and neurotransmitters' mechanisms; and between compounds to be discovered on levels yet unknown.

The Contributions of Genetic Research

The area of genetics has shown amazing advances in recent years (Watson, Tooze & Kurtz, 1983). These advances are expected to eventually allow us to pinpoint the site of genetic disorders (that is, disorders that are caused by information encoded within DNA) and to find ways to reverse the pathological process at the source. For purposes of this chapter, the question is whether any depressive disorder or predisposition to depressive symptoms will be traceable to a specific gene, or combination of genes, or whether it will be found to occur mostly in normal genotypes. Moreover, if genetic influences are found for specific types of depression, are the markers found in a large enough proportion of affected families to make the identification of affected genes practical?

Studies of familial aggregation have shown strong evidence of genetic influences in bipolar disorder as well as increased risk of nonbipolar depressive disorder in families with a history of bipolar disorder (Andreasen, in press). At the very least, this line of research provides information for affected individuals regarding a higher risk of having children with depressive disorder. However, specific risk estimates appear to be quite variable. For example, in one study, the age-corrected proportion of affected offspring of two affected parents dropped from 74 to 57 percent when the largest family was omitted (Gershon et al., 1982). The generalizability of these rates to the general population is hard to estimate.

At present, neither high-risk markers nor genetically linked errors of metabolism have been isolated for depression.

The identification of affected individuals within specific pedigrees could lead to further studies of biological differences and perhaps to intervention studies with the affected individuals to determine whether biological, environmental, or psychological interventions are able to reduce expression of the pathological process. Scarr and McCartney (1983) proposed a theory of genotype-environment effects, which can help guide this line of work.

If a single gene or combination of genes could be found, one could study their biological effects and treat inborn errors of metabolism, by supplying deficient metabolites or missing proteins or by suggesting strict diets of nutrients that cannot be metabolized (Watson, Tooze & Kurtz, 1983, p. 212). Other potential interventions might include identifying sperm and egg cells with disorder-linked genes, separating out those that are free from such genes, and doing in vitro fertilization to ensure that progeny without the gene were born. (This would allow parents with the gene to have children without fear of their inheriting the disorder.) Ways of learning how to reduce penetrance would include determining which kinds of naturally occurring environmental intervention reduce gene expression by comparing those individuals with the gene who exhibit the disorder with those who do not. One could then use this information to create preventive environments. Once this is possible, one could identify fetuses with marker genes and provide those with such genes with especially designed prophylactic environments, training programs, and vocational counseling to reduce the likelihood of occurrence of episodes, or to reduce the intensity, duration, and frequency of episodes.

The more reliably the disorder can be identified, the more likely it is that genetic factors can be studied. For example, genetic factors related to bipolar illness are easier to study than those related to major depression or dysthymia. Therefore, at least for now, successful identification of genetic markers is unlikely to have a major impact on the most prevalent forms of depression.

Finding the gene related to a disorder does not signal the end of the process (Roberts, 1990). In 1989, the cystic fibrosis gene was found. Plans for the biggest genetic screening program to date were begun. One simple mutation causes most cases of the disease. About 75% of those who carry the abnormal gene have this mutation. But as investigators attempted to identify the remaining mutations, they found that the remaining cases appear to be related to many rare mutations. The fear now is that most will be "private" mutations, occurring in just one individual. A panel meeting in March 1990 at the National Institutes of Health (NIH) decided that widespread screening was premature, and recommended it only for those with a family history of the disease.

For now, given the imperfect test, if one partner tests positive and one negative, there is no way to tell if the latter carries the disease gene by means of an unidentified mutation. This would leave 1 in 15 couples in "genetic limbo."

The NIH panel agreed on the following guidelines: If genetic screening is ever instituted,

— it should be voluntary and confidential;
— it should be available to all who want it (the panel advised against testing newborns and children);
— informed consent should be required;
— laboratory quality assurance should be mandatory;
— adequate education and counseling should be available before testing is offered.

Encouraging reports regarding the discovery of genetic linkage of bipolar illness to loci on chromosome 11 and the X chromosome have been contradicted by subsequent findings. In 1987, a landmark article in *Nature* reported linkage between this disorder and DNA markers on the short arm of chromosome 11 in an Old Amish pedigree (Egeland *et al.*, 1987). Two articles in the same issue (Detera-Wadleigh et al., 1987; Hodgkinson et al., 1987) reported clear evidence that manic-depressive illness was *not* linked to chromosome 11 in other pedigrees, which was interpreted to mean that the predisposition might be attributable to different genes in different families. Still another article reported linkage between X-chromosome markers and bipolar affective illness in Israeli pedigrees (Baron et al., 1987).

Later, however, further question regarding linkage in chromosome 11 was raised by the addition of more members to the sample of the originally studied Amish pedigree (Kelsoe et al., 1989). This greatly reduced the probability of linkage to a single gene in chromosome 11 (Barinaga, 1989). Ciaranello and Ciaranello (1991) explained:

> Repeat diagnoses of the original core pedigree led them to reclassify two individuals without changing the LOD [log of odds] scores. However, the addition of more complete genotyping on ten unaffected members (who had been typed with only a single marker in the original study), plus the inclusion of two family members who were clinically unaffected in the first study but developed affective illness during the follow-up period and several new family members, all combined to drastically reduce LOD scores to −9.31 for HRAS1 and −7.75 for INS. Both scores are highly significant for the exclusion of linkage (P. 153).

In terms of the X chromosome linkage, Berrettini et al. (1990) tested linkage of X-chromosome markers of the q28 region to manic-depressive linkages in 14 pedigrees. He and his team found no evidence of linkage or heterogeneity in the pedigrees they studied. At best, this study indicates that this linkage is not as common as previously thought.

In their review, Ciaranello and Ciaranello (1991) also mentioned a study by Neiswanger et al. (1990) that excluded linkage in three large families with unipolar affective disorder to certain suspected loci on both chromosome 11 and X.

One of the strengths of genetic approaches is their ability to be tested and specific hypotheses refuted. This part of the scientific approach is well exemplified by the rapidity with which apparently revolutionary findings have been found to be invalid.

As was the case in earlier times, when such new concepts as psychodynamic approaches, behavioral approaches, and pharmacological approaches to treatment were expected to have major effects on mental health advances, the current excitement regarding the short-term application of genetic and biological approaches to depression may be greater than is warranted. There is no doubt that the conceptual and technological advances that have resulted in the biological revolution in psychiatry will allow us to examine mental and behavioral variables in ways that were previously impossible. It is not at all clear that this more detailed look at genetic variables will render obsolete other approaches to the treatment or prevention of mental disorders.

The most likely scenario in the future is a combination of approaches (see Chapter 23). For example, if reliable genetic or other biological markers of high risk are found, they could be used to identify populations that would be offered interventions designed to reduce the likelihood of clinical episodes of depression. Studies that attempt to specify the biological changes that occur when psychological interventions are successful in terminating or averting a depressive episode would be most exciting.

The conceptual changes occurring in the general public as biological and genetic approaches to depression get more press could have potentially damaging effects (especially if they turn out to be wrong, and thus produce unnecessary worries). It is believed that changing the attribution of these disorders from victim-blaming popular beliefs (e.g., that if they tried hard enough or changed their attitude, they would be well) to the notion of depression as an illness, and possibly a genetic illness, will be beneficial. However, extreme versions of the genetic perspective could reinforce the equally maladaptive belief that certain people or families have "bad blood," that the pathology is part of the very fiber of their being, and thus, that they can do nothing to get rid of the "underlying defect."

Even if we were to find single genes or combinations of genes that are linked to specific types of depression, the attempt to eradicate them could have unforeseen effects. Such genes might be part of the source of more subtle personality traits, such as "temperament." If those aspects are prevented from occurring as genotypes, more than just depression might be prevented. Socially beneficial products of greater sensitivity to environmental hardships, to injustice, or to beauty might be lost in the process.

Part II

Steps in Research on Preventive Interventions

4. Identifying the Target: What Do You Intend to Prevent?

To know if we have prevented depression, we must be able to identify instances of depression and count them. This will allow us to determine if the quantity of new occurrences of depression is being reduced. Such a goal presupposes that one can reliably identify the condition. As it turns out, there are several definitions of *depression*, and these definitions do not all agree on who is *depressed*.

On "Depression"

Depressed *mood* is a common emotion, usually of short duration, experienced by almost all individuals at some time or other. The person experiencing it may or may not be able to connect it to specific events. Although generally experienced as unpleasant, it appears to be of little significance by itself.

Depression *as a symptom* can be a sign of distress, generally connected to unhappy events, illnesses, or other stressful conditions. Often, additional symptoms are associated with the symptom of depression, such as trouble concentrating, reduced motivation, and so on. Several scales have been constructed to reflect depressive symptomatology as a continuous variable. These scales assume that the experience of depression can be conceptualized as a continuum, with greater or lesser levels of severity.

Depression *as a syndrome* has been carefully described in recent years. Minimal criteria for major depression syndrome have been specified. When enough other specific symptoms accompany depressed mood, and when the combination of symptoms lasts longer than a specified period, the syndrome of depression is said to be present (see Chapter 2). Conceptually, a syndrome is an entity that is either present or absent in an individual. Thus, it is generally measured as a dichotomous variable. A major depressive syndrome may be present due to a number of triggers, such as bereavement (Clayton, 1987), and is not necessarily conceptualized as a disorder.

Depression *as a disorder* is a clinical entity, which, again, is understood as being either present or absent. Generally, to meet criteria for the disorder, the syndrome must be present. In addition, several other criteria must be met. For example, in the case of a DSM-III-R major depressive episode, a major depressive syndrome must be present, but, in addition, one must rule out organic factors, uncomplicated bereavement, the absence of psychotic symptoms when the mood symptoms are not present, and the absence of psychotic disorders (DSM-III-R, pp. 222–23). This definition of depression is most compatible with the idea that clinical depression is an illness. The constantly revised delineation of the disorder reflects attempts to hone the definition of this entity so as to isolate it as a disease, with clear prognosis, family history, and, ideally, an etiology that will point to specific therapeutic and preventive strategies.

Relationships among Different Types of Depression

The similarities among the different kinds of depression described above suggest that similar mechanisms may be operating in each case. The human capacity to experience depressed mood appears to be a characteristic of normal individuals. Reactivity to negative events appears, again, to be a sign of normal functioning. When the frequency, duration, and intensity of depressed mood states become excessive and interfere with daily functioning, these states are labeled by health professionals as a psychological or emotional problem, or a mental disorder. As these states worsen, and begin to be accompanied by biological abnormalities, they resemble physical illnesses.

There is a fair amount of controversy regarding whether "depression" is a unitary phenomenon, and its identified manifestations are a matter of degree, or whether there are many types of depression, and the apparent similarities between them are more a matter of confusion created in part by the use of inexact language. It is possible, of course, that depressed mood is essentially similar across all its manifestations, but that many paths may trigger such mood, including trivial fluctuations in the state of the organism (passing mood states), reactions to specific environmental stress, long-lasting ways of responding to life that result in chronic depressed states, and abnormal physiological functioning (due to the ingestion of depressogenic substances, secondary to other illnesses, or due to specific biological abnormalities that are related primarily to depressed states). Three alternative mechanisms explaining the relationships between depressed mood and abnormal physiological process can be postulated: abnormal physiological functioning could be the cause of the depressed state; the depressed state could trigger the pathological process; or there could be a reciprocal interaction between the two. The second and third alternatives allow for the possibility that preventing depressed states could also prevent the physiological pathology.

Which Type of "Depression" Should We Prevent?

The clearest argument can be made for preventing depression as a syndrome and as a disorder. Major depressive episodes have been defined specifically enough to permit their identification with a satisfactory degree of reliability. Since a major depressive syndrome is an essential element of the episode, a reduction in the incidence of major depressive syndromes would result in a reduction of major depressive episodes. Major depressive episodes are recognized as an important mental heath problem. They comprise a large segment of mental health visits, and they are the target of serious research efforts dedicated to improving its treatment (Rehm, in press). Well-documented reductions in the incidence of major depressive episodes would be recognized as a major contribution to the mental health field.

Depressive symptomatology is another possible target for prevention efforts. If depressive symptoms are viewed as a gateway toward clinical episodes of depression, the reduction of such symptoms ought to reduce the incidence of clinical episodes. Clinical episodes of depression involve several symptoms that must be present at a high enough intensity and for a long enough duration. Preventive programs that successfully increase a person's ability to manage moods so that frequency, intensity, and duration of symptoms are reduced could theoretically forestall such episodes. Lewinsohn and colleagues (Lewinsohn, Hoberman & Rosenbaum, 1989) pointed out that although not all individuals with high scores on depression scales meet the criteria for depressive disorders, the opposite tends to be true. In other words, persons with depressive disorders are likely to have high scores on a depression scale. This suggests that high levels of depression are necessary, though not sufficient, to trigger a depressive episode. There may be an individually defined threshold of depressive symptoms past which the person becomes highly likely to develop some kind of dysfunction, including a depressive disorder. Thus, preventing high levels of depressive symptoms may prevent depressive disorders and perhaps other types of dysfunction.

Measuring the effect of preventive programs focused on depressive symptoms would not be difficult. Scores on self-report scales have been used in several community studies to determine the level of depression in a population. Cutoff scores have been used to determine the prevalence of depressive phenomena in such studies. For example, Roberts (1987, p. 51) reviewed studies reporting from 9 percent to 29 percent prevalence rates for depressive symptomatology when a score of 16 or more on the Center for Epidemiological Studies Depression scale is used to define significant depression. Reductions in the incidence of persons scoring above the cutoff on such scales would be evidence of preventive effects.

There is controversy about the value of preventing high levels of depressive symptomatology—is it a worthy or important goal for prevention? Some clinicians feel that using resources to reduce depressive feelings would be wasteful, especially when persons with severe mental disorders are going without treatment. These critics describe such efforts as dealing with the "problems in living" inherent in human experience, rather than tackling true "diseases" such as major depression.

Supporters of broad-based efforts at prevention point out that high levels of depression can themselves have a widespread negative impact in our population. For example, there is now evidence that high levels of depression, even if not meeting criteria for depressive disorders, can significantly reduce the level of functioning. Such a reduction can be as marked as that produced by diagnosable depression and major chronic physical illnesses such as hypertension, diabetes, advanced coronary artery disease, angina, arthritis, back problems, lung problems, and gastrointestinal disorder (Wells et al., 1989). Other data indicate that mothers with moderate levels of depression are more likely to engage in aggressive behavior toward their children than are mothers with high levels of depression, who are more likely to passively neglect their children (Zuravin, 1989).

Other arguments for learning how to prevent depressive symptoms come from the literature on substance abuse. There is now evidence that persons with a history of depression are more likely to smoke and less likely to quit successfully (Anda et al., 1990; Glassman et al., 1990). The high levels of depression in other substance abusers suggest that this mechanism may be operating in the use of "harder" drugs as well (Batki, Sorensen, Gibson & Maude-Griffin, 1988; Batki, Sorensen, Faltz & Madover, 1989).

It is very possible that high levels of depressive symptoms have pervasive effects on the population at large, affecting not only individual ability to deal with the stresses of life but also interpersonal relationships. In the latter case, for instance, one can imagine depressive symptoms diminishing the pleasure usually derived from a relationship, decreasing motivation to work on the relationship, altering one's assessment of the relationship by ignoring its positive aspects and exaggerating its negative facets, and reducing the hope that the relationship will improve. These mechanisms may increase the probability of divorce, producing further stress and depression on the couple as well as on any offspring.

Recommendations

Given the documented impact of depressive disorders and states of high depressive symptoms, we suggest that research studies on the prevention of depression target both types of depression: clinical episodes meeting accepted criteria, and high scores on symptom scales. It is possible that some interventions will be particularly effective for one but not the other; some will be effective for both; and some will have an immediate effect on depressive levels, and only a longer range effect on reducing clinical episodes. With some interventions, full-blown clinical episodes might indeed be preventable, but high depression levels might still be present in participants. Unless both types of depression are measured, these possibilities will not be detectable.

In addition, it is important that the impact of both types of depression on other aspects of functioning be examined. Although most clinicians would argue that a clinical depression is more disruptive and therefore more worthy of intervention (therapeutic or preventive), high levels of depression symptoms, in part because of their pervasiveness, may have greater adverse effects on human life.

Different interventions may have effects on elements of a person's life beyond his or her mood state. Certainly, an intervention that both reduces symptom levels and produces effects on job productivity or the ability to engage in healthier interpersonal relations would be preferable to one that affects only how participants feel and little else. One can also imagine interventions that reduce the experience of depression but produce deleterious effects on other aspects of persons' lives, such as irresponsible behavior, drug abuse (including abuse of prescription or other legal drugs), or other behavior that is likely to result in feelings of guilt. Eventually, the field ought to develop a core battery of instruments that measure basic aspects of human functioning, so that preventive interventions can be compared with each other regarding the breadth of their effect.

5. Choosing a Theory to Guide the Intervention: What Mechanisms Are Involved?

To prevent an episode of depression, one must use a strategy that addresses one or more of the following factors:

1. *the* mechanism that produces the depressive episode.
2. the triggers that activate the mechanisms that produce the episode.
3. the processes that take place between the onset of the triggering event and the beginning of the pathological process. Ideally, these processes can be attenuated so that they do not reach a threshold past which the pathological mechanism is activated.
4. the processes that occur once the pathological mechanism is activated. Interventions might be able to normalize the individual's state at early stages of the pathological processes, so that, even if the mechanism involved has reached pathological levels, it restabilizes quickly. This would result in reduced intensity, duration, and frequency of overtly dysfunctional episodes.

The choice of preventive strategies is influenced by theoretical formulations and the feasibility of interventions based on these formulations. Current progress in each area of research is the limiting factor on whether the theoretical approach can guide practical prevention strategies.

The first set of strategies, which focuses on the mechanisms of depressive disorders, has generally applied to uniquely individual factors, such as psychological or biological processes. Psychological mechanisms that have been suggested include psychodynamic theories of depression, such as the classic description of depression as anger turned toward the self, the cognitive theories that focus on ways in which persons interpret their reality, and the behavioral theories regarding the level of response-contingent positive reinforcement. Biological mechanisms have posited abnormalities at the synaptic level (such as the availability of neurotransmitters), the endocrine system, or even the genetic code. None of these theorized mechanisms has yet been found to be either necessary or sufficient for depressive disorders.

The second set of factors, which is comprised of triggers that may activate the more proximal causes of dysfunction, again has many candidates. The most influential conditions for depression include stressful life events and direct physical insults. Stressful life events are events that do not directly damage the individual's physical organism but that have an impact on the person's objective or symbolic resources as well as his or her burdens. They include discrete events such as financial loss, loss of loved ones through separation or death, changes in social status (including positive changes, such as career advancement), or chronic stress, such as living in a high-crime area, in poverty, or with a physical illness. Although poverty has long been believed to produce cases of clinical depression, only recently has epidemiological work been able to pinpoint the extent of its specific influence (Bruce et al., 1991). The work of Brown and Harris (1978) on the social origins of depression identified four factors that increased vulnerability to stressful events and placed Caucasian women in England at greater risk for clinical depression: the absence of a close, intimate, confiding relationship; the loss of one's mother before age eleven; three or more children under fifteen years living at home; and the absence of a job outside the home.

Physical insults to the organism include iatrogenically produced depressive episodes (say, as a result of antihypertensive medication), physical disability as a result of an accident or illness, or environmental factors such as the availability of light in the case of seasonal affective disorder. Interesting speculation about the effect of social changes on physical factors has been advanced: Ehlers, Frank and Kupfer (1988) suggested that the social losses, such as that of a marital partner, may increase the probability of depression in part by disrupting the individual's daily routine, leading to the dysregulation of circadian rhythms.

There are also theoretical frameworks that explicitly combine environmental and individual factors (both psychological and biological). For example, Akiskal and McKinney (1973; Whybrow, Akiskal & McKinney, 1984) described clinical depression as a final common path to adaptive failure of the organism: heredity and temperament, developmental and characterologic parameters, precipitating stressors (such as life events and biological insults), and modulating parameters (such as age, sex, and endocrine status) are presumed to affect neurochemistry and neurophysiological arousal, which in turn can produce (and be affected by) brain dysfunction (at the limbic-diencephalic level), which produces (and is affected by) the depressive syndrome. There is now sufficient evidence showing that environmental triggers can increase the probability of depressive episodes. Nevertheless, neither social nor physical factors appear to be either necessary or sufficient to initiate clinical episodes of depression.

The third strategy refers to attenuating processes that lead to depressive episodes before a hypothetical threshold is crossed. Whatever will eventually be discovered regarding depressive dysfunctions, it appears that, in most cases, these episodes take some time to reach clinical levels. This suggests that monitoring levels of depression and keeping them from becoming intense might reverse whatever process is caused by environmental factors. Although in a few cases, the trigger must be identified to normalize the process (for example, if a medication is responsible for the depression), in most cases, the trigger will either be unknown, categorically unalterable (such as the loss of a loved one), or practically difficult to change (such as chronic illness, chronic poverty, or occupational stress). In such cases, professionals need not give up or decide to wait until the chronic condition changes. Instead, they could focus the preventive interventions on the mood itself. The intervention could be conceptualized as an additional factor modulating the individual's mood states and counteracting the influence of the other factors. It is important to note that the etiological factors and the preventive factors need not address the same domains. Thus, this strategy is pragmatic. If depressive symptoms are attenuated and depressive episodes are made less frequent, the preventive intervention is effective, even if it addresses mechanisms other than those involved in the episode's initiation.

The fourth strategy involves teaching individuals at high risk for depressive episodes ways to normalize their own mood state early in the course of the pathological process. The difference between this strategy and the former is mainly conceptual. In the third strategy, the intent is to keep the depressive process from going over a certain (generally unknown) threshold. The fourth strategy assumes that, at times, the threshold might be crossed, but that the individual might be able to reduce its intensity without professional care so that the (now clinical) depression subsides below the threshold. In practice, this might mean that a person is able to "catch" the depression as it begins to affect daily functioning, and to reverse it, so that he or she is able to function well again.

Choosing a Theory That Suggests a Practical Intervention

Research on preventive intervention requires a focus on those theories that address modifiable factors. These interventions can focus on the individual, the family, or the larger social and physical environment. In general, the more expansive the intervention, the more difficult it is to implement reliably. On the other hand, social and community interventions are theoretically more likely to have an impact on population rates of disorders, such as incidence. Physically invasive interventions, such as the use of pharmacotherapy, have generally not been suggested for preventive programs, in part because the level of risk inherent in such interventions has been considered higher than is warranted for use in nondysfunctional populations. Thus, the main focus of preventive studies to date relies on psychological interventions, in which the individual is taught methods designed to manage one's own mood or is given services or support designed to reduce social or emotional stress.

6. Identifying High-Risk Groups: For Whom Is the Intervention Appropriate?

In general, the less expensive and the less potentially harmful the intervention, the more widely it can be implemented. As the intervention becomes more expensive, and as it becomes more potent, it becomes increasingly important to limit its reach to the population most at risk.

To make this point most forcefully, let's consider the following example: assume that ten percent of the population is at lifetime risk for a specific depressive disorder. A community-wide mass media intervention consisting of ten half-hour segments regarding methods to maintain one's mood within normal limits which could be seen by anyone, preferably at a time of his or her choosing, could be proposed as reasonable. However, an intervention that requires universal attendance at three weekly individual sessions for a year or more would not be a reasonable use of people's time and public monies. Note that this holds even if the former method produces a small effect size (say, a reduction from ten percent to nine percent in the incidence of depressive disorders) and the latter method produces a large effect size (say, a reduction from ten percent to three percent in incidence).

The factors that need to be considered include the cost per affected person, the amount of coercion involved, the proportion of those not at risk who would have to undergo the preventive procedure, and the likelihood of negative effects (for example, causing unnecessary fear of becoming depressed to the ninety percent of the population who are unlikely to become clinically depressed).

In the example above, we assume that the ten percent risk rate is all the information we have, and that we are unable to identify those within the population who are at higher (or highest) risk. If we were able to find that a certain segment of the population had an eighty percent chance of becoming depressed, it would be easier to justify a concerted effort at reaching those most at risk. The danger here lies in possibly producing negative effects by identifying the individual persons. For example, would they be more likely to be shunned by prospective marital partners if they are identified as highly likely to become depressed, and if so, could this fact itself increase their likelihood of becoming depressed?

Societal Risk

Another factor to be taken into account involves the benefit to be derived by society by focusing on certain populations. These estimates necessarily involve comparisons that can be emotionally difficult to specify. If they are not made explicitly, however, they will be made by default. Given the few resources devoted to mental health and the even smaller number of these devoted to prevention of psychological problems, it seems prudent to examine the choice of populations carefully.

Suppose, for example, that an effective preventive intervention for depression were developed which significantly reduces the occurrence of depressive episodes for at least a ten-year period. Suppose, further, that it could be applied throughout the life span and worked reasonably well for both genders. Two projects are put forward, and only one can be funded: the first targets elderly men in nursing homes; the second targets 18- to 24-year-old women pregnant with their first child.

Even if the risk for depression were the same for both populations, the repercussions of depressive episodes within the next ten years would be much greater for the women about to begin their childbearing years. When focusing on the individuals themselves, the decisions and the achievements of the next ten years are going to have a major effect on the women's lives for much longer than the decisions and achievements of the men in the nursing homes. Going beyond the individuals themselves, there are sufficient data now to indicate that maternal depression can have serious repercussions on the welfare of their children.

From a societal point of view, then, risk involves more than just reducing the number of depressive episodes in the individuals targeted for intervention. Ramifications in terms of person-years of health, the effect on other individuals to whom the person is related, and the effect on productivity and overall contributions to the welfare of the society also need to be taken into account.

Several other aspects of identifying targets of depression prevention projects are beginning to be gleaned. For example, the role of depression on substance abuse, which has been clinically discussed for many years, is gaining empirical support. Studies reporting the role of depression on smoking are beginning to show that persons with a history of depression are more likely to smoke and less likely to quit successfully (Glassman et al., 1990). Studies also show that other substance abusers have a high prevalence of depression (Batki et al., 1989). If depression is related to substance abuse in general, alcohol consumption may also be related to depression. Given the high relationship between alcohol use and automobile accidents, criminal behavior, and violence, it is not too far-fetched to see how depression may have a widespread effect on several highly noxious aspects of our society. Once again, targeting those most likely to become involved in substance abuse, accidents, crime, and violence may be the best use of depression prevention efforts.

The choices to be made are real. The difficulty of making these choices is also very real. One runs into the quagmire of labeling one person's life as more important, or at least more influential than another's. Do these differences make one less worthy than another for societal support?

One possible way to reduce the difficulty involved in making this type of decision is to make preventive interventions as universal as possible, and so inexpensive as to make it unreasonable to deny their implementation. Whether such universal and inexpensive interven-

Table 6.1. Comparing Incidence in an Experimental Group with a Control Group: Sample Size Required per Group when Using the z Statistic with Power $(1 - \beta) = .80$ and $\alpha = .05$ (One-Tailed)

Incidence in Experimental Group	Incidence in Control Group								
	.10	.15	.20	.25	.30	.35	.40	.45	.50
.05	342	110	59	38	27	21	17	13	11
.10		539	156	78	48	33	25	19	15
.15			712	197	95	57	38	28	21
.20				860	231	108	64	42	30
.25					984	258	119	69	45
.30						1083	280	128	73
.35							1157	295	133
.40								1206	305
.45									1231

Source: These estimates are based on Table 13.B (pp. 216–217) in *Designing Clinical Research: An Epidemiologic Approach,* by S. B. Hulley and S. R. Cummings (Baltimore: Williams & Wilkins, 1988).

Note: Estimates do not include the continuity correction, and thus slightly underestimate sample size.

tions can be sufficiently effective to have a major impact on the incidence (and therefore the prevalence) of depression remains to be seen.

The Need to Identify Groups at Imminent High Risk

Risk factors, as reported in the literature, are generally *lifetime* risk factors. When conducting a study on the outcome of a prevention intervention for depression, imminent high risk factors are needed, for example, risk factors predicting to one-year incidence. In other words, high-risk screening scales must be truly able to predict which individuals from a population are likely to develop a clinical episode of depression in the short run (Miranda, Muñoz & Shumway, 1990). Otherwise, the level of annual incidence, even in a group with a high lifetime risk for depression, will not provide sufficient statistical power to properly test the hypothesis of whether the intervention prevents major depressive episodes.

Table 6.1 provides estimates of the sample size needed for a one-tailed test according to different levels of incidence. The sample sizes refer to the final sample size. Estimates of dropout rates will necessarily increase the initial sample size required.

7. Designing the Intervention: How Do You Propose to Prevent the Target Condition?

Several factors contribute to the form of preventive interventions: theoretical factors, technological factors, economic factors, and cultural factors.

Theoretical Factors

The mechanisms hypothesized to underlie or trigger depressive episodes are generally fundamental to the design of an intervention. Thus, a biologically oriented professional might consider interventions that bring hormonal or other psychologically related substances within normal limits; a genetically oriented investigator might seek to identify genes related to depressive disorders and attempt changes in the genes or the substances controlled by the identified genes that would lower risk; and a socially oriented investigator might focus on social stressors and social supports to reduce depressive episodes.

Technological Factors

Once theoretical factors have established the potential targets for intervention, issues of technological feasibility must be considered. For example, psychological interventions of an educational nature depend on pedagogical techniques that work. If the instructors are not able to teach the participants in the intervention the skills that are theorized to decrease the probability of depression, the theory cannot be tested nor the intervention implemented. Similarly, if socioeconomic status, racial discrimination, gender discrimination, biological dysregulation, or genetic factors are considered to be contributors to the risk for depression, unless methods that reliably modify these factors are available, interventions focused on them cannot be given a fair test.

The response to this issue, of course, is not to give up the goal of prevention. Rather, this awareness should lead to greater efforts to develop methods that successfully modify those factors postulated to mediate depression.

Economic Factors

Once theoretical approaches have been chosen, and once the technology for addressing them has been developed, issues of cost need to be taken into account. The cost of interventions will always be a factor in terms of feasibility.

With regard to preventive interventions, issues of cost revolve around the following factors:

— the absolute cost for the service provider, and the availability of the resources for the prevention program;
— the relative cost for the service provider, and the decision to divert resources from current services (usually treatment services), with the expectation that such redirecting of resources will produce a greater overall impact in terms of increased health and reduced dysfunction;
— the cost of the recipient of the services, including the monetary cost, time involved in receiving the service, and the response cost involved (in terms of having to travel to a specific location, to undergo uncomfortable procedures, and the overall amount of effort involved in receiving the intervention).

Cultural Factors

The acceptability of any form of intervention will vary across population groups because of many factors, including conscious philosophical stances, nonconscious biases, lack of knowledge, lack of resources, and differences in perceived cost.

We found a number of instances in which *philosophical stances* either hindered or helped in our work. A woman explicitly objected to the use of deep muscular relaxation training because she felt that it was a form of "yoga," that yoga was a non-Christian practice, and she, as a Christian, refused to engage in such a practice. This deeply held belief was not assuaged by assurances that relaxation training as we taught it was not part of training in yoga, and that we did not intend to teach yoga to participants. Sometimes, of course, such explicit beliefs are helpful in terms of making the skills taught more acceptable. Another woman, who described herself as a Baptist, stated that what we were teaching in the Depression Prevention Course was what the Bible taught, only we were using other words. Again, we said that it was not our intent to teach a religious method, but that if the materials we were sharing with the participants in the course suited their religious values, we were very glad.

Biases regarding whether it is helpful (or harmful) to address emotional or psychological issues were probably related to whether people chose to enter the study, whether they chose to participate in the course, and how much they disclosed to the instructor and other participants. Our stance was that participants in the course could share as much or as little about their personal situation as they wanted. The rationale for the course was that learning the self-control methods and applying them to their lives was the active ingredient: self-disclosure, by itself, was not necessary to benefit from the course. All personal matters discussed were to remain confidential. However, participants were free (and, in fact, encouraged) to discuss the self-control methods with family or friends.

Lack of knowledge includes such basic elements as the ability to speak the language in which the intervention is administered and the ability to read materials. It may also include how to obtain information in an educational setting (many of our Spanish-speaking participants had very few years of schooling) or how to participate in group discussion.

Lack of resources is yet another factor and includes such elements as having enough money to take the bus to the location of the program, having someone to care for one's children, or being able to take the time to attend the intervention. An explicit focus on ways to make preventive interventions more accessible, ideally at any place and time of the participant's choosing, is critical to the program's success.

Relative perceived cost refers to such issues as whether attending a psychological intervention is going to result in stigma from one's peers (versus, for example, increased status as someone who has learned something others may not have learned). Competing uses of one's time, including perception of preventive activities as appropriate for family participation, will play a major role in the utilization of preventive services.

The method of delivery may have differential effects on the acceptability of an intervention. For example, the same message given by a physician, a minister, or a rock star would have different impact on an atheist, a believer, or a rebellious adolescent. Similarly, messages using the mass media, computers, or print are likely to have differing impact on diverse audiences.

General Recommendations

Preventive interventions need to be short enough to be practical, yet intensive enough to be effective. One cannot expect a brief intervention to have major long-term effects in preventing depression. On the other hand, a costly, time-consuming, comprehensive intervention is unlikely to be widely adopted, not only because resources for such an intervention are unlikely to be allocated, but also because it may be hard to find recipients who would make the necessary time commitment.

Comparisons with treatment approaches are useful here. If the preventive intervention takes as long as treatment, and if our ability to identify high-risk groups is limited, then it is reasonable to ask whether we should implement such a program preventively as opposed to merely waiting until individuals become depressed and then treating them. Of course, comparisons of this sort are usually not so simple: such factors as the impact of depression on one's health, family, and work life also need to be taken into account, as well as the likelihood that one would seek treatment if depressed. If preventive interventions are more acceptable than treatment, if earlier intervention is more effective than later intervention, and if the impact of even moderate levels of depression is pervasive, prevention may still be preferable.

Prevention providers also need to consider whether they are merely "preaching to the converted." Does the program reach those who traditionally underutilize mental health services? Does this underutilization result from their own lack of interest or because the program excludes them from participation (e.g., by lack of language-appropriate services)? Similarly, the level of risk of those who obtain the services should be examined. Ideally, those at highest risk should be sought out by prevention services.

Examples of Preventive Intervention

One of the best designed community prevention studies in terms of its sampling procedure was conducted by Vega et al. (1987). A screening-enumeration process was used to obtain a county-wide probability sample of low-income Mexican-American women between 35 and 50 years of age. This door-to-door method was intended to produce a representative sample of the high-risk population that had been identified in earlier epidemiological studies. The interventions were performed by indigenous Hispanic natural helpers ("servidoras") trained to carry out a one-to-one contact condition (the "linkperson" mode) and an educational group (the "merienda educativa" condition). Both intervention conditions used a social learning-based approach focused on instrumental, problem-solving techniques to cope with the stresses that low-income Hispanic women face.

Participants located through the door-to-door enumeration method were screened out of the study if their depression score was above a certain level. Thus, the study explicitly focused on those initially exhibiting low levels of depression, and attempted to prevent high levels. Those with scores below the cutoff point were randomly assigned to either of the two experimental conditions or to the no-intervention control condition. Results from this study have not yet been published. A paper presented at an NIMH-sponsored workshop (Valle, 1990) suggested that the subgroup with the lowest initial depression levels showed significantly lower depression scores at follow-up when compared with similar controls.

Unfortunately, evaluation of diagnostic status at one year was not carried out. Thus, only effects on symptom levels will be available. In addition, the use of high symptom scores to screen out participants in a prevention trial may be unadvisable, because those with high scores, but not meeting diagnostic criteria, may be at particularly high risk for clinical depression and other disorders. The following section will address this issue in more detail.

Preventing Depression by Reducing Symptoms

A number of studies have attempted to reduce depressive symptoms in populations considered to be at risk for depression (either disorders or high levels of symptoms). In general, they have shown positive results in terms of symptom reduction, which parallel those of treatment outcome trials. These studies usually invite the target population to take part in the intervention offered on the basis of such factors as age, life events, socioeconomic conditions, or other demographic variables, rather than diagnostic status. Some projects are designed to identify and exclude those with clinical depression and refer them for therapy; others take all who wish to participate.

The role of such projects in the mental health services spectrum is controversial. Some have described this type of service as "therapy for subclinical depression." Some have derided it as services for the "worried well." However, after noting that high symptom scores are necessary but not sufficient for depressive disorders, Lewinsohn, Hoberman, and Rosenbaum (1988) suggest that high depressive symptom scores may reflect a nonspecific negative affect (perhaps akin to the concept of "demoralization" (Frank, 1973) that can be triggered by, among other factors, stressful events. This negative affect can increase the likelihood of a variety of medical and psychiatric disorders, including depressive disorders. However, the specific progression from negative affect to depressive disorder depends on other characteristics of the person (e.g., sex, age, history of depression) that elicit the range of systemic disturbances constituting a depressive episode. Acute negative affect, then, could serve as a trigger in persons who are predisposed to depressive disorder. Chronic negative affect could be a constant high-risk marker.

This line of reasoning suggests that interventions that teach persons to manage negative mood so that its intensity, duration, and frequency are reduced may help prevent depressive disorders as well as other disorders. Two questions will need to be answered: First, are there methods that have been shown to reduce depressive symptoms reliably in nonclinical populations? Second, do these reductions prevent depressive disorders? The answer to the first question is clearly affirmative. The second question remains unanswered.

We will now describe several studies aimed at symptom reduction to illustrate the range of approaches that have been tested.

A study from Australia (Raphael, 1977) assessed 200 widows applying for widow's pensions and selected 64 believed to be at high risk of "morbidity" according to four indices: perceived nonsupportiveness in the bereaved's social network, traumatic circumstances of the death, highly ambivalent relationship with the deceased, and a concurrent life crisis. Widows were randomly assigned to the experimental (n = 31) or control (n = 33) conditions. The intervention consisted of individual sessions by the investigator, a dynamically trained psychiatrist, using a model of "selective ego support for ego processes stressed by the crisis experience." This involved expression of grieving affects and facilitation of the mourning process with review of positive and negative aspects of the relationship. The sessions took place at the widow's own home, and averaged four sessions per widow, ranging from one to nine. All intervention ended by three months after the husband's death. Outcome was determined using a general health questionnaire sent by the university medical school (without reference to the intervenor) thirteen months following the spouse's death. Comparisons across randomized conditions are reported in terms of "good" or "bad" outcomes, and were significant at the .02 level. Those with initial high levels of perceived nonsupportiveness showed the greatest differences in outcome. Of specific interest for this book is the report that outpatient medical treatment for depression was sought by four in the control group and three in the intervention condition and that four control condition participants required hospitalization for depression, compared with none in the intervention group.

The Michigan Department of Mental Health (Tableman, 1987) Stress Management Training project deserves special attention because, unlike most other projects, it is essentially a service program that has been carefully evaluated. It is not merely a research program that exists only while research funds support it. Its focus is on enhancing the management of stress by women on public assistance. Groups of six to twelve women attend ten weekly two-and-a-half to three-hour sessions. Transportation and child care are provided. The groups meet in churches or community centers, explicitly avoiding meeting in mental health centers to reduce fear of stigma. The group teaches cognitive restructuring and behavioral training to increase self-esteem and decrease learned helplessness. Two projects involving white and African American women in different geographical locations have shown significant differences on depression symptom scores when experimental and control groups are compared immediately following intervention and at six months follow-up.

An interesting hybrid of prevention and treatment interventions is the "Coping-with-Depression Course" (CWD) developed by Lewinsohn and colleagues in Eugene, Oregon (Brown & Lewinsohn, 1984; Lewinsohn, 1987; Lewinsohn, Hoberman & Clarke, 1989). Lewinsohn (1987) described the course as a cognitive-behavioral educational experience, which is advertised as a course in newspapers, radio, and TV, and which has minimal exclusion criteria (mainly severe disorders, including bipolar disorder). People receiving treatment for depression may participate. Obviously, such a course tends to attract persons for whom depression is perceived as a problem: in its early forms, approximately eighty percent of the participants met criteria for diagnosis of depression. The course has its own text, *Control Your Depression* (Lewinsohn et al., 1986), is highly structured, time-limited, and focused on skill-training. A book describing it in detail is available (Lewinsohn, Antonuccio, Steinmetz & Teri, 1984). Several studies have shown consistent reduction in depressive symptoms, with continued improvement effects evident at least up to six-month follow-ups.

Steinmetz, Lewinsohn, and Antonuccio (1983) examined preintervention variables that predict improvement with the CWD course. Eight predictors account for 56 percent of the variance in posttreatment scores: lower scores are predicted by lower pretreatment depression level, expectation of improvement, initial satisfaction with major life roles, *not* receiving concurrent treatment, perceived social support, *not* having physical problems, *not* having a history of suicidal attempts, and having greater perceived mastery over one's life. In sum, those with healthier status initially appear to benefit most from the intervention.

Adaptations of the Coping-with-Depression Course are being developed for the elderly (Steinmetz, Zeiss & Thompson, 1987) and for adolescents (Clarke, 1990). The Depression Prevention Course (Muñoz, 1984) used in the Depression Prevention Research Project also traces its lineage to Lewinsohn's work.

The studies mentioned thus far are adaptations of treatment approaches that have been used for preventive, community-based (versus clinic-based) interventions. Nevertheless, they still have a clinical flavor to them, with the focus resembling what a person seeking therapy would receive. This is both a strength and a weakness. The strength is that extrapolation from clinical experience makes it more likely that effects on depressive symptomatology will be similar to those found in the larger treatment outcome literature. The weakness is that one could ask whether it is better to just wait until the targeted individuals become clinically depressed, and then offer them these services. After all, if one is going to offer a high-risk group the same services as one would offer a clinically depressed individual, and if only some proportion (usually less than half) of the high-risk group is likely to develop a clinical episode, isn't it more advisable to save the intervener's time and use it for those who actually become depressed? Two questions are raised by this line of thinking: (1) Are there other interventions that are not just variants of psychotherapy which might reduce depression levels? And (2) are there more efficient ways to deliver prevention services that would make them more practical?

Two studies can serve as illustrations of the first issue: services focused on areas not generally addressed in psychotherapy, but that appear to be relevant to depressive symptom levels.

Bloom, Hodges & Caldwell (1982) randomly assigned 100 newly separated persons to an intervention condition and fifty to a no-treatment control group. The six-month-long intervention was designed on the basis of an analysis of the literature that identified the major stressful elements in the separation experience. Paraprofessionals with volunteer counseling experience served as "program representatives," contacting participants on a regular basis, developing opportunities for social interaction, and referring to the program's "study groups." Five such groups were available: career planning and employment, legal and financial issues, child-rearing and single-parenting, housing and homemaking, and socialization and personal self-esteem. The study groups were led by professionals in relevant fields. The average number of contacts with the representatives was ten (range: 1–

37). Participation in each of the study groups varied from only four people using the housing and homemaking group to forty-four using the socialization group. Of nine dependent measures of adjustment, five significant differences favoring the intervention group were found, including a measure of "neurasthenia." Differences persisted at eighteen- and thirty-month follow-ups (Bloom, 1985, p. 76).

The Michigan Prevention Research Center has conducted a randomized trial with 928 recently unemployed adults (Caplan et al., 1989). The intervention included a training seminar in job seeking with a problem-solving process emphasizing protection against setback and positive social reinforcement. The experimental condition yielded significantly greater percentages of employed persons at four weeks and four months after the intervention than the control condition (a self-administered booklet). The reemployed had significantly less depression scores than the unemployed group, as well as less anxiety and anger and better self-esteem and rated quality of life.

The two preventive intervention projects noted above originate from the perspective of "stressful life events." For a comprehensive review of this research and its implications for prevention, see Bloom (1985).

The second issue, that of developing ways to make provision of preventive services more efficient and more practical, will require going beyond the traditional mental health model, which assumes that professionals will provide service directly. We will need to make available interventions that can be used by consumers at their convenience (both in terms of time and location). Chapter 22 addresses these options in greater detail.

8. Designing the Study: How Will You Measure the Effects of the Intervention?

In the last four chapters we addressed basic issues involved in launching a prevention program: stipulating the condition to be prevented, specifying the mechanisms hypothesized to be responsible for the appearance and duration of the condition, identifying the groups within the population that are most susceptible to the condition, and delineating the intervention intended to prevent the condition. In this chapter, we turn to the process of evaluating the effects of the preventive intervention on the target condition. As in other chapters, our focus will be on depression.

Elements of Outcome Studies

The basic logic behind the scientific evaluation of an intervention is to compare the effect of the intervention with the effect of either another intervention or no intervention at all (Hulley & Cummings, 1988). However, if we merely compared changes following an intervention administered to those who choose to take part in it with changes in those who did not receive the intervention because of lack of interest, any differences found could be due to differences between these two groups that have little or nothing to do with the intervention. For this reason, we recommend that outcome studies randomly assign individuals *who are interested in the intervention* to experimental and control conditions. Experimental conditions refer to those conditions that are intended to produce the preventive effect, while control conditions are either interventions that are not expected to have a preventive effect (but control for the attention or information given to participants in the experimental condition), or no interventions at all (generally termed "no-intervention control"). Such studies are called "randomized controlled trials."

At this stage in the development of methods to evaluate depression prevention interventions, several issues must be considered.

Appropriate Participants for Studies of Prevention

It is very important that prevention studies in the area of depression clearly include individuals who are *not* suffering from clinical episodes of depression. The danger is that money and time supposedly allocated to *prevention* research might be used to pursue studies of *treatment* outcome. Treatment outcome studies should definitely be supported, but not in the guise of prevention trials.

This proviso implies that some screening method be used to identify those persons who are already experiencing a clinical episode of depression. Such people should be referred for treatment. Failure to refer them for treatment raises ethical concerns: preventive interventions do not explicitly involve a therapeutic contract or close monitoring of individuals' symptoms. In addition, in a randomized preventive trial some participants may not receive any type of intervention. For those who are not clinically depressed, not receiving an experimental preventive intervention involves no risk. Those who are clinically depressed, however, ought to be informed of the availability of treatments for their condition, and encouraged to use them. If, in addition to referral to treatment, access to the prevention intervention were allowed, it might be of interest to track the level of depression throughout the intervention. Given that many clinically depressed people do not seek treatment, even when referred, it would be good to examine possible "treatment effects" of preventive interventions. If these preventive interventions were found to have these welcome "side effects," they might attain greater priority for funding. Still, such effects would not be preventive in the strict sense.

Components of Outreach

One of the differences between treatment services and preventive services involves who seeks whom. Generally, clinical services are offered to people who request them, usually because they are experiencing discomfort or pain. Preventive services, especially in the mental health field, are not yet advanced enough or available enough to have become as commonplace as dental checkups or childhood immunizations. Therefore, preventive mental health services require a strong outreach component. It is especially important to include in a preventive trial segments of the population that are not generally included in treatment studies and that underutilize treatment services. In the United States, these populations include those with low incomes, minorities, and non-English-speaking persons (Hough et al., 1987).

Longitudinal Follow-up

Preventive interventions are intended to have enduring effects. Unlike treatment interventions, which are intended to bring to an end a pathological process that is currently present, preventive interventions are intended to bring into play a process that will protect the individual from future clinical episodes. Therefore, it is important that changes be measured not only immediately after the intervention takes place, but for a long enough interval to ascertain whether the effects are enduring.

The length of the follow-up depends on the intervention. For example, imagine an intervention focused on the effect of marital satisfaction on depression. The intervention consists of educating adolescents about the realities of marriage, including having greater control over when one marries, choosing a marriage partner, information about how to avoid conceiving a child before one is ready to devote the time and resources needed to care for it adequately, and so on. Such an intervention would ideally result in a significant proportion of the adolescents delaying marriage for several years. Measurement of marital satisfaction could therefore not take place for long after the intervention ended. The effect of marital satisfaction on depression would also need to wait. In a way, the more far-reaching the intervention in terms of the participants' lives, the more important that long-term follow-ups take place, and the less likely that there will be large numbers of such studies. The amount of commitment required on the part of researchers and funding agencies is considerable.

To make such studies practical, researchers can include relatively short-term measures of change. For example, the number of marriages (and/or pregnancies) in the experimental group could be compared with control groups within the usual grant period. Subjective feelings of control over one's life and level of depressive symptoms could also be assessed to determine whether these factors have been affected. Examination of these findings could help policymakers decide whether to implement such interventions without waiting too many years. Researchers could also publish these findings to justify continued support for their research program.

The Measurement of Theorized Mediating Variables

Most interventions attempt to have an impact on factors that are hypothesized to have an effect on depression. These factors are believed to mediate changes in depression levels, that is, to play an intermediary role between the intention to maintain a healthy mood and the actual achievement of such a mood state. For example, various theories assign such elements as self-esteem, internal control, "rational" thinking, level of reinforcement, or ego strength as roles in the development of depression. Preventive interventions based on such theories are expected to produce their preventive effects by first affecting these elements. Thus, to properly test the theory, it is imperative that the proposed elements be measured.

Several outcomes are possible:

1. The mediating variables change, and depression is prevented. This outcome is the most supportive of the theory. Although it is possible that some other element, not measured, might have been the true cause of the preventive effect, the results of the experiment are consonant with the original hypothesis. In addition, the tested intervention has been found to be effective: both theory and practice have been advanced.
2. The mediating variables change, but there is no measurable effect on depression. This pattern suggests that the intervention successfully modified its intended target, but that these changes were not related to the ultimate goal of the intervention, that is, depression. The theory has not been supported, nor has the intervention been found to be effective for the prevention of depression.
3. The mediating variables do not change, but preventive effects are detected. This pattern suggests that other aspects of the intervention may have produced the preventive effects. The results do not support the theory, but the intervention has been found to be effective. Further research to identify the active ingredients responsible for the preventive effect are clearly in order. This type of result can be very influential in modifying theories of depression.
4. The mediating variables do not change, and neither is there a preventive effect. This can be the most demoralizing result for the prevention professional. Of course, these results are also consonant with the theory in that, if the intervention did not produce the intended effects on the mediating variables, a preventive effect ought not to have occurred. The logical next step is to change the intervention so that it does affect the mediating variables.

The Measurement of Moderator Variables

Moderator variables are factors that change the effect of mediating variables on the outcome variable. Such variables can amplify or nullify the effect of mediators. For example, let's say that a certain preventive intervention teaches participants how to think constructively when major disappointments occur in their lives. These changes in thinking style might be detectable only when negative life events occur (Metalsky et al., 1982). These changes in thinking might not have a noticeable effect on depression if both groups being compared have too low a level of life changes. It is only when major negative life events occur, and they are included in the analysis, that changes in thinking style would be found to have a protective effect.

True Experiments versus Quasiexperimental Designs

There is some controversy surrounding the advisability of conducting true experiments (Campbell & Stanley, 1963), such as randomized controlled trials, at this time in the development of the preventive mental health field. The argument could be made that we first need systematic research programs that examine in detail such factors as interest in prevention services, recruitment methods, adaptation of interventions to narrowly defined high-risk groups (including cultural and linguistic issues), development and norming of measures for each of the identified groups, and single-group studies to determine elements of the intervention that need further work. On the other hand, there is no substitute for a randomized controlled trial to answer the question of whether the preventive intervention was significantly better than no intervention or a comparison condition (Price & Smith, 1985).

Whether or not true experiments are "premature" is ultimately a matter of judgment. Researchers need to decide if the potential benefits of testing preventive interventions for depression sooner rather than later outweigh the risks of having inconclusive effects because the measurement and the intervention methods have not been sufficiently developed.

Part III

The San Francisco Depression Prevention Research Project

9. Overview of the Depression Prevention Research Project

In this chapter, we will illustrate the steps described in Part II by sharing our experiences in conducting the San Francisco Depression Prevention Research Project (DPRP).

Identifying the Target

For the randomized trial of the Depression Prevention Research Project, we chose to target both depressive symptoms and depressive disorders, namely major depression and dysthymia. Since this was, to our knowledge, the first randomized controlled prevention trial focused on depression, we had no data on the effectiveness of preventive interventions.

Several important pieces of information were unavailable at the time we designed the study:

1. Rates of incidence of major depression were relatively hard to find, and differed widely from study to study (Boyd & Weissman, 1982). The Epidemiological Catchment Area incidence data were not available at the time. They have since been reported (Eaton et al., 1989).
2. The effect of cognitive-behavioral intervention for the treatment of depression was very promising, but it had not yet been used for prevention, nor had it been properly evaluated in a population of primary care patients, most of whom, of course, had physical illnesses. (Having a physical illness has generally been an exclusionary criteria in depression treatment outcome studies.)
3. Intervention studies with low-income and minority populations were rare, and often reported high dropout rates. Most treatment outcome studies have been conducted with white middle-class populations.

In sum, we were extrapolating along a number of dimensions simultaneously. Thus, it made sense to target depression both in the form of depressive symptoms and depressive disorders in the first depression prevention trial.

Choosing a Theory to Guide the Intervention

The DPRP was based on a social learning conception (Bandura, 1969, 1977) of depression derived primarily from the work of Peter M. Lewinsohn (Lewinsohn, 1975; Zeiss, Lewinsohn & Muñoz, 1979), and that of the varied types of cognitive and behavioral therapies (Beck, Rush, Shaw & Emery, 1979; Ellis, 1962; Ellis & Harper, 1961; Kelly, 1955; Mahoney & Thoresen, 1974).

The syndrome of depression was conceptualized as consisting of a number of related symptoms stemming from an overall deterioration in mood state. A reciprocal process was hypothesized involving mood, thoughts, and behaviors: specific thoughts and behaviors increase or decrease the likelihood of depressed mood, and depressed mood in turn increases the likelihood that depressive thinking and behavior will occur. This description permits thoughts and behaviors to play roles as either triggers or sustainers of the depressive process or both. Reducing thoughts and behaviors related to depressed mood is hypothesized to attenuate levels of depressive symptoms, until they reach normal proportions. Although several classes of thought and behavior pattern can be defined as being common in depressed persons, and although a generalized method of intervention is suggested by this approach, social learning theory also emphasizes individual differences. Thus, individuals are expected to have idiosyncratic thoughts and behavior patterns that are most powerfully connected with depressed mood.

A self-control emphasis was also important in the conceptualization of depression and its prevention in the DPRP. Persons were considered to be at greater risk for depression if they engaged in maladaptive styles of self-monitoring, self-evaluation, and self-reinforcement (Rehm, 1977). Thus, part of the intervention would need to address the person's ability to identify different levels of mood in themselves, to recognize thoughts and behaviors, and to make a conscious connection among these factors. Then, interventions could be implemented that were designed to decrease depressogenic thoughts and behaviors and to engage in healthy levels and types of such cognitions and actions. These interventions could then be judged in terms of their effectiveness in changing the thoughts and actions as well as in producing relatively better mood states.

Some comments regarding the biological and environmental aspects of depression are in order here. We assume that biological mechanisms are involved in all human functioning. Thoughts, behaviors, and emotions are, at one level, biological events in the central nervous system. At an even more basic level, they involve atomic and subatomic interactions governed by the laws of physics. At a higher level of analysis, these phenomena can be characterized as psychological processes, such as those described in theories of learning, memory, motivation, social interaction, and so on. Moving farther up the hierarchy of levels of analysis, it is clear that the social and physical environment, including such aspects as economic, historical, and cultural influences, can affect rates of depression, if nothing else because of the stresses it induces.

From our clinical experience and our reading of the clinical and research literature on depression, it appears to us that the capacity to experience depressed mood is a normal human ability. Accordingly, all normal human beings can experience depressed mood. Given sufficient stress, deprivation, or physical insults, all humans are capable of severe depressed states. At the same time, it is very clear that some individuals are at much higher risk for depression than others, and that some individuals, even when they succumb to depressive episodes, can bounce back relatively quickly, while others become mired in them. There is now sufficient information from twin and other family studies that a family history of depression is a risk factor for depression. At least some of this risk appears to be genetic, as strongly supported by monozygotic twin adoption studies (Andreasen, in press), in which relatives of bipolar probands appear to have increased risk not only of bipolar disorder but also of unipolar depression. However, it is very likely that major depressive syndromes may stem from several sources, only one of which may be the genetic susceptibility connected to bipolar disorder.

Another fairly clear aspect of depression is the disruption of bodily functions that accompanies the depressive syndrome: psychomotor retardation, lack of energy, inability to enjoy formerly pleasurable activities, problems with sleep, and problems with appetite. This suggests a fairly pervasive biological dysregulation, which could be the result of either the severe and persistent depressed mood or a more basic dysregulation, underlying both the somatic symptoms and the depressed mood. Of course, it is also possible that there is a reciprocal interaction between reactive mood states and longer lasting biological processes. If this were the case, regardless of which process is chronologically earlier in a particular episode, their inextricable relationship could augment their individual intensity and duration. Psychological interventions designed to dampen their reciprocal effects by systematically reducing the negative mood state would be expected to help normalize whatever biological processes are involved in most episodes of major depression. Similarly, interventions designed to act directly on biological mechanisms could be expected eventually to modify mood states as well as related cognitive and behavioral processes. Support for these ideas can be found in the literature on treatment outcome, which shows very clearly that episodes of major depression commonly seen in outpatient settings can be treated very effectively with either pharmacotherapy or psychological interventions focused specifically on the depressed state (Hollon & Najavits, 1988; Hollon, Shelton & Loosen, 1991; Rehm, in press; Weissman, Jarrett & Rush, 1987). As far as prevention efforts are concerned, psychological methods, being less physically invasive, having no physical side effects, and being usable when needed by the individual, are currently more advisable.

A metaphor that we find helpful to use in discussing various approaches to the treatment of depression is that the mechanism involved in depression resembles a massive machine run by numerous sets of gears, each of which has its own handle. When depression strikes, this large machine begins to slow down, as though the works were "gummed up." When treating depression, the therapist grabs hold of the handle that he or she has learned to manipulate, and slowly begins to turn the particular set of gears connected to that handle. As these gears pick up speed, the entire machinery begins to speed up, until the entire machine is running properly. The pharmacotherapist works with the biological gears, the cognitive therapist with thoughts, the behavioral therapist with activities, and so on. If they are effective at changing their target, the depression should lift.

Preventive interventions are intended to give the participants a basic understanding of the depression mechanism, and teach them to turn certain handles themselves. Ideally, the individual will keep the machine running at a good speed, so that it does not slow down at all. And if it begins to do so, due to stress, illness, and so on, the individual can turn the crank more conscientiously, to forestall a full-blown episode.

Identifying High-Risk Groups

The choice of the high-risk population in the Depression Prevention Research Project was influenced by various factors. First, data from several studies indicated that there was a high prevalence of depressive disorders in primary care populations. We assumed that it was unlikely that individuals made the decision to seek medical help only once they met clinical criteria for depression. More likely, the probability of seeking such help increased as depressive symptoms increased. Thus, people becoming depressed, but not yet clinically depressed, would be likely to go to primary care clinics. This suggested that not only the prevalence but also the incidence would be high in primary care settings. At the time the study was being planned (1982), only reports of the prevalence of depressive symptoms and depressive episodes in primary care settings were available. Thus, it was difficult to predict the rates of incidence.

In addition to the rates of depressive symptomatology and depressive disorders in primary care settings, there was a growing literature on high rates of depressive symptoms in low income and minority populations. In a review of studies using the Center for Epidemiological Studies—Depression Scale (CES-D), Roberts (1987) reported the highest proportions of high symptomatology (using the traditional cutoff score of 16) in African American and Latino samples. Moreover, he reported that socioeconomic status accounted for most of this effect. In studies conducted by Vega (1980), non-English-speaking Latinos in California had higher levels of depressive symptoms than did English-speaking Latinos. Thus, minority status, poverty, and inability to speak English all contributed to higher depressive symptoms and, possibly, to having a greater risk of crossing over the threshold for depressive disorders.

Finally, a growing literature pointed out that the utilization of mental health services for depression was much lower than the prevalence would suggest. In the general population, only twenty percent of those meeting DSM-III criteria for depression sought mental health care. Minorities were less likely to seek such help than whites: in the UCLA ECA study, of those meeting DSM-III criteria, Mexican Americans were half as likely as whites to seek mental health care (11% of Mexican Americans versus 22% of non-Hispanic whites). In addition, primary care physicians greatly underrecognized clinical depression in their patients: rates of recognition hovered around thirty-three percent across studies. Further, the physicians in the clinics we were about to study reported to us that, even when depression was recognized, many of them had stopped referring their patients to treatment because they found that the patients did not follow through.

These factors indicated that a primary care clinic serving low-income, predominantly minority patients would be likely to have a high incidence of depression. Similarly, persons attending such a clinic would be less likely to obtain mental health treatment if they became clinically depressed. These factors alone suggested that this population is a reasonable sample for a prevention study.

In terms of future applications, having a working prevention program based in a primary care setting seemed ideal for the possible adoption of the preventive service. We hoped to be able to proceed with a working preventive program once the study was over.

Designing the Intervention: The Depression Prevention Course

The intervention that was evaluated in the DPRP was an eight-session course given in a weekly two-hour meetings of a group of no more than ten participants led by one instructor. The Depression Prevention Course (Muñoz, 1982) included a number of cognitive-behavioral techniques focusing on three main areas: thoughts, increasing pleasant activities, and interpersonal skills. The primary source for these techniques was the book *Control Your Depression*, by Peter M. Lewinsohn, Ricardo F. Muñoz, Mary Ann Youngren, and Antonette M. Zeiss (1978, 1986). This book included the therapeutic procedures used in a randomized controlled depression treatment trial conducted earlier by the authors (Zeiss, Lewinsohn & Muñoz, 1979). The Depression Prevention Course materials were designed to be taught to persons who were not clinically depressed, deliberately making available to them the same self-control skills that depressed persons learned in treatment. The DPRP would evaluate whether teaching these skills had a measurable effect on depression symptoms and episodes of clinical depression.

We decided to have the instructors be doctoral level psychologists. Two large jumps had already been made by (1) using these methods for prevention in nondepressed persons, rather than for treatment in clinically depressed persons, and (2) applying them to a population of medical patients, many of them low-income minorities, rather than to white middle class patients with no significant medical problems. We hoped that the effectiveness of the intervention would be increased by having instructors with advanced training in psychology similar to that of the therapists in the study in which these methods had been tested previously (Zeiss, Lewinsohn & Muñoz, 1979).

To assure that the intervention was implemented in a replicable fashion, we prepared a written protocol consisting of two parts: Outlines for Participants and Lecture Notes for Instructors. Appendix A contains excerpts from each of these parts for each of the eight sessions.

Designing the Study

The specifics of the design, sampling, measures, and procedures are detailed in Chapter 10. Among the elements that were high in our priority list as we designed the DPRP were:

1. The study was to be a true preventive study, and thus did not include individuals who were already in need of treatment. We used a diagnostic instrument to screen for (and refer for treatment) those who were clinically depressed or who had other psychiatric disorders.
2. The study was to include those portions of the community that were generally underserved. Thus, we chose to work in primary care clinics, including public sector clinics with low-income and minority populations. We also included persons using the clinics who were not English-speaking. The main study included Spanish-speaking individuals, the largest non-English-speaking group in the clinics. We also conducted a pilot study in Chinese (Cantonese and Mandarin).
3. The sample was to be followed beyond the period immediately after the intervention. We conducted follow-ups at posttreatment, six months, and twelve months after the initial screening.
4. The theorized mediating variables to which preventive effects were to be attributed were assessed. The logic was that in addition to merely testing for preventive effects, the variables that ostensibly mediated the effect would be measured to determine if they were affected by the intervention. Whether or not effects on these mediators were related to effects on depression variables would also be measured. The mediating variables in the DPRP included thoughts, expectations, assumptions, pleasant activities, and social activities.
5. Moderator variables, such as social support and life events, were also examined to determine if they had an impact on the results.
6. The design was to be a true experiment, in which the assignment to a condition would be made only when volunteers had completed all screening procedures and had demonstrated that they would be participating in the study. Assignment would be done randomly, so that we would be able to attribute changes, if any, to the intervention and not to self-selection factors.

10. Methods

This chapter explains the procedures and measures utilized in the San Francisco Depression Prevention Research Project (DPRP).

The Procedure of the DPRP

Recruitment

Given the previously documented finding that ethnic minorities report higher levels of depressive symptomatology and may be in greater need of preventive interventions, we paid particular attention to reaching an ethnically diverse sample at the outset of the study.

Recruitment for the DPRP occurred at three primary care sites: (1) University of California at San Francisco Moffitt Hospital Internal Medicine Clinic (UCSF group); (2) San Francisco General Hospital General Medical Clinic (SFGH-ENG Group); and (3) San Francisco General Hospital Family Practice Clinic (SFGH-SPAN Group). All three clinics were included in the recruitment effort to better represent the population seeking public medical services in San Francisco.

The UCSF and SFGH General Medical Clinics serve primarily older and chronically ill patients. Because of their location, UCSF serves more white and economically less impoverished San Francisco residents, and SFGH General Medical Clinic serves many more African Americans with lower income. The SFGH Family Practice Clinic serves young families with their children. Because of the large immigrant Latino community in the immediate vicinity of SFGH, this clinic also serves a large number of Spanish-speaking women and their children. Recruitment at this clinic targeted Spanish-speaking patients only. For them, the study was administered entirely in Spanish (including assessments and intervention). Both UCSF and SFGH General Medical Clinics also serve some Asian/Pacific Islander patients, but they are small in number as compared with the other ethnic groups. It is likely that many of the Asian/Pacific Islander residents who use public health services prefer to use the ones in their community (such as those located in the San Francisco Chinatown) rather than traveling to either UCSF or SFGH.

The number of prospective participants partaking in the screening and the presence of differences across recruitment sites are further assessed in the next chapter.

Screenings

Prospective participants were initially screened in person or by mail. In-person recruitment was conducted by DPRP interviewers who approached patients waiting to see their physicians in the various clinics. If patients were interested in being screened for participation in the study, they were administered the Demographics Questionnaire and the Center for Epidemiological Studies–Depression Scale (CES-D; Radloff, 1977). Recruitment by mail targeted patients who had a clinic appointment in the preceding six months, to whom the first screening measures were sent.

All participants signed a consent form at the time of the first screening. In it, the study aim was described as "to understand depression in medical outpatients. We want to know (1) how people control their feelings of depression naturally, (2) whether we can teach people ways to control them even better, and (3) how their mood affects their health."

Criteria for continuation with further screening included: (1) age between 18 and 69; (2) literacy in English or Spanish (so they could complete the study questionnaires and the homework assigned in the class intervention); (3) having a medical chart open for at least six months (thereby allowing for detection of change in medical condition while participating in the study); (4) not terminally ill (as determined by the physician); and (5) not currently receiving mental health treatment.

All second screenings occurred in person. This interview entailed the administration of the Beck Depression Inventory (BDI; Beck et al., 1979) and the NIMH Diagnostic Interview Schedule (DIS; Robins et al., 1981). The latter produced DSM-III diagnoses on most Axis I major disorders, including major depression and dysthymia. Participants were paid ten dollars for this interview. For all participants of the second screening, their medical chart was reviewed to assess their medical diagnosis/diagnoses, number of outpatient visits and/or hospitalization days.

The final screening included a series of paper-and-pencil and orally administered measures, and participants were once again paid ten dollars for participation in this screening. These instruments assessed recent life events (Sarason, Johnson & Siegel, 1978), family history of psychological disorders (Muñoz, 1983), social desirability (Crowne &

Marlowe, 1960), positive and negative affect (Affect-Balance Scale; Bradburn, 1969), quality of life (Flanagan, 1978), and those examining various cognitions and behaviors that were the targets of the experimental intervention: the Personal Beliefs Inventory, Subjective Probability Questionnaire, and Cognitive Events (Muñoz, 1977), Pleasant Activities Schedule (Lewinsohn, Biglan & Zeiss, 1976), Social Activities Questionnaire, and the Assertion Questionnaire (Zeiss, Lewinsohn & Muñoz, 1979).

At the completion of the screening process, those meeting the inclusionary criteria were offered participation in the depression prevention trial. In addition to age, literacy, and absence of terminal illness, other inclusionary criteria were: (1) not meeting DSM III/DIS criteria for current diagnosis (within the last six months) of major depression, bipolar disorder, drug or alcohol abuse and/or dependence, or lifetime diagnosis of organic brain syndrome or schizophrenia; or (2) not judged to be inappropriate for the class or in need of immediate treatment (e.g., suicidal); and (3) the ability to attend the eight-week sessions if assigned to the class conditions. Those meeting current diagnosis or judged to be in need of clinical treatment were referred for mental health treatment.

Randomization and Randomized Conditions

Upon agreeing to randomization, the participants were randomly assigned (with stratification by language and sex) to Class, Control (no intervention) and Video (information-only control) conditions. The Class condition involved an eight-week, two-hour per week intervention, in which participants were taught social learning, self-control techniques to improve their mood and prevent depression. The Video condition participants were administered a forty-minute videotape presentation briefly covering the methods discussed in the classes, and the Control condition received no intervention. Since the Class condition was the primary intervention of interest, a randomization ratio of 2:1:1 for Class:Video:Control conditions was used. The randomized SFGH-SPAN group was assigned to either the Class or the Control condition, because the videotape was not available in Spanish.

Follow-up Assessments

All randomized participants were administered post-testing upon completion of the intervention. We will refer to this assessment as the "post-follow-up." In addition, follow-up assessments were conducted at designated times after their initial administration: at six months and twelve months. Most of the measures were administered at all three follow-up assessments points, except for demographics and family history of psychological disorders, as these were, by and large, not expected to change. The DIS was readministered only at one-year follow-up to obtain incidence data. A listing of the instruments administered at each timeline is presented in Table 10.1.

Interviewers administering the follow-up instruments were blind to the condition of assignment. Participants were paid ten dollars for the post- and six-months follow-up interviews. At one-year follow-up, they were paid twenty dollars, as the interview involved the readministration of the DIS, extending its length to two hours from the usual one hour. To encourage Class condition participants to attend all/many class sessions, a bonus system was instituted and presented at the beginning of the class sessions and implemented at follow-up assessments. At postintervention follow-up, this was an "all-or-none system." Those who attended all class sessions were given a bonus of eight dollars in addition to the regular ten-dollar payment. If any class

Table 10.1. Measures Administered by Assessment Period

Measure	Pre	Follow-up		
		Post	6 Months	12 Months
Demographics	x			
Family history of psychiatric disorder	x			
Center for Epidemiologic Studies–Depression Scale (CES-D)	x	x	x	x
Beck Depression Inventory (BDI)	x	x	x	x
Diagnostic Interview Schedule (DIS)	x			x
Quality of Life	x	x	x	x
Affect-balance (AB)	x	x	x	x
Medical chart review	x			x
Physical Symptoms Checklist	x	x	x	x
Personal Beliefs Inventory (PBI)	x	x	x	x
Subjective Probability Questionnaire (SPQ)	x	x	x	x
Cognitive Events Schedule (CES)	x	x	x	x
Pleasant Activities Schedule (PAS)	x	x	x	x
Social Activities Questionnaire (SAQ)	x	x	x	x
Assertion Questionnaire (AQ)	x	x	x	x
Life Experiences Survey (LES)	x		x	x
Crowne-Marlowe Social Desirability	x	x	x	x

was missed, no bonus was offered. At six-months and one-year follow-up, a different system was instituted. Class participants were paid an additional one dollar for every class they attended. Participants were thus encouraged to attend all sessions, but if one or a few were missed, monetary incentive was still provided for continued attendance.

The Instruments of the DPRP

Next, we present the measures utilized in the DPRP. Copies of previously unpublished measures (e.g., the cognitive-behavioral instruments) may be found in Appendix B.

Demographics

The Demographics Questionnaire was designed to assess basic sociodemographic characteristics of the medical patients. These included sex, age, marital status, ethnicity, education, occupation, income, and health status information. In addition, the current utilization of mental health/alcohol and drug treatments was assessed, as it served as an exclusionary criterion.

A Family History of Psychiatric Disorder

The presence of a family history of psychological disorder was assessed by a measure specifically constructed for this study (Muñoz, 1983). It inquired if the participant's biological parents, maternal and paternal grandparents, and siblings had ever suffered from emotional illness. If any of these relatives was reported as having a history of emotional illness, the participant was coded as positive for a family history of psychiatric disorder. Of the 228 participants who completed this instrument, 88 (or 38.60%) indicated a presence of family history of psychiatric disorder, while the remaining 140 did not.

Symptoms of Depression

We used two measures of depressive symptomatology: the CES-D (Radloff, 1977) and the BDI (Beck et al., 1961). While both assessed depressive level, the CES-D has been used often in community-based epidemiological studies, whereas the BDI was preferred in clinical trials.

The CES-D consisted of twenty items; sixteen reflected symptoms of depression and four reflected positive mood (which were reversed during scoring). The items were rated from 0 to 3 by the respondent, with a possible range of 0 to 60, where higher scores signified greater levels of depression. The usual cutoff score for "significant" levels of depressive symptoms was 16. The CES-D does not identify specific depressive disorders; it is not a diagnostic tool. We shall comment on this later in the chapter. In a representative national survey, the CES-D mean was found to be 8.7 (standard deviation [SD] = 8.4) (Sayetta & Johnson, 1980).

In tests conducted in household interview surveys and psychiatric settings, the CES-D was found to have very high internal consistency and adequate test-retest reliability. Validity was established by patterns of correlations with other self-report measures, by correlations with clinical ratings of depression, and by relationships with other variables that support its construct validity (Radloff, 1977). Its psychometric properties in nonwhite populations have also been assessed and found to be good (for example, see Kuo, 1984; Roberts, 1980; Roberts & Vernon, 1983; Ying, 1988).

The test-retest reliability of the instruments used in the DPRP was assessed by comparing the preintervention score with the post-, six-months, and one-year follow-up scores in Control condition participants. CES-D scores at the three follow-up points were found to be significantly correlated with the pre-CES-D score (Pearson's $r = .59$, $p = .001$, $n = 43$, with the post-follow-up score; $r = .53$, $p = .001$, $n = 44$, with the six-months follow-up score; $r = .39$, $p = .01$, $n = 45$, with the one-year follow-up score). In addition, the coefficient alpha measuring internal consistency of the CES-D was found to be .81 ($n = 552$). Respondents with a family history of psychiatric disorders reported a significantly higher level of CES-D score than those without a family history (mean of 21.03 and 17.16, respectively, $t = 2.25$, $df = 225$, $p = .03$).

The development of the BDI was based on the rationale that depression consisted of characteristic attitudes and symptoms that may be assessed on a self-report scale. Beck (1967) observed his depressed patients and identified twenty-one characteristic categories of attitudes and symptoms. He then developed a graded series of four self-evaluative statements for each category, which were chosen on the basis of their relationship to overt behavioral manifestations of depression. They were ranked to reflect the range of severity of the symptom, from neutral to maximal severity. Numerical values from 0 to 3 were assigned to each statement to indicate the degree of severity. The final BDI score was obtained from summing item scores. In 1978, the BDI was revised to improve the clarity of the statements (Beck et al., 1979). The revised BDI was used in our study.

Many studies assessing the psychometric properties of the BDI were reviewed by Beck, Steer, and Garbin (1988). They reported the internal consistency of the BDI to range from coefficient alpha = .73 to .92; test-retest reliability Pearson's r ranged from .48 to .86. They also found its concurrent validity with other measures of depression and its construct validity with other measures of psychopathology to be high.

Alpha reliability of the BDI was found to be .89 (n = 268) in our study. Using only DPRP Control condition participants, the test-retest reliability of the BDI score at post-, six-months, and one-year follow-up was compared with the pre-score. The results for these tests at the various time periods were: Pearson's r = .64, p = .001, n = 43; r = .70, p = .001, n = 44; and r = .55, p = .001, n = 45, respectively. As in the case of the CES-D, those with a family history of psychiatric disorders reported a higher level of depression as measured by the BDI than those who did not have a comparable history (means of 16.36 and 13.27, respectively, t = 2.47, df = 225, p = .01).

Although the two measures of depressive symptomatology had been found to be significantly correlated (in our study, Pearson's r = .64, p = .001, n = 295), studies examining the factor structure of the two scales show they tapped different aspects of depression. The CES-D items were found to address primarily the affective aspect of depression, and secondarily somatic and interpersonal symptoms (e.g., Radloff, 1977; Roberts, Vernon & Rhoades, 1989; Ying, 1988). On the other hand, the BDI items focused primarily on depressive cognitions (Beck et al., 1988; Louks, Hayne & Smith, 1989), consistent with its author's interest in cognitive treatment of depression. When we subjected the CES-D and BDI items to a factor analysis, the results supported previous findings. Four factors with an eigenvalue greater than 1 were created, three of which composed solely of CES-D (positive affect) or solely of BDI items (cognitive and somatic). The only exception was the affect factor, which consists primarily of CES-D items (ten such items) and only three BDI items. The CES-D items were more strongly loaded (from .75 to .40) than the BDI items (.36 to .25) to the affect factor. Thus, inclusion of these two measures allowed for the specification of the dimension of depression most affected by the experimental intervention. If change occurred primarily on the CES-D but not on the BDI, this would imply success in modification of affect. On the other hand, if change occurred primarily on the BDI, the implication is that the locus of change lies primarily with the cognitive and somatic symptoms.

Methods

DSM-III Diagnoses

Diagnoses of major depression, dysthymia and other clinical syndromes were made using the DIS (Robins et al., 1981), a computer-scored structured interview designed to be conducted by lay interviewers. The investigators received training in its use from its developers, and, in turn, trained the DPRP staff. In addition to disqualifying those prospective participants already clinically depressed before the intervention, the DIS was used to identify participants who became clinically depressed during the one-year follow-up. Robins et al. (1981) reported data supporting the validity of the instrument.

Measures of depressive symptomatology and clinical diagnosis were included to assess depression as a continuous phenomenon as well as a discrete entity. Previous findings had shown the CES-D and BDI to hold a less than perfect relationship to DSM-III diagnosis of major depression (Myers & Weissman, 1980b; Oliver & Simmons, 1984; Roberts & Vernon, 1981; Roberts et al., 1989). In our study, we found a significant difference in depression symptom level (as measured by the CES-D and BDI) for those who did and did not meet DIS/DSM-III diagnosis of major depression, current (i.e., within the last six months). Compared with those who did not meet diagnostic criteria, those currently suffering from major depression reported significantly more depressive symptoms on both the CES-D (mean = 18.15 and 29.41, respectively, $t = -5.49$, $df = 294$, $p = .0001$) and BDI (mean = 13.76 and 25.73, respectively, $t = -7.74$, $p = .0001$).

While the intent of our intervention was to reduce the symptom level and incidence of clinical disorder, it was also possible that only one would be significantly affected. Inclusion of both types of measures helped to determine whether symptom level, incidence, or both were reduced by the intervention.

The relationship of a family history of psychiatric disorder and major DIS/DSM-III lifetime clinical diagnoses was also assessed. Chi-Square tests revealed a nonsignificant relationship with organic brain syndrome, bipolar illness, schizophrenia, alcohol and drug abuse and/or dependence. A significant positive relationship between a family history of psychiatric illness and major depression (Chi-Square = 15.05, $df = 1$, $p = .0001$) and dysthymia (Chi-Square = 4.36, $df = 1$, $p = .04$) was found. The proportion of respondents meeting diagnostic criteria for major depression ever in their lifetime were 34.48 percent and 12.86 percent, respectively, for those with and without a family history. The corresponding proportions meeting criteria for dysthymia were 13.79 percent and 5.71 percent.

Psychological Well-being

Psychological well-being was assessed by Flanagan's (1978, 1979) Quality of Life Score and Bradburn and Caplovitz's (1965) positive and negative Affect-Balance Scores.

Upon collecting more than 6,500 critical incidents from nearly 3,000 people of various ages, races, and backgrounds from different regions of the United States, Flanagan (1978, 1979) reduced these to fifteen major life components, and constructed an item assessing overall life quality which was adopted for the study.

The test-retest reliability of the overall life quality item in the DPRP was as follows: at post-follow-up, Pearson's r= .32, p = .04, n = 42; at six-months follow-up, r = .74, p = .001, n = 43; at one-year follow-up, r = .31, p = .05, n = 40. Life quality was significantly negatively correlated with depressive level (with both the CES-D and BDI, r = −.48, p = .0001, n = 226). Those who met current diagnostic criteria for major depression also reported significantly poorer life quality than their nondepressed counterparts (mean life quality = 2.39 versus 3.04, t = 3.32, df = 224, p = .001, with higher scores on a five-point scale signifying better perceived quality of life). Finally, persons with a family history of psychiatric illness reported poorer life quality than those who did not have such a history (mean = 2.73 and 3.05, respectively, t = −2.07, df = 217, p = .04).

The Affect-Balance Scale measured psychological well-being as a function of two independent dimensions: positive and negative affect (Bradburn, 1969; Bradburn & Caplovitz, 1965). It was postulated (and found) that the two dimensions were relatively independent of each other. Two scores were derived from the scale, the AB+ and AB− scores, obtained by summing the items measuring positive and negative affect, respectively.

In studies of urban and suburban populations, Bradburn (1969) found the AB+ to be significantly correlated with social contact and active interest in the world, while AB− was associated with poor health and high anxiety, which were replicated in later studies (e.g., Andrews & Withey, 1976; Harding, 1982). He also reported high test-retest reliability over a three-day period; for AB+, r = .83, and for AB−, r = .81, with n = 174.

In the DPRP, the test-retest reliability of AB+ was .65 (p = .001, n = 44) at post-, .69 (p = .001, n = 44) at six-months, and .46 (p = .002, n = 45) at twelve-months follow-up. For AB−, the test-retest reliability coefficient was .68 (p = .001, n = 44) at post-, .61 (p = .001, n = 44) at six-months, and .34 (p = .02, n = 45) at one-year follow-up. Internal consistency for AB+ was found to be .71 (n = 228), and .75 (n = 228) for

AB−. AB+ was significantly negatively correlated with CES-D (r = −.34, p = .0001) and BDI scores (r = −.40, p = .0001), while AB− was significantly positively correlated with CES-D (r = .55, p = .0001) and BDI (r = .53, p = .0001), n = 234 in all cases. Participants suffering from current major depression also scored significantly lower than those who did not meet diagnostic criteria on AB+ (mean = 2.30 versus 2.89, respectively, t = −2.03, df = 232, p = .001) but higher on AB− (mean = 3.38 versus 1.82, respectively, t = 5.26, df = 232, p = .0001). While AB+ was not significantly correlated with a family history of psychiatric disorder, AB− was, with those who had such a history scoring significantly higher than those who did not (means of 2.56 and 1.78, respectively, t = 3.35, df = 225, p = .001).

As in the case of depressive symptomatology, two measures of psychological well-being were utilized. The positive and negative affect scores were significantly correlated with the quality of life item, r = .38, and r = −.51 (p = .001, n = 224), respectively, yet they were conceptually different. The life quality item, following a series of questions requiring the respondent to rate the importance of various domains of their life and the extent to which the needs in these areas were met, involved a cognitive appraisal that was relatively long-term and stable. Affect-Balance, as its name implied, on the other hand, focused on the emotional experience of the respondent, and was likely to be more short-term and fluctuating, as it inquired about one's mood "during the past few weeks." This distinction had been repeatedly upheld in the literature (Abbey & Andrews, 1986; Andrews & McKennell, 1980; Campbell, Converse & Rodgers, 1976; McKennell, 1978; McKennell & Andrews, 1980). Inclusion of both measures allowed for the determination of whether the intervention modified short-term affective or more long-term cognitive appraisal of one's life, or both.

Physical Symptoms Checklist

The Physical Symptoms Checklist was derived from the standard review of systems section of a complete medical history (DeGowin & DeGowin, 1976) and the Hopkins Symptoms Checklist (Lipman, Covi & Shapiro, 1979). The Checklist consisted of thirty items, and was scored by adding the number of items currently experienced by the participant.

The test-retest reliability of the Physical Symptoms Checklist score from initial screening to post-, six-months, and one-year follow-ups was found to be good; Pearson's r = .63 (p = .001, n = 43) at post-; r = .73 (p = .001, n = 44) at six-months; r = .50 (p = .001, n = 45) at one-year follow-up. Coefficient alpha was high, i.e., .89 (n = 223). Presence of larger numbers of symptoms was positively correlated with high depressive symptomatology (with CES-D, $r = .42$, and with BDI, $r = .48$, $p = .0001$, $n = 236$ in both cases). Respondents who met diagnostic criteria for current major depression were found to report higher numbers of physical symptoms than those who did not (mean = 11.30 versus 7.54, $t = 3.40$, respectively, $df = 234$, $p = .001$). The number of physical symptoms did not hold a significant relationship with AB+, but was significantly negatively correlated with life quality ($r = -.31$, $p = .0001$, $n = 226$), and positively correlated with AB− ($r = .29$, $p = .0001$, $n = 234$). Those with a family history had a mean of 9.40 symptoms versus 7.29 symptoms for those without such a history ($t = 2.49$, $df = 225$, $p = .01$)

Review of the Medical Chart

We reviewed the medical chart for those participants who completed the DIS for the number of outpatient visits and hospitalizations in the previous year. When thirty randomly selected charts were reviewed by a second auditor, complete reliability was found (i.e., 100 percent agreement).

The number of outpatient visits was positively correlated with number of physical symptoms ($r = .24$, $p = .0003$, $n = 215$). Contrary to expectation, the number of hospitalizations was negatively correlated with CES-D score ($r = -.14$, $p = .02$, $n = 260$) and AB− ($r = -.16$, $p = .02$, $n = 210$). This means that fewer hospitalizations were marginally correlated with greater depressive level and negative affect. The medical chart review variables did not vary by presence of a family history of psychiatric disorders, nor presence of current major depression.

Cognitive-Behavioral Measures

Six cognitive-behavioral (C-B) scales were utilized in this study. The three measures used to assess cognition were the Personal Beliefs Inventory (PBI; Muñoz, 1977), the Subjective Probability Questionnaire (SPQ; Muñoz, 1977), and the Cognitive Events Schedule (CES; Muñoz, 1977). The behavioral variables were the Pleasant Activities Schedule (PAS; MacPhillamy & Lewinsohn, 1971), the Social Activities Questionnaire (SAQ; Youngren, 1978; Youngren, Zeiss & Lewinsohn, 1975; Zeiss, Lewinsohn & Muñoz, 1979), and the Assertion Questionnaire (AQ; Youngren, 1978; Youngren, Zeiss & Lewinsohn, 1975).

The Personal Beliefs Inventory (PBI) measured the extent of "irrational beliefs" (Ellis, 1962; Ellis & Harper, 1961) held. It was designed to test the hypothesis that psychological difficulties (i.e., depression in this case) stemmed from such maladaptive or dysfunctional beliefs. Muñoz (1977) developed the thirty-item PBI, Form M-1 by adopting fifteen belief items from Hartman's (1968) Personal Beliefs Scale (but excluded the behavioral and symptom-related items), and the other fifteen items from beliefs inventories furnished by Gerald Kranzler of the University of Oregon. The version of the PBI used in the DPRP was PBI, Form M-2, and consisted of thirteen items found to discriminate most between a depressed and nondepressed sample in Muñoz's (1977) study. The "most discriminating items" were those to which the depressed group (in the original study) responded significantly differently in the predicted direction from the nondepressed controls.

The PBI items were scored on a five-point scale, reflecting (1) high disagreement to (5) high agreement. All items indicated maladaptive beliefs, and higher scores (obtained by adding the ratings) reflected greater dysfunctional beliefs. The possible range of scores was from 13 to 65. Depressed individuals were expected to score higher than nondepressed people.

Muñoz (1977) reported a significant difference ($p < .001$) in the predicted direction at initial assessment among the three groups he studied, with the depressed group scoring significantly higher than the two nondepressed groups. The one-month test-retest correlations on the total scores of the PBI, Form M-1 were significant at .001 level, with $r = .74$ ($n = 34$) for the depressed group, and $r = .60$ ($n = 24$) and $r = .69$ ($n = 18$) for the nondepressed groups (Muñoz, 1977; Zeiss et al., 1979). In the current study, the test-retest reliability of the PBI, Form M-2, was poor at post-follow-up, with Pearson's $r = .23$, $p = .14$, $n = 44$; but improved at six-months, $r = .36$, $p = .02$, $n = 44$, and one-year follow-up, with $r = .53$, $p = .001$, $n = 45$. Its coefficient alpha was .63 ($n = 227$) in our study.

The Subjective Probability Questionnaire (SPQ) measured optimism, the extent to which one believed a positive statement was true now or was likely to become true (these items made up the SPQ+ subscale), and pessimism, the extent to which one believed a negative statement was true now or was likely to become true (these items made up the SPQ− subscale).

This scale was inspired in part by Beck's "primary triad" (Beck, 1967): a negative view of the world, self, and future served as the source of depressed mood. Eighty items were generated by Muñoz (1977) to fall into three dichotomous categories: positive-negative, self-world, and present-future. Respondents indicated the chances, from 0 to 100, that each of the 80 statements was true. For the DPRP, the SPQ Short Form was used. This included only the thirty items found to be most discriminating between the depressed and nondepressed individuals (i.e., p

< .001) in Muñoz's (1977) original study. Of these, seventeen items made up the SPQ+ subscale, and thirteen made up the SPQ− subscale. The mean score of each subscale was calculated, with a possible range of 0 to 100 for each (0 to 100 percent probability).

Muñoz (1977) found depressed people to score significantly lower on SPQ+ but higher on SPQ− when compared with nondepressed people. The originally reported test-retest reliability at one month was high ($p = .001$), especially for the depressed group. The test-retest reliability of the SPQ+ and SPQ− in the DPRP control group was as follows: for SPQ+, at post, Pearson's $r = .58$, $p = .001$, $n = 44$, at six months, $r = .49$, $p = .001$, $n = 44$, and at one year, $r = .41$, $p = .005$, $n = 45$; for SPQ−, at post, $r = .21$, $p = .17$, $n = 44$, at six months, $r = .43$, $p = .004$, $n = 44$, and at one year, $r = .25$, $p = .09$, $n = 45$. Coefficient alpha was .86 for SPQ+ ($n = 225$) and .64 for SPQ− ($n = 228$).

The Cognitive Events Schedule (CES) measured the frequency of covert reinforcement and punishment, that is, the rate with which individuals experienced positive and negative thoughts in the preceding thirty days. Muñoz (1977) developed the CES to parallel the PAS, hypothesizing that depressed individuals reinforced themselves less not only objectively but also subjectively (mentally) by generating lower levels of positive thoughts, and punished themselves more by generating higher levels of negative thoughts.

The CES asked respondents to report the frequency of occurrence of 64 thoughts over the past thirty days. Frequency was indicated on a three-point scale [1—thought did not occur in the past thirty days; 2—thought occurred a few times (one to six times); and three—thought occurred often (seven or more times)]. The twenty-one items assessing positive thought were summed to yield the CES+ score (with a possible range of 21 to 63), and the forty-three items assessing negative thought were summed to yield the CES− score (with a possible range of 43 to 129).

In his study of depressed and nondepressed people, Muñoz (1977) found depressed people to score significantly ($p < .05$) lower on CES+ but higher on CES− than nondepressed people. The test-retest reliability of the CES+ and CES− scores in the DPRP Control condition participants were as follows; for the positive thought score: from pre- to postassessment, Pearson's $r = .70$, $p = .001$; from pre- to six-months follow-up, $r = .61$, $p = .001$; and from pre- to one-year follow-up, $r = .70$, $p = .001$, $n = 44$ in all cases. For the negative thought scores, the relationships at the three time periods were $r = .55$, $p = .001$; $r = .58$, $p = .001$; and $r = .58$ and $p = .001$, $n = 44$ in all cases. Coefficient alpha was .85 for CES+ ($n = 223$) and .91 for CES− ($n = 221$).

The Pleasant Activities Schedule (PAS) assessed the number of pleasant activities and their subjective enjoyability in the last month. It was a 49-item subset of the 320-item Pleasant Events Schedule (MacPhillamy & Lewinsohn, 1971). The original scale was designed to operationalize the concept of "reinforcement" in a person's life. Lewinsohn and colleagues (Lewinsohn & Graf, 1973; Lewinsohn & Libert, 1972; Lewinsohn & MacPhillamy, 1974; MacPhillamy & Lewinsohn, 1974) found depressed people scored significantly lower on the PES than nondepressed psychiatric control patients. A subset of the 49 items found to be associated with mood for at least 10% of the sample were identified by Lewinsohn, Biglan, and Zeiss (1976) and adopted by the DPRP.

The scoring of the PAS items was the same as that of the CES+ and CES− items. The range of possible PAS scores was from 49 to 147. The test-retest reliability of the PAS items at post-follow-up was r = .74, p = .001 (n = 43); at six-months follow-up, r = .70, p = .001 (n = 44); and at one-year follow-up, r = .47, p = .001 (n = 44). The coefficient alpha for PAS was .93 (n = 219).

The 46-item Social Activities Questionnaire examined the extent of interpersonal interactions in the last thirty days. It was constructed on the basis of face validity from Youngren, Zeiss, and Lewinsohn's (1975) 160-item Interpersonal Events Schedule, with some of the items derived from Watson and Friend (1969). Youngren (1978) found depressed patients scored significantly lower on the SAQ than normal controls.

The method for the scoring of the SAQ was the same as that for the PAS, CES+, and CES−. Youngren (1978) reported test-retest reliabilities to range from .61 and .71. in the DPRP, the test-retest reliabilities were .76 (p = .001, n = 44) at post-, .76 (p = .001, n = 44) at six-months, and .63 (p = .001, n = 44) at one-year follow-up. Its coefficient alpha was .89 (n = 213).

The 42-item Assertion Questionnaire assesses the extent to which someone disclosed feelings, fear, ignorance, and opinion, solicits another person's perception, and turned down requests in the last thirty days. Like the SAQ, it was also rationally derived (i.e., using face validity) from the Interpersonal Events Schedule. Many of the scale's items were adopted from Gambrill and Richey (1975). While Youngren (1978) did not find a significant difference in AQ scores between depressed and nondepressed people, it was included in the DPRP to test if assertive people do indeed demonstrate superior mood to nonassertive people. If this failed to be supported by the data at preintervention, it was to be deleted from succeeding analyses.

Again, the AQ was scored the same way as the CES+, CES−, PAS, and the SAQ, with the range of possible scores being 42 to 126. Youngren (1978) reported test-retest reliabilities ranging from .61 to .64. In the DPRP, the test-retest reliability was .59 (p = .001) at post-, r = .54 (p = .02) at six-months, and r = .53 (p = .001) at one-year follow-up, with n = 44 at all points. In addition, its items had high internal consistency (alpha = .92, n = 218).

By and large, the cognitive-behavioral variables were not related to family history of psychiatric illness. The exceptions were the presence of a positive relationship with SPQ− (t = 3.10, df = 226, p = .01; with mean scores of 31.02 and 25.02 for those with and without a family history) and CES− (t = 4.12, df = 225, p = .0001; with mean scores of 66.81 and 58.58 for those with and without a family history). Contrary to expectation, family history was also positively correlated with assertion. Those who had a family history of psychiatric illness reported greater assertiveness (t = 2.15, df = 225, p = .03; with mean scores of 64.91 and 61.49 for those with and without a family history).

The cognitive-behavioral variables were not related to medical utilization variables, that is, number of outpatient visits and hospitalizations in the last year. Most of them, however, were correlated with number of physical symptoms reported: higher PBI, SPQ−, and CES− scores were positively related to having more physical symptoms (r = .15, p = .03, n = 215; r = .31, p = .0001, n = 215; and r = .34, p = .0001, n = 213); while higher SPQ+ and PAS scores were negatively correlated with physical symptoms (r = −.20, p = .003, n = 215; and r = −.17, p = .02, n = 213, respectively).

All of the cognitive-behavioral variables held significant relationships in the predicted direction with the outcome measures (CES-D, BDI, presence of major depression, life quality, AB+ and AB−). The only exception was the Assertion Questionnaire, which was not correlated with CES-D, BDI, presence of major depression, and life quality, but held a positive correlation with both AB+ (r = .23, p = .001) and AB− (r = .19, p = .01, n = 234 in both cases). This finding was contrary to the original theoretical conception. We shall return to this briefly.

In addition to assessing the relationship of individual cognitive-behavior variables with the outcome variables, multivariate analysis (multiple regressions) were also conducted to assess the ability of cognitive-behavioral variables to predict to performance on the outcome measures. This served as an additional check on the soundness of the basis for the experimental intervention of this study. The results are presented in Tables 10.2 through 10.7.

Table 10.2 shows 37 percent of the variance in the pre-CES-D score was accounted for by the cognitive-behavioral variables [F (8,224) = 17.96, p = .0001]. Using a one-tailed test, variables that significantly predicted to pre-CES-D score were (in the order of their standardized

Table 10.2. Multiple Regression Analysis of Cognitive-Behavioral Variables Predicting to Pre-CES-D Score

Variable	Standardized Beta	P Value
CES−	.29	.001
CES+	−.16	.01
PBI	.06	.15
SAQ	.05	.27
SPQ−	.22	.001
SPQ+	−.09	.10
AQ	−.01	.46
PAS	−.17	.03

Notes: Adjusted R-Square = .37, F (8,224) = 17.96, p = .0001. See Table 10.1 for a key to abbreviations.

Table 10.3. Multiple Regression Analysis of Cognitive-Behavioral Variables Predicting to Pre-BDI Score

Variable	Standardized Beta	P Value
CES−	.34	.01
CES+	−.18	.01
PBI	.10	.03
SAQ	−.02	.42
SPQ−	.18	.01
SPQ+	−.11	.03
AQ	.08	.11
PAS	−.15	.04

Notes: Adjusted R-Square = .46, F (8,224) = 25.90, p = .0001. See Table 10.1 for a key to abbreviations.

beta size): CES− (standardized beta = .29, p = .001), SPQ− (standardized beta = .22, p = .001), CES+ (standardized beta = −.16, p = .01), PAS (standardized beta = −.17, p = .03).

Turning to the prediction of the pre-BDI score, Table 10.3 shows the total variance accounted for by the cognitive-behavioral variables was 46 percent, F (8,224) = 25.90, p = .0001. With the exception of the Social Activities and Assertion Questionnaires, all of the predictor variables were significant at the .05 level (using a one-tailed test).

Table 10.4 presents the results of a probit analysis using the cognitive-behavioral variables to predict the presence of current (within six months) major depression. While the overall model was not

Table 10.4. Probit Analysis of Cognitive-Behavioral Variables Predicting to the Presence of Current Major Depression

Variable	Regression Coefficient	Standard Error	t
PBI	.01	.02	.53
SPQ+	−.01	.01	−.53
SPQ−	.01	.01	.72
PAS	.01	.01	.73
SAQ	−.01	.01	−.58
AQ	.01	.01	.62
CES+	−.04	.02	−2.17
CES−	.03	.01	3.28

Notes: Intercept = 2.73, Standard Error = 1.16, Pearson Goodness-of-Fit-Chi-Square = 212.69, df = 218, p = .59. See Table 10.1 for a key to abbreviations.

Table 10.5. Multiple Regression Analysis of Cognitive-Behavioral Variables Predicting to Pre-Quality of Life Score

Variable	Standardized Beta	P Value
CES−	−.32	.01
CES+	.19	.01
PBI	.07	.10
SAQ	.21	.01
SPQ−	−.08	.11
SPQ+	.11	.06
AQ	.02	.42
PAS	.01	.47

Notes: Adjusted R-Square = .32, F (8,217) = 14.33, p = .0001. See Table 10.1 for a key to abbreviations.

significant, using a one-tailed test, lower scores on CES+ (p = .05) and higher scores on CES− (p = .001) were significantly predictive to current diagnosis of major depression.

The amount of variance accounted for in overall life satisfaction level by cognitive-behavioral variables was 32 percent [F (8,217) = 14.33, p = .0001]. As Table 10.5 shows, CES− (standardized beta = −.32, p = .01), CES+ (standardized beta = .19, p = .01), and SAQ (standardized beta = .21, p = .01) emerged as significant predictors, using a one-tailed test.

The positive Affect-Balance score was also significantly predicted by the cognitive-behavioral variables (Table 10.6). Here, 37 percent of the

Table 10.6. Multiple Regression Analysis of Cognitive-Behavioral Variables Predicting to Pre-Positive Affect-Balance Score

Variable	Standardized Beta	P Value
CES−	−.04	.29
CES+	.16	.01
PBI	.02	.37
SAQ	−.02	.41
SPQ−	−.05	.24
SPQ+	.14	.02
AS	−.05	.24
PAS	.43	.01

Notes: Adjusted R-Square = .37, F (8,224) = 17.81, p = .0001. See Table 10.1 for a key to abbreviations.

Table 10.7. Multiple Regression Analysis of Cognitive-Behavioral Variables Predicting to Pre-Negative Affect-Balance Score

Variable	Standardized Beta	P Value
CES−	.46	.01
CES+	−.09	.10
PBI	−.06	.12
SAQ	−.14	.04
SPQ−	.02	.39
SPQ+	.02	.38
AQ	.24	.01
PAS	−.17	.03

Notes: Adjusted R-Square = .37, F (8,224) = 18.04, p = .0001. See Table 10.1 for a key to abbreviations.

variance was accounted for, F (8,224) = 17.81, p = .0001. Increasing positive affect was predicted by higher scores on PAS (standardized beta = .43, p = .01), CES+ (standardized beta = .16, p = .01), and SPQ+ (standardized beta = .14, p = .02), again using a one-tailed test.

Turning to negative Affect-Balance score (Table 10.7), the cognitive-behavioral variables accounted for 37 percent of the variance, F (8,224) = 18.04, p = .0001. Using a one-tailed test, in the order of the standardized beta size, the significant predictors were: CES− (standardized beta = .46, p = . 01), AQ (standardized beta = .24, p = .01), PAS (standardized beta = −.17, p = .03), and SAQ (standardized beta = −.14, p = .04).

Contrary to expectation, scoring higher on assertion was predictive of higher negative affect rather than lower negative affect. Also, unexpectedly, respondents scoring higher on assertion were more likely to have a family history of psychiatric illness. As noted previously, AQ was also not significantly correlated with most of the outcome variables. A reexamination of the assertion items suggested that while some may be viewed as describing appropriate assertive behavior, others could be interpreted as overly demanding, critical, and complaining. Since performance on this measure was contrary to expectation at preintervention, we did not feel justified in retaining it in further analyses.

In summary, the cognitive-behavioral variables significantly predicted to depressive level and emotional well-being at the outset of the study. Higher frequencies of negative cognition and lower frequencies of positive cognition were also predictive of the presence of current major depression. With the exception of assertion, in all cases, the direction of the relationship was as expected.

Environmental Variable: Life Events

One area not directly addressed in the intervention but likely to mediate mood was that of life events. The practice of the cognitive-behavioral techniques taught in the intervention, such as engaging in more pleasant and social activities, made it likely that more positive and fewer negative events would occur.

The Life Experiences Survey (LES) assessed "positive and negative life experiences as well as individualized . . . impact of events" (Sarason, Johnson & Siegel, 1978). Participants indicated the occurrence (or nonoccurrence) of events in the last year (zero to six months or seven to twelve months). In addition, they rated on a seven-point scale, ranging from extremely negative (−3) to extremely positive (+3), the impact of the events that did occur. In the DPRP, the item score has been recoded to range from 0 to 6, with 0 indicating extremely negative impact, 3 representing no impact, and 6 representing extremely positive impact. The positive life events sum score was based on the sum of positive event ratings within either the zero- to six months-period or seven- to twelve-months period, while the negative life event sum score was based on the absolute value of the sum of the negative events ratings during these two time periods. Since the post-follow-up assessment occurred within six months of the initial prescreening for most participants, the LES was readministered only at the six- and twelve-months follow-up assessments.

Many of the LES items were based on existing life events measures, particularly the Schedule of Recent Experiences (SRE, Holmes & Rahe, 1967). Others were added because they were judged to be events that occur frequently and may have exerted a significant impact on the person experiencing them. Of the fifty-seven items, the forty-seven designed for use in the general population were adopted by the DPRP. Excluded were the additional ten items designed for students. Four additional questions (inquiring about experiences of being mugged, robbed, car quit running, and involuntarily taking someone into one's house) were added as they may be particularly relevant for the urban, poor, minority populations.

Sarason et al. (1978) reported the test-retest reliability at five to six weeks to be high ($p = .001$). They also found significant correlation of negative life event scores with anxiety and BDI score. The test-retest reliability was not assessed in the DPRP, as positive and negative events sums across time points were unlikely to be related, given the long time lapsed between each assessment period. Alpha coefficient could not be determined given the many items that did not occur (rated as "3," that is, "no impact").

The relationship of life event ratings and outcome variables was tested. It was anticipated that more recent life event ratings (for the last six months) were likely to hold a relationship to the current depressive level, life quality, and affect-balance scores because of the comparability of time period under consideration. However, life event ratings over six months ago were less likely to be related to outcome. The results of the correlational analysis showed that while positive events sum in the last seven to twelve months was not significantly correlated to most of the outcome measures, the other life event sums were. Higher positive life events sum in the last six months was negatively correlated with BDI ($r = -.13$, $p = .05$, $n = 236$) and positively correlated with positive affect ($r = .36$, $p = .001$, $n = 234$). Higher negative life events sum in the last six months was positively correlated with both measures of depressive symptomatology (for CES-D, $r = .30$, $p = .001$, $n = 236$; for BDI, $r = .26$, $p = .001$). It was also positively correlated with negative affect ($r = .28$, $p = .001$, $n = 234$). Those with a family history of psychiatric illness were more likely to report higher negative life event sums than those without such a history (means of 6.02 versus 4.45, respectively, $t = 2.02$, $df = 226$, $p = .05$). Negative life events sum for the previous seven to twelve months was significantly correlated with all outcome variables: with CES-D, $r = .30$, $p = .001$;

with BDI, $r = .24$, $p = .001$; with life quality, $r = -.23$, $p = .001$; with positive affect, $r = -.13$, $p = .05$; and with negative affect, $r = .23$, $p = .001$ ($n = 226$ or more in all cases). In addition, while level of positive events sum did not vary by presence of current major depression, those who suffered from this diagnosis did report a higher negative life events sum, both in the last six months and during the seven to twelve months prior, than the nondepressed group (for the last six months, mean = 7.14 versus 4.60, respectively, $t = 2.49$, $df = 234$, $p = .01$; for the previous seven to twelve months, mean = 5.02 versus 3.30, respectively, $t = 2.00$, $df = 234$, $p = .05$).

Life events scores did not vary by medical chart review variables (i.e., number of outpatient visits and hospitalizations). Negative life events sum in the last six months and during the previous seven to twelve months were found to be significantly positively correlated with number of physical symptoms reported ($r = .38$, $p = .0001$; and $r = .32$, $p = .0001$, $n = 215$ in both cases).

The Crowne-Marlowe Social Desirability Scale

The Crowne-Marlowe Social Desirability Scale was developed to assess the degree to which respondents present themselves in a favorable, socially desirable light to achieve social approval (Crowne & Marlowe, 1960). Strong social desirability need might compromise the accuracy of the responses on the other measures. Respondents with high scores on social desirability may be more likely to deny symptoms and to assert greater emotional well-being than they actually experienced.

The authors of this social desirability scale stated, "For inclusion in the scale, an item had to meet the criterion of cultural approval . . . and was required to have minimal pathological or abnormal implications if responded to in either the socially desirable or undesirable direction" (Crowne & Marlowe, 1960). Judges were employed to rate the social desirability of fifty items. Items that did not meet at least 90 percent interrater agreement were subsequently deleted. The remaining items were presented to undergraduate students. A total of thirty-three items were retained that discriminated at the .05 level or better between high and low total scores. Of these, fourteen, which composed two clusters of "assert good items" (items 1, 2, 5, 6, 7, 9, and 14) and "deny bad items" (items 3, 4, 8, 10, 11, 12, and 13) (Caplan et al. 1975), were selected for the DPRP. A "true" response to the former or a "false" response to the latter contributed one point to the overall social desirability score, and the higher the final score, the greater the need for social desirability.

Crowne and Marlowe (1960, 1964) found their social desirability score to be significantly correlated with the MMPI validity scales ($p < .05$). The test-retest correlation at one month with college students was found to be .89 (Crowne & Marlowe, 1960). In the DPRP, the test-retest reliability was found to be $r = .75$ ($p = .0001$) at post, $r = .71$ ($p = .0001$) at six months, and $r = .65$ ($p = .0001$) at one year, $n = 44$ in all cases. The coefficient alpha for the "assert good" subscale was .65 ($n = 227$), and .69 for the "deny bad" subscale ($n = 228$).

The Crowne-Marlowe social desirability score was found to be significantly negatively correlated with BDI and AB− ($r = -.15$, $p = .03$ and $r = -.39$, $p = .0001$, respectively), and positively correlated with life quality ($r = .29$, $p = .0001$), suggesting that persons with a stronger social desirability tendency reported less depression and more satisfaction with their lives. Social desirability was not found to be significantly associated with the presence of current major depression, number of physical symptoms reported, number of outpatient visits, or number of hospitalizations.

Instrument Translation

All instruments used in the study were translated by a team of Spanish-speaking mental health professionals/students. The measures were translated into Spanish, and then independently back-translated into English by a group blind to the original English version. The original and the back-translated English versions were then compared. Variations were discussed and reconciled by the team. In the case of the DIS, a previous Spanish version (Karno et al., 1983) was also consulted.

11. Characteristics of the Samples at Initial Screenings

As noted in the previous chapter, the recruitment for the DPRP occurred at three sites: The University of California at San Francisco Moffit Hospital Internal Medicine Clinic (UCSF group), San Francisco General Hospital General Medical Clinic (SFGH-ENG Group), and San Francisco General Hospital Family Practice Clinic (SFGH-SPAN Group). We will examine the comparability of the three groups at the outset of the study, and whether they may be combined into one group when testing for the effect of the experimental intervention. In addition, this chapter assesses the presence of differences between randomized and nonrandomized groups, and comparability across the three randomization conditions. The generalizability of the results of the intervention is partly dependent on the degree to which the randomized group is similar to the nonrandomized group (with the exception of performance on depression and depression-related measures, given that the absence of current clinical depression is a major exclusionary criterion), and the success of the randomization process in creating comparable Class, Control, and Video conditions. Finally, given the multiethnic composition of the sample, we also examine presence of ethnic differences in performance on the major variables.

Variation across Recruitment Sites

We begin by assessing the rate of acceptance and continuation through the three screening sessions by group. Table 11.1 presents the number of patients recruited at the three clinics who participated in the initial three screenings. Of the 707 who were recruited and partook in the first screening, 41.30 percent (n = 292) went on to the second screening. Of these, in turn, 79.72 percent (n = 232) participated in the third screening. Chi-Square tests revealed a significant overall group difference in acceptance rate from the first to the second screening (Chi-Square = 22.25, df = 2, p = .001). More specifically, the SFGH-ENG and SFGH-SPAN groups had a significantly higher acceptance rate (51.42% and

Characteristics of the Samples at Initial Screenings

Table 11.1. Number of Participants at Three Screenings

	UCSF	SFGH-ENG	SFGH-SPAN	Total
Screening 1	339	247	121	707
Screening 2	110	127	55	292
Screening 3	87	103	42	232
Randomization	62	60	28	150

Note: UCSF = University of California, San Francisco, Internal Medicine Clinic. SFGH-ENG = San Francisco General Hospital, English-speaking patients (from General Medicine Clinic). SFGH-SPAN = San Francisco General Hospital, Spanish-speaking patients (from Family Practice Clinic).

45.45%) into the second screening than the UCSF group (32.45%). No difference was found between the two SFGH language groups. The Chi-Square statistic for the SFGH-ENG and UCSF comparison was 21.34, df = 1, p = .0001; for the SFGH-SPAN and UCSF comparison, it was 6.56, df = 1, p = .01. For the pairwise comparisons, the alpha level of significance was set at .0167 (i.e., .05 divided by three contrasts).

This difference was likely to be due to the method of recruitment. Those recruited by mail (e.g., all of the respondents in the UCSF group) were less likely to continue with further screening. Completing the first screening for them meant mailing the first screening measures. However, participation in the second assessment required a face-to-face interview, a considerably greater effort on their part. Those recruited in person (most of the SFGH respondents) completed the first screening measures in the hospital, and had already met a representative of the the DPRP team. This contact facilitated their return for further assessments. We found no difference across the three groups in the rate of continued participation from the second to third screening or from third screening to randomization.

Since the three clinics were chosen to ensure the diversity of our primary care sample, it is not surprising that they differed on the major demographic characteristics assessed. These are presented in Tables 11.2 and 11.3 for all screened at these three sites. Table 11.3 also examines the presence of differences in family history of psychiatric disorders across sites.

Table 11.2 shows the results of overall F tests assessing the presence of differences across the three groups on continuous demographic variables. The F-value was significant at the .001 level in all cases. Subsequently, pairwise comparisons were conducted, using the Scheffé posthoc test, with the alpha level of significance set at .0167 (.05

Table 11.2. Demographic Characteristics across Recruitment Sites (for Continuous Variables)

Variable	Group 1 (UCSF)	Group 2 (SFGH-ENG)	Group 3 (SFGH-SPAN)	Overall Test			Significant Contrasts*		
				df	F	p	Groups	t	p
Age	48.53 (14.28)	50.71 (11.53)	42.86 (14.44)	2,696	13.97	0.001	1 > 3	3.99	.001
	n = 333	n = 245	n = 121				2 > 3	5.27	.001
Years in U.S.**	25.19 (16.58)	18.71 (16.76)	9.14 (9.21)	2,267	34.94	0.001	1 > 3	8.51	.001
	n = 98	n = 59	n = 113				2 > 3	4.08	.001
Years in San Francisco	21.90 (16.93)	21.79 (15.27)	8.34 (8.71)	2,690	38.79	0.001	1 > 3	11.06	.001
	n = 332	n = 242	n = 119				2 > 3	10.63	.001
Education	13.29 (3.69)	11.38 (3.44)	8.74 (4.08)	2,678	66.60	0.001	1 > 2	6.36	.001
	n = 326	n = 245	n = 110				1 > 3	10.35	.001
							2 > 3	5.91	.001
Income (in thousands)***	15.28 (13.84)	6.82 (6.03)	9.02 (6.93)	2,576	42.07	0.001	1 > 2	8.85	.001
	n = 255	n = 224	n = 100				1 > 3	5.65	.001
							2 < 3	−2.75	.02

Note: See Table 11.1 for a key to abbreviations.
*Scheffé posthoc test used, with significance level of alpha = 0.05/3 contrasts.
**Ascertained for foreign-born participants only.
***For 1983–84.

divided by three contrasts). Table 11.3 reports the findings of chi-square tests examining the presence of differences across the three groups on categorical demographics variables. Here also we found the three groups to differ (significant overall chi-square value); thus pair-wise comparisons, as previously discussed, were conducted.

Age, Sex, Marital Status, Ethnicity

The UCSF and SFGH-ENG groups were significantly older than the SFGH-SPAN group (mean ages of 48.53, 50.71 and 42.86, respectively). The three groups differed significantly in the proportion of men and women represented, with the SFGH-SPAN group being most heavily dominated by women (80.16%), followed by the UCSF group (66.57%), and the SFGH-ENG group having relatively fewer women than men (46.56%). The three groups also differed significantly in marital status. The SFGH-SPAN group was most likely to be married (53.72%), while the SFGH-ENG group was most likely to be formerly married, that is, separated/divorced/widowed (50.20%), and the UCSF group was almost equally divided among never married, married, once-married participants. In terms of ethnic composition, as anticipated, the UCSF group was most heavily represented by white patients (62.23%), while the SFGH-ENG group had the largest group of African Americans (44.49%), followed by whites (30.62%), and the SFGH-SPAN group was almost entirely Latino (96.64%). Asian/Pacific Islanders made up a little over 10 percent, and Native-Americans made up less than 5 percent of the sample of UCSF and SFGH-ENG patients.

In general, these sample characteristics reflected those found in the respective clinics. A survey of the UCSF Internal Medicine Clinic (Pérez-Stable, 1991) showed that of the 10,227 patients who used the clinic in 1988, 38 percent were male and 68 percent were female. The ethnic composition was 12 percent Asian, 15 percent African American, 10 percent Latino, 50 percent white, and 12 percent "Other." The mean age was 48 years.

Of the patients seen at the SFGH General Medical Clinic between May and October 1984, 6,213 were between the ages of 20 and 64, with a median age of 48. A little over half were male (52.61%). In terms of ethnic composition, 35.09 percent were African American, 26.33 percent were white, 17.53 percent were Latinos, 8.97 percent were Asians, and 12.09 percent were grouped under "Other."

An internal study conducted in the Family Practice Clinic in 1981 (O'Connor, 1984) showed approximately three-fourths of patients between ages 18 and 69 to be female, with a median age of about 35. Across all age groups, half of the patients were Latino.

Table 11.3. Demographic Characteristics across Recruitment Sites (for Categorical Variables)

Variable	Group 1 (UCSF)	Group 2 (SFGH-ENG)	Group 3 (SFGH-SPAN)	Overall Test			Significant Contrasts*			
				Chi-Sq	df	p	Groups	Chi-Sq	df	p
SEX										
Male	112 (33.43%)	132 (53.44%)	24 (19.84%)	44.85	2,700	.001	1 vs. 2	23.38	1,580	.001
Female	223 (66.57%)	115 (46.56%)	97 (80.16%)				2 vs. 3	37.56	1,366	.001
Total	335	247	121				1 vs. 3	7.85	1,454	.01
MARITAL STATUS										
Never married	106 (31.27%)	52 (21.05%)	18 (14.87%)	37.32	4,702	.001	1 vs. 2	13.57	2,583	.001
Now married	112 (33.04%	71 (28.75%)	65 (53.72%)				2 vs. 3	21.85	2,365	.001
Formerly married	121 (35.69%)	124 (50.20%)	38 (31.41%)				1 vs. 3	19.27	2,457	.001
Total	339	247	121							
EMPLOYED										
Yes	150 (44.25%)	55 (22.27%)	32 (26.67%)	34.05	2,703	.001	1 vs. 2	30.35	1,584	.001
No	189 (55.75%)	192 (77.73%)	88 (73.33%)				1 vs. 3	11.45	1,457	.001
Total	339	247	120							

UNEMPLOYMENT STATUS**										
Looking for work	20 (10.81%)	46 (25.99%)	23 (27.38%)	99.44	8,437	.001	1 vs. 2	30.22	4,357	.001
Student	18 (9.73%)	1 (0.56%)	7 (8.33%)							
Homemaker	20 (10.81%)	15 (8.48%)	35 (41.67%)				2 vs. 3	63.97	4,256	.001
Disabled	83 (44.87%)	88 (49.72%)	14 (16.67%)							
Retired	44 (23.78%)	27 (15.25%)	5 (5.95%)				1 vs. 3	59.77	4,264	.001
Total	185	177	84							
ETHNICITY										
Asian/Pacific Islander	35 (10.84%)	32 (13.06%)	0	504.45	8,678	.001	1 vs. 2	91.58	4,563	.001
African American	36 (11.15%)	109 (44.49%)	1 (0.84%)							
Latino	37 (11.45%)	20 (8.16%)	115 (96.64%)				2 vs. 3	271.85	4,339	.001
White	201 (62.23%)	75 (30.62%)	0							
Native American	14 (4.33%)	9 (3.67%)	3 (2.52%)				1 vs. 3	282.22	4,437	.001
Total	323	245	119							
FAMILY HISTORY OF PSYCHIATRIC DISORDERS										
Yes	38 (43.68%)	36 (36.00%)	14 (34.15%)	1.58	2,225	.46				
No	49 (56.32%)	64 (64.00%)	27 (65.85%)							
Total	87	100	41							

Note: See Table 11.1 for a key to abbreviations.

*Scheffé posthoc test used, with significance level of alpha = 0.05/3 contrasts.

**For unemployed participants only.

The Length of Residence in the United States and San Francisco

Of the three groups, the SFGH-SPAN included the most immigrants (n = 113), followed by UCSF (n = 98) and SFGH-ENG (n = 59). Of these immigrants, those in the SFGH-SPAN group had lived in the United States for an average of a little over 9 years, significantly shorter than those in the UCSF (25.19 years) and SFGH-ENG groups (18.71 years). This difference accounted for the fact that, regardless of their place of birth, UCSF and SFGH-ENG patients had lived in San Francisco close to 22 years, while SFGH-SPAN patients had been in the city for only a little more than 8 years.

Education, Income, and Employment Status

The three groups differed from one another in terms of education, annual household income (in 1983–84), and employment status. The UCSF group was the most highly educated (13.29 years) and received the highest annual income ($15,280). The SFGH-ENG group was better educated than the SFGH-SPAN group (mean of 11.38 years versus 8.74 years); however, its annual income fell below that of the latter ($6,820 versus $9,020). This is likely to be due to the fact that the (older) SFGH-ENG group suffered more from debilitating physical illness than the SFGH-SPAN group, and was unable to maintain employment. This is substantiated by the finding regarding employment status reported in Table 11.3, that is, while both groups included approximately over three-fourths of unemployed patients, the SFGH-ENG group had a higher proportion of disabled patients (49.72%) than the SFGH-SPAN group (16.67%). For the latter, being unemployed was likely to reflect not disability but being a homemaker (8.48% of SFGH-ENG versus 41.67% of SFGH-SPAN unemployed groups). In contrast, only about half of the UCSF patients were unemployed, and of these, 10.81 percent were housewives.

A Family History of Psychiatric Disorder

Table 11.3 also shows comparable rates of self-reported family history of psychiatric disorder across the three recruitment sites.

Outcome Variables: Level of Depression and Psychological Well-being

Turning to the outcome variables (Table 11.4), the SFGH-SPAN group scored significantly higher on the initial CES-D (mean of 23.25) than

Table 11.4. Initial Levels of Depression and Psychological Well-being across Recruitment Sites

Variable	Group 1 (UCSF)	Group 2 (SFGH-ENG)	Group 3 (SFGH-SPAN)	Overall Test			Significant Contrasts*		
				df	F	p	Groups	t	p
CES-D	19.53 (13.63) n = 310	19.01 (12.49) n = 240	23.25 (14.13) n = 104	2,651	3.94	0.02	1 < 3 2 < 3	−2.46 −2.71	0.01 0.02
BDI	14.21 (9.84) n = 108	16.37 (10.27) n = 129	16.09 (10.61) n = 54	2,288	1.44	0.24			
AB+	2.82 (1.72) n = 87	2.82 (1.57) n = 101	2.83 (1.63) n = 41	2,226	0.001	0.99			
AB−	2.48 (1.74) n = 87	1.88 (1.68) n = 101	1.67 (1.70) n = 41	2,226	4.36	0.01	1 > 2 1 > 3	2.41 2.55	0.05 0.03
Quality of Life	3.02 (1.08) n = 82	2.82 (1.13) n = 99	3.05 (1.07) n = 39	2,217	1.05	0.35			

Note: See Table 11.1 for a key to abbreviations.
*Scheffé posthoc test used, with significance level of alpha = 0.05/3 contrasts.

both the UCSF and the SFGH-ENG groups (mean of 19.53 and 19.01, respectively), but no group differences were found on the BDI. This was consistent with Roberts et al.'s finding that Latinos score more depressed on the CES-D than the general population (Roberts, 1981; Roberts & Vernon, 1983). In addition to reflecting the stresses of immigrating to a new country, this may also be due to the greater proportion of women represented in this group, who generally score higher than men on the CES-D. While the three groups did not differ on positive affect, the UCSF group reported experiencing more negative affect in the past few weeks than the two SFGH groups. No differences were found in their ratings of their life quality.

DSM-III/DIS Clinical Diagnoses

Tables 11.5 and 11.6 report lifetime diagnosis and current diagnosis by groups. By and large, the three groups did not differ in lifetime prevalence of major DSM-III diagnoses. The major exceptions were organic brain syndrome (SFGH-SPAN group reported a higher prevalence rate than the UCSF group, likely to be an artifact of poorer educational level), alcohol abuse and/or dependence (SFGH-ENG reported a higher prevalence rate than both the UCSF and SFGH-SPAN groups), drug abuse and/or dependence (SFGH-ENG group reported a higher prevalence rate than the SFGH-SPAN group), and tobacco dependence (again, SFGH-ENG reported a higher prevalence rate than the SFGH-SPAN group).

The lifetime prevalence rates across the recruitment sites for major diagnoses were: 7.75 percent for organic brain syndrome, 1.37 percent for bipolar disorder, 19.52 percent for major depression, 10.62 percent for dysthymia, 0.68 percent for schizophrenia, 32.19 percent for alcohol abuse and/or dependence, and 7.53 percent for drug abuse and/or dependence.

Turning to current (within the last six months) diagnoses of these major disorders, the prevalence rates across the recruitment sites for these major diagnoses were: 7.53 percent for organic brain syndrome, 0.68 percent for bipolar disorder, 15.07 percent for major depression, 0.68 percent for schizophrenia, 7.53 percent for alcohol abuse and/or dependence, and 2.05 percent for drug abuse and/or dependence. No group differences were found.

Physical Health and Medical Chart Review

Table 11.7 presents the results of comparing the three groups on the number of physical symptoms they currently experience, their subjec-

Table 11.5. Lifetime Prevalence Rates of Selected DIS/DSM-III Diagnoses across Recruitment Sites

Diagnosis	Group 1 (UCSF) (n = 110)	Group 2 (SFGH-ENG) (n = 127)	Group 3 (SFGH-SPAN) (n = 55)	Overall Test			Significant Contrasts*			
				df	Chi-Sq	p	Groups	df	Chi-Sq	p
Organic brain syndrome	4 (3.85%)	9 (7.20%)	9 (16.36%)	2,281	7.98	0.02	1 vs. 3	1,157	7.51	0.01
Major depression	25 (22.73%)	18 (14.17%)	14 (25.45%)	2,289	4.26	0.12				
Major depression, single episode	5 (4.55%)	1 (0.79%)	3 (5.45%)	2,289	4.06	0.13				
Major depression, recurrent	19 (17.27%)	14 (11.02%)	10 (18.18%)	2,289	2.48	0.29				
Dysthymia	9 (8.18%)	15 (11.81%)	7 (12.73%)	2,289	1.14	0.57				
Bipolar disorder	1 (0.91%)	2 (1.57%)	1 (1.82%)	2,289	0.29	0.86				
Schizophrenia	0	1 (0.79%)	1 (1.82%)	2,289	1.82	0.40				
Alcohol abuse and/or dependence	25 (22.73%)	56 (44.09%)	13 (23.64%)	2,289	14.60	0.001	1 vs. 2	1,235	11.96	0.001
							2 vs. 3	1,180	6.82	0.01
Drug abuse and/or dependence	8 (7.27%)	14 (11.02%)	0	2,289	6.71	0.04	2 vs. 3	1,180	6.57	0.01
Obsessive-compulsive disorder	8 (7.27%)	9 (7.09%)	2 (3.64%)	2,289	0.92	0.63				
Phobic disorders	25 (22.73%)	31 (24.41%)	16 (29.09%)	2,289	0.81	0.67				
Agoraphobia	11 (10.00%)	16 (12.60%)	4 (7.27%)	2,289	1.22	0.54				
Simple phobia	16 (14.55%)	21 (16.54%)	13 (23.64%)	2,289	2.19	0.34				
Social phobia	4 (3.64%)	6 (4.72%)	1 (1.82%)	2,289	0.90	0.64				
Somatization disorder	1 (0.91%)	1 (0.79%)	2 (3.64%)	2,289	2.58	0.28				
Panic disorder	2 (1.82%)	3 (2.36%)	0	2,289	1.28	0.53				
Antisocial personality	8 (7.27%)	11 (8.66%)	2 (3.64%)	2,289	1.45	0.48				
Tobacco dependence	48 (43.64%)	73 (57.48%)	15 (27.27%)	2,289	14.69	0.001	2 vs. 3	1,180	14.02	0.001
Pathological gambling	2 (1.82%)	3 (2.36%)	0	2,289	1.28	0.53				
Sexual dysfunction	36 (32.73%)	34 (26.77%)	18 (32.73%)	2,289	1.21	0.55				

Note: See Table 11.1 for a key to abbreviations.

*Scheffé posthoc test used, with significance level of alpha = 0.05/3 contrasts.

Table 11.6. Current (within Last Six Months) Prevalence Rates of Selected DIS/DSM-III Diagnoses across Recruitment Sites

Diagnosis	Group 1 (UCSF)	Group 2 (SFGH-ENG)	Group 3 (SFGH-SPAN)	Overall Test df	Chi-Sq	p
Major depression	17 (15.45%)	15 (11.81%)	12 (21.82%)	2,289	3.02	0.22
Bipolar disorder	1 (0.91%)	0	1 (1.82%)	2,289	2.00	0.37
Schizophrenia	0	1 (0.79%)	1 (1.82%)	2,289	1.82	0.40
Alcohol abuse and/ or dependence	7 (6.36%)	13 (10.24%)	2 (3.64%)	2,289	2.75	0.25
Drug abuse and/or dependence	3 (2.37%)	3 (2.36%)	0	2,289	1.46	0.48

Note: See Table 11.1 for a key to abbreviations.

tive ratings of health status, and the extent to which they have been concerned about their health in the past month. The SFGH-ENG group reported experiencing significantly more symptoms (mean of 9.47) than the UCSF group (mean of 6.75). Similarly, the UCSF group reported a superior health status to both SFGH groups. On a scale of 1 to 4, ranging from (1) excellent health to (4) poor health, the mean health rating for the UCSF group was 2.47, while for the SFGH-ENG and SFGH-SPAN groups it was 3.02 and 2.96, respectively. With regard to the level of concern (with higher scores reflecting greater concern), the SFGH-ENG expressed significantly more worry about their health than either of the UCSF and SFGH-SPAN groups in the last month. Ultimately, of the three groups, the UCSF group reported the best physical health, the SFGH-ENG group reported the worst, and the SFGH-SPAN group occupied an intermediate position.

Table 11.8 presents the results of the medical chart review. We assessed the number of outpatient visits and hospitalizations for the previous year. The three groups varied on the number of outpatient visits and hospitalizations. Specifically, the two SFGH groups reported more frequent outpatient visits than the UCSF group (the mean for the SFGH-ENG and SFGH-SPAN groups was 6.62 and 6.36, respectively, and 4.69 for the UCSF group.) In terms of the number of hospitalizations, we found the three groups to differ. The SFGH-ENG group was hospitalized more frequently (mean = 0.67) than either the UCSF group (mean = 0.14) or the SFGH-SPAN group (mean = 0.07). These findings suggest the SFGH-ENG group used medical services most frequently, followed by the SFGH-SPAN group, and, lastly, by the UCSF group.

Table 11.7. Initial Physical Health across Recruitment Sites

Variable	Group 1 (UCSF)	Group 2 (SFGH-ENG)	Group 3 (SFGH-SPAN)	Overall Test			Significant Contrasts*		
				df	F	p	Groups	t	p
Number of physical symptoms	6.75 (5.85) n = 87	9.47 (6.67) n = 103	7.51 (5.60) n = 41	2,228	4.78	0.01	1 < 2	−3.02	0.01
Health status	2.47 (0.84) n = 330	3.02 (0.82) n = 244	2.96 (0.71) n = 120	2,691	36.63	0.001	1 < 2 1 < 3	−7.96 −5.64	0.001 0.001
Health concern	5.63 (3.15) n = 313	7.02 (3.08) n = 239	6.05 (3.56) n = 113	2,662	12.93	0.001	1 < 2 2 > 3	−5.01 2.65	0.001 0.01

Note: See Table 11.1 for a key to abbreviations.
*Scheffé posthoc test used, with significance level of alpha = 0.05/3 contrasts.

Table 11.8. Medical Utilization across Recruitment Sites

				Overall Test			Significant Contrasts*		
Variable	Group 1 (UCSF)	Group 2 (SFGH-ENG)	Group 3 (SFGH-SPAN)	df	F	p	Groups	t	p
Number of outpatient visits	4.69 (3.33)	6.62 (3.41)	6.36 (3.90)	2,262	9.27	0.001	1 < 3	−2.70	0.01
	n = 105	n = 116	n = 44				2 < 3	−4.15	0.001
Number of hospitalizations	0.14 (0.47)	0.67 (1.05)	0.07 (0.26)	2,258	16.89	0.001	1 < 2	−4.82	0.001
	n = 105	n = 112	n = 44				2 > 3	5.65	0.001

Note: See Table 11.1 for a key to abbreviations.
*Scheffé posthoc test used, with significance level of alpha = 0.05/3 contrasts.

Cognitive-Behavioral Variables

By and large, the three groups did not differ on the cognitive-behavioral variables targeted by the intervention (the Personal Beliefs Inventory, the Subjective Probability Questionnaire, the Pleasant Activities Schedule, and the Social Activities Questionnaire). The only exception was the finding that the SFGH-ENG group scored significantly higher than the SFGH-SPAN group on CES+ ($t = 2.63$, $p = .01$) (Table 11.9).

Life Events and Social Desirability

In addition to the cognitive-behavioral mediating variables and the outcome variables, we asked about the presence and impact of life events the participants had experienced in the last year, and assessed the participants' level of social desirability. The results are presented in Table 11.10.

For life events, four indicators were examined: the impact of positive life events and negative events in the last six months, and seven to twelve months. The impact score was calculated as follows: the number of positive/negative life events identified per time period multiplied by the impact of the event (ranges from 0 [no impact] to 3 [extreme positive/negative impact]). The three groups were found to vary on the impact of positive life events in the last six months ($p = .05$). Pairwise comparisons using a significance level of .0168 showed the SFGH-SPAN group to report marginally greater positive life events than the UCSF group. The groups did not vary on the other life events indicators.

In terms of social desirability, the SFGH-SPAN group scored significantly higher than the UCSF group, which may reflect Latinos' strong emphasis on interpersonal politeness and being "bien educado," or well-behaved.

In summary, group differences were found on demographic variables, physical health, and medical utilization. The prevalence of major psychiatric diagnoses, outcome measures (including depressive levels, affect, and quality of life), cognitive-behavioral, and environmental variables were similar for the three groups. In all cases, the presence of an overall difference (significant F) was followed by pairwise comparisons, with the .05 significance level divided by the three comparison tests. Despite the more conservative test, it is likely that, given the numerous tests conducted, significant differences will be found by chance. Thus, variation on the nondemographic variables found at the initial screening ought to be viewed with caution. Given the similarity

Table 11.9. Initial Cognitions and Behaviors across Recruitment Sites

Variable	Group 1 (UCSF)	Group 2 (SFGH-ENG)	Group 3 (SFGH-SPAN)	Overall Test			Significant Contrasts*		
				df	F	p	Groups	t	p
PBI	38.32 (8.01) n = 87	39.12 (7.87) n = 103	41.39 (9.03) n = 42	2,229	2.04	0.13			
SPQ+	63.78 (16.05) n = 87	65.09 (16.82) n = 102	64.72 (17.90) n = 42	2,228	0.15	0.86			
SPQ−	25.99 (13.02) n = 87	27.06 (15.62) n = 102	29.56 (14.96) n = 42	2,228	0.85	0.43			
CES+	44.77 (8.52) n = 86	45.20 (8.74) n = 103	41.02 (8.40) n = 41	2,227	3.67	0.03	2 > 3	2.63	0.01
CES−	60.95 (14.70) n = 86	61.73 (15.80) n = 103	62.59 (14.64) n = 41	2,227	0.17	0.85			
PAS	106.19 (15.17) n = 86	108.41 (16.15) n = 103	103.90 (17.24) n = 41	2,227	1.26	0.29			
SAQ	71.02 (10.96) n = 86	73.68 (12.44) n = 103	71.10 (13.03) n = 42	2,228	1.37	0.26			

Note: See Tables 10.1 and 11.1 for keys to abbreviations.
*Scheffé posthoc test used, with significance level of alpha = 0.05/3 contrasts.

Table 11.10. Life Events and Social Desirability across Recruitment Sites

Variable	Group 1 (UCSF)	Group 2 (SFGH-ENG)	Group 3 (SFGH-SPAN)	Overall Test			Significant Contrasts*		
				df	F	p	Groups	t	p
Life Events + Sum (0–6 months)	2.44 (2.99) n = 87	3.29 (4.14) n = 102	4.15 (4.39) n = 41	2,227	3.02	0.05	1 < 3	−2.38	0.02
Life Events − Sum (0–6 months)	4.10 (4.99) n = 87	5.59 (6.53) n = 102	5.61 (5.38) n = 41	2,227	1.80	0.17			
Life Events + Sum (7–12 months)	1.20 (2.47) n = 87	1.59 (2.48) n = 102	1.80 (2.93) n = 41	2,227	0.96	0.38			
Life Events − Sum (7–12 months)	3.03 (4.53) n = 87	4.00 (4.95) n = 102	3.73 (5.48) n = 41	2,227	0.94	0.39			
Crowne-Marlowe	7.06 (3.30) n = 86	7.50 (3.17) n = 103	8.67 (2.64) n = 41	2,227	3.70	0.03	1 < 3	−2.71	0.01

*Scheffé posthoc test used, with significance level of alpha = 0.05/3 contrasts.

across the groups on the nondemographic variables, including those to be directly targeted in the study, the three groups were combined, and further discussions will not continue to differentiate them. The presence of demographic differences supports the need of sampling from several primary care clinics to approximate the actual ethnic diversity of San Francisco and to improve the generalizability of the findings.

Variation between the Randomized and Nonrandomized Groups

Of the 232 who participated in the third screening, 210 completed the instruments. Of these, a total of 150 participants were randomly assigned into the three intervention conditions. The primary reason for exclusion from randomization was meeting DSM-III/DIS criteria for psychiatric diagnosis (73.17%). Others were excluded because they appeared in need of treatment (e.g., marked low mood or suicidality), even though they did not meet diagnostic criteria. Only 6 percent of those eligible for randomization refused to continue. How did the randomized group differ from those who were not randomized?

Demographic Variables

As Tables 11.11 and 11.12 demonstrate, the randomized and the nonrandomized patients did not differ on demographic variables, except for age. The randomized group was significantly older (mean of 52.46) than the nonrandomized group (47.19).

A Family History of Psychiatric Disorder

Table 11.12 shows a smaller proportion of the randomized group to have a family history of psychiatric illness (Chi-Square = 13.30, df = 1,225, p = .001).

Outcome Variables: Levels of Depression and Psychological Well-being

Table 11.13 shows the randomized and nonrandomized groups differed significantly on all outcome variables. As expected (due to the exclusion of participants who met the criteria for major depression and other disorders), those who were screened out scored higher on the CES-D and BDI (on the CES-D, the mean scores were 21.37 versus

Table 11.11. Demographic Characteristics by Randomization (for Continuous Variables)

Variable	Randomized	Nonrandomized	t	df	p
Age	52.46 (12.03) n = 149	47.19 (13.86) n = 550	4.59	264.51	0.001
Years in U.S.*	18.30 (15.67) n = 61	16.70 (15.72) n = 209	0.70	268	0.49
Years in San Francisco	21.25 (15.45) n = 150	19.06 (16.17) n = 543	1.49	691	0.14
Education	12.18 (3.50) n = 144	11.78 (4.13) n = 537	1.17	260.3	0.24
Income** (in thousands)	10.84 (8.51) n = 133	10.95 (11.70) n = 446	−0.12	295.02	0.91

*Ascertained for foreign-born participants only.
**For 1983–84.

15.04; and on the BDI, the mean scores were 19.27 versus 11.98). In addition, the randomized group experienced more positive (means of 3.07 versus 2.35) but less negative affect (means of 1.64 versus 2.89) than the nonrandomized group in the past few weeks. The randomized group gave a higher rating for their quality of life than the nonrandomized group (mean of 3.13 and 2.55, respectively, with 1 reflecting poor and 5 indicating excellent quality of life).

DSM-III/DIS Clinical Diagnoses

Table 11.14 presents lifetime prevalence rates for the remaining diagnoses, after deleting organic brain syndrome and schizophrenia (because respondents with lifetime histories of these diagnoses were excluded from the randomized group). The table shows the randomized groups to report significantly lower lifetime prevalence rates than the nonrandomized group on the following diagnoses: major depression; major depression, recurrent type; dysthymia; tobacco dependence; phobia; social phobia; panic disorder; and alcohol and drug abuse and/or dependence. The randomized group suffered from fewer psychiatric disorders than the nonrandomized group as a result of their not meeting certain DIS/DSM-III exclusionary criteria, as previously discussed.

Since all respondents meeting diagnostic criteria for current major

Table 11.12. Demographic Characteristics by Randomization (for Categorical Variables)

Variable	Randomized	Nonrandomized	Chi-Sq	df	p
SEX					
Male	57 (38.00%)	211 (38.16%)	0.001	1,701	0.97
Female	93 (62.00%)	342 (61.84%)			
Total	150	553			
MARITAL STATUS					
Never married	27 (18.00%)	149 (26.75%)	4.95	2,704	0.08
Now married	59 (39.33%)	189 (33.93%)			
Formerly married	64 (42.67%)	219 (39.32%)			
Total	150	557			
EMPLOYED					
Yes	48 (32.21%)	189 (33.93%)	0.16	1,704	0.69
No	101 (67.79%)	368 (66.07%)			
Total	149	557			
UNEMPLOYMENT STATUS*					
Looking for work	21 (21.65%)	68 (19.48%)	6.56	4,441	0.16
Student	3 (3.09%)	23 (6.59%)			
Homemaker	11 (11.34%)	59 (16.91%)			
Disabled	39 (40.21%)	146 (41.83%)			
Retired	23 (23.71%)	53 (15.19%)			
Total	97	349			
ETHNICITY					
Asian/Pacific Islander	15 (10.14%)	52 (9.65%)	2.52	4,682	0.64
African American	35 (23.65%)	111 (20.59%)			
Latino	36 (24.32%)	136 (25.23%)			
White	54 (36.49%)	222 (41.19%)			
Native American	8 (5.40%)	18 (3.34%)			
Total	148	539			
FAMILY HISTORY OF PSYCHIATRIC DISORDERS					
Yes	44 (29.73%)	43 (54.43%)	13.30	1,225	0.001
No	104 (70.27%)	36 (45.57%)			
Total	148	79			

*For unemployed participants only.

depression, bipolar disorder, alcohol and drug abuse and/or dependence have been excluded from the randomized group, comparisons between the randomized and nonrandomized groups on these variables are not presented.

Characteristics of the Samples at Initial Screenings

Table 11.13. Initial Levels of Depression and Psychological Well-being by Randomization

Variable	Randomized	Nonrandomized	t	df	p
CES-D	15.04 (11.05) n = 149	21.37 (13.66) n = 505	−5.81	293.9	0.0001
BDI	11.98 (7.96) n = 150	19.27 (10.97) n = 141	−6.45	254.2	0.0001
AB+	3.07 (1.59) n = 150	2.35 (1.62) n = 79	3.23	227	0.001
AB−	1.64 (1.66) n = 150	2.89 (1.56) n = 79	−5.50	227	0.0001
Quality of Life	3.13 (1.07) n = 145	2.55 (1.06) n = 76	3.83	219	0.0001

Note: See Table 10.1 for a key to abbreviations of measures.

Table 11.14. Lifetime Prevalence Rates of Selected DIS/DSM-III Diagnosis by Randomization

Diagnosis	Randomized (n = 150)	Nonrandomized (n = 142)	Chi-Sq	df	p
Major depression	14 (9.33%)	43 (30.28%)	20.38	1,290	0.001
Major depression, single episode	2 (1.33%)	7 (4.93%)	3.16	1,290	0.08
Major depression, recurrent	11 (7.33%)	32 (22.54%)	13.42	1,290	0.001
Dysthymia	9 (6.00%)	22 (15.49%)	6.93	1,290	0.01
Bipolar disorder	1 (0.67%)	3 (2.11%)	1.13	1,290	0.29
Alcohol abuse and/or dependence	34 (22.67%)	60 (42.25%)	12.82	1,290	0.001
Drug abuse and/or dependence	5 (3.33%)	17 (11.97%)	7.81	1,290	0.01
Obsessive-compulsive disorder	9 (6.00%)	10 (7.04%)	0.13	1,290	0.72
Phobic disorders	28 (18.67%)	44 (30.99%)	5.96	1,290	0.02
Agoraphobia	13 (8.67%)	18 (12.68%)	1.24	1,290	0.27
Simple phobia	21 (14.00%)	29 (20.42%)	2.12	1,290	0.15
Social phobia	2 (1.33%)	9 (6.34%)	5.04	1,290	0.03
Somatization disorder	1 (0.67%)	3 (2.11%)	1.13	1,290	0.29
Panic disorder	0	5 (3.52%)	5.37	1,290	0.02
Antisocial personality	8 (5.33%)	13 (9.15%)	1.60	1,290	0.21
Tobacco dependence	60 (40.00%)	76 (53.52%)	5.36	1,290	0.02
Pathological gambling	4 (2.67%)	1 (0.70%)	1.67	1,290	0.20
Sexual dysfunction	49 (32.67%)	39 (27.46%)	0.94	1,290	0.33

Physical Health and Medical Chart Review

As Table 11.15 indicates, the randomized group reported significantly fewer physical symptoms than the nonrandomized group. However, the two groups did not differ in their subjective ratings of their physical health and concern over their health. In addition, Table 11.16 shows the two groups had similar medical chart review results, that is, they had comparable numbers of outpatient visits and hospitalizations in the previous year.

Cognitive-Behavioral Variables

As expected, the randomized and nonrandomized groups differed significantly on most of the cognitive-behavioral variables. As Table 11.17 indicates, the difference in the Personal Beliefs score showed the nonrandomized group held more maladaptive beliefs than the randomized group (means of 40.92 and 38.31, respectively). Compared with the nonrandomized group, the randomized group also assigned higher probabilities to positive items (means of 67.01 and 59.95, respectively) but lower probability levels to negative items (means of 25.16 versus 30.74, respectively), indicative of their holding more positive views of themselves and the world. Similarly, the former reported, on the average, having more positive (45.34 versus 42.33) but fewer negative thoughts (58.09 versus 68.16) during the last month. In addition, the randomized group engaged in more pleasant activities (mean of 108.86 versus 102.86) and more social activities (73.46 versus 69.98) than the nonrandomized group in the past month. All of these differences are consistent with the nonrandomized group's being more depressed than the randomized group. These results also support the hypothesized relationship between the cognitive-behavioral measures and depression.

Table 11.15. Initial Physical Health by Randomization

Variable	Randomized	Nonrandomized	t	df	p
Number of physical symptoms	7.18 (6.02) n = 150	9.80 (6.46) n = 81	−3.69	229	0.002
Health status	2.66 (0.83) n = 150	2.77 (0.86) n = 544	−1.40	692	0.16
Health concern	5.90 (3.27) n = 145	6.29 (3.25) n = 520	−1.25	663	0.21

Table 11.16. Medical Utilization by Randomization

Variable	Randomized	Nonrandomized	df	t	p
Number of outpatient visits	6.06 (3.75) n = 141	5.52 (3.35) n = 124	263	1.23	0.22
Number of hospitalization	0.35 (0.74) n = 138	0.37 (0.87) n = 123	259	−0.18	0.86

Table 11.17. Initial Cognitions and Behaviors by Randomization

Variable	Randomized	Nonrandomized	t	df	p
PBI	38.31 (7.86) n = 150	40.92 (8.52) n = 82	−2.34	230	0.02
SPQ+	67.01 (15.90) n = 150	59.95 (17.20) n = 81	3.13	229	0.002
SPQ−	25.16 (13.54) n = 150	30.74 (15.73) n = 81	−2.82	229	0.005
CES+	45.34 (8.54) n = 150	42.33 (8.71) n = 80	2.52	228	0.01
CES−	58.09 (13.57) n = 150	68.16 (15.82) n = 80	−5.06	228	0.0001
PAS	108.86 (14.96) n = 150	102.86 (17.24) n = 80	2.75	228	0.01
SAQ	73.46 (11.74) n = 149	69.98 (12.34) n = 82	2.12	229	0.04

Note: See Table 10.1 for a key to abbreviations.

Life Events and Social Desirability

Compared with the nonrandomized participants, the randomized group reported a significantly lower positive life event sum seven to twelve months before the screening (mean = 2.02 versus 1.25, respectively, df = 118.98, t = 1.96, p = .05). This was contrary to expectation. As no other differences on life events were found between the randomized and nonrandomized groups (as Table 11.18 shows), this may have been due to chance. The two groups did not differ on social desirability.

In conclusion, the randomized and nonrandomized groups differed most markedly on the cognitive-behavioral and outcome variables. The differences found are likely to be a result of excluding certain partici-

Table 11.18. Life Events and Social Desirability by Randomization

Variable	Randomized	Nonrandomized	df	t	p
Life Events + Sum (0–6 months)	3.25 (3.97) n = 150	2.80 (3.65) n = 82	230	−0.83	0.41
Life Events − Sum (0–6 months)	4.80 (6.07) n = 150	5.33 (5.13) n = 82	230	0.67	0.50
Life Events + Sum (7–12 months)	1.25 (2.10) n = 150	2.02 (3.24) n = 82	118.98	1.96	0.05
Life Events − Sum (7–12 months)	3.29 (4.59) n = 150	4.17 (5.34) n = 82	230	1.32	0.19
Crowne-Marlowe	7.74 (3.16) n = 150	7.18 (3.19) n = 80	228	1.29	0.20

pants from randomization due to the presence of a current diagnosis of major depression, bipolar disorder, alcohol and drug abuse and/or dependence, or lifetime diagnosis of organic brain syndrome or schizophrenia. Those excluded from the study held more maladaptive beliefs and more negative views of themselves and the world, experienced more negative but fewer positive thoughts, and engaged in fewer pleasant and social activities. They also reported higher levels of depressive symptoms, poorer life quality, a greater probability of having a family history of psychiatric illness, and experienced more negative and less positive affect than the randomized group. The only finding that was contrary to expectation was their having experienced more positive life events in the seven to twelve months before the screening.

Variation by Randomization Condition

Upon agreeing to be randomized, the study participants were randomly assigned to a Class, Control (no intervention), and Video (information only) conditions. A total of 72 participants were assigned to the Class condition, 30 to the Video condition and 48 to the Control condition (the smaller number of participants in the Video condition is due to its unavailability to Spanish-speaking participants). Randomization successfully resulted in the comparability of the three conditions on the variables of interest before the intervention.

Characteristics of the Samples at Initial Screenings

Demographic Variables

Tables 11.19 and 11.20 present the demographic characteristics of the three randomized conditions. We found no differences across the groups, except in terms of ethnicity. The pairwise comparisons revealed no two conditions to vary significantly.

A Family History of Psychiatric Disorder

Table 11.20 also shows the randomized group to vary in the prevalence of family history of psychiatric disorder. However, pairwise comparisons (with significance level for alpha = .05/3) revealed no two groups to be significantly different from each other. Possible effects of a difference in family history across the conditions would have acted against our hypotheses, because the Class condition had almost twice the rate of family history than the Control conditions.

Outcome Variables: Level of Depression and Emotional Well-being

As is seen in Table 11.21, the three conditions did not differ on the outcome variables at initial assessment.

Table 11.19. Demographic Characteristics by Randomization Condition (for Continuous Variables)

Variable	Class	Control	Video	df	F	p
Age	50.82 (13.45) n = 72	52.48 (11.63) n = 48	54.93 (11.30) n = 30	2,147	1.17	0.31
Years in U.S.*	12.92 (11.86) n = 72	12.81 (10.36) n = 48	12.40 (9.83) n = 30	2,147	0.02	0.98
Years in San Francisco	22.01 (15.23) n = 72	19.06 (15.81) n = 48	22.93 (15.55) n = 30	2,147	0.74	0.48
Education	12.56 (3.42) n = 70	11.61 (4.09) n = 46	12.07 (2.51) n = 29	2,142	1.03	0.36
Income** (in thousands)	11.19 (9.66) n = 63	10.58 (7.63) n = 43	10.44 (7.11) n = 27	2,130	0.10	0.90

*Ascertained for foreign-born participants only.
**For 1983–84.

Table 11.20. Demographic Characteristics by Randomization Condition (for Categorical Variables)*

Variable	Class	Control	Video	Overall Test Chi-Sq	df	p
SEX						
Male	26 (36.11%)	17 (35.42%)	14 (46.67%)	1.20	2,147	0.55
Female	46 (63.89%)	31 (64.58%)	16 (53.33%)			
Total	72	48	30			
MARITAL STATUS						
Never married	14 (19.44%)	8 (16.66%)	5 (16.67%)	1.00	4,145	0.91
Now married	29 (40.28%)	20 (41.67%)	10 (33.33%)			
Formerly married	29 (40.28%)	20 (41.67%)	15 (50.00%)			
Total	72	48	30			
EMPLOYED						
Yes	18 (25.35%)	17 (35.42%)	13 (43.33%)	3.45	2,146	0.18
No	53 (74.65%)	31 (64.58%)	17 (56.67%)			
Total	71	48	30			
UNEMPLOYMENT STATUS**						
Looking for work	13 (25.49%)	5 (17.24%)	3 (17.65%)	4.21	8,88	0.84
Student	2 (3.92%)	1 (3.45%)	0			
Homemaker	5 (9.80%)	5 (17.24%)	1 (5.88%)			
Disabled	21 (41.18%)	11 (37.93%)	7 (41.18%)			
Retired	10 (19.61%)	7 (24.14%)	6 (35.29%)			
Total	51	29	17			
ETHNICITY						
Asian/Pacific Islander	6 (8.45%)	4 (8.51%)	5 (16.67%)	15.62	8,139	0.05
African American	14 (19.72%)	13 (27.66%)	8 (26.67%)			
Latino	16 (22.54%)	18 (38.30%)	2 (6.66%)			
White	31 (43.66%)	11 (23.40%)	12 (40.00%)			
Native American	4 (5.63%)	1 (2.13%)	3 (10.00%)			
Total	71	47	30			
FAMILY HISTORY OF PSYCHIATRIC DISORDERS						
Yes	28 (38.89%)	10 (20.83%)	6 (20.00%)	6.11	2,147	0.05
No	44 (61.11%)	38 (79.17%)	24 (80.00%)			
Total	72	48	30			

*No pairwise comparisons were significant, and thus are not reported (Scheffé post-hoc test used, with significance level of alpha = 0.05/3 contrasts).

**For unemployed participants only.

Table 11.21. Initial Levels of Depression and Psychological Well-being by Randomization Condition

Variable	Class	Control	Video	df	F	p
CES-D	15.57 (11.38) n = 72	15.77 (11.39) n = 48	12.67 (9.62) n = 30	2,146	0.87	0.42
BDI	12.58 (8.63) n = 72	12.23 (6.82) n = 48	10.16 (7.92) n = 30	2,147	1.01	0.37
AB+	3.14 (1.54) n = 72	2.71 (1.79) n = 48	3.47 (1.28) n = 30	2,147	2.28	0.11
AB−	1.81 (1.73) n = 72	1.60 (1.71) n = 48	1.30 (1.39) n = 30	2,147	0.99	0.37
Quality of Life	3.01 (1.07) n = 70	3.04 (1.06) n = 47	3.55 (0.99) n = 29	2,143	2.92	0.06

Note: See Table 10.1 for a key to abbreviations.

DSM-III/DIS Clinical Diagnoses

Table 11.22 shows the three conditions did not differ on lifetime prevalence of major diagnoses. Again, organic brain syndrome and schizophrenia are deleted from the table, as respondents meeting those diagnoses were excluded from randomization.

Physical Health and Medical Chart Review

As Tables 11.23 and 11.24 indicate, the three conditions did not differ in number of physical symptoms reported, health status or health concern, nor in the number of outpatient visits and hospitalizations.

Cognitive Behavioral Variables

As Table 11.25 shows, the three conditions did not differ on any of the cognitive-behavioral variables.

Life Events and Social Desirability

Finally, as Table 11.26 shows, the three conditions also did not differ on these variables.

All in all, except for an overrepresentation of Latinos in the Control but underrepresentation in the Video condition (due to the un-

Table 11.22. Lifetime Prevalence Rates of Selected DIS/DSM-III Diagnoses by Randomization Condition

Diagnosis	Class (n = 72)	Control (n = 48)	Video (n = 30)	Overall Test Chi-Sq	df	p
Major depression	8 (11.11%)	1 (2.08%)	4 (13.33%)	3.40	2,147	.14
Major depression, single episode	1 (1.39%)	0	1 (3.33%)	1.56	2,147	.46
Major depression, recurrent	6 (8.33%)	1 (2.08%)	3 (10.00%)	2.48	2,147	.29
Dysthymia	6 (8.33%)	2 (4.17%)	1 (3.33%)	1.36	2,147	.51
Bipolar disorder	1 (1.39%)	0	0	1.09	2,147	.58
Alcohol abuse and/ or dependence	15 (20.83%)	11 (22.92%)	8 (26.67%)	0.41	2,147	.81
Drug abuse and/or dependence	1 (1.39%)	2 (4.17%)	2 (6.67%)	1.98	2,147	.37
Obsessive-compulsive disorder	3 (4.17%)	3 (6.25%)	3 (10.00%)	1.29	2,147	.53
Phobic disorders	13 (18.06%)	12 (25.00%)	2 (6.67%)	4.20	2,147	.12
Agoraphobia	6 (8.33%)	6 (12.50%)	1 (3.33%)	1.98	2,147	.37
Simple phobia	10 (13.89%)	9 (18.75%)	1 (3.33%)	3.83	2,147	.15
Social phobia	2 (2.78%)	0	0	2.20	2,147	.33
Somatization disorder	0	1 (2.08%)	0	2.14	2,147	.34
Panic disorder	0	0	0			
Antisocial personality	4 (5.56%)	2 (4.17%)	2 (6.67%)	0.24	2,147	.89
Tobacco dependence	30 (41.67%)	14 (29.17%)	16 (53.35%)	4.65	2,147	.10
Pathological gambling	2 (2.78%)	2 (4.17%)	0	1.24	2,147	.54
Sexual dysfunction	20 (27.78%)	21 (43.75%)	8 (26.67%)	3.96	2,147	.14

Table 11.23. Initial Physical Health by Randomization Condition

Variable	Class	Control	Video	df	F	p
Number of physical symptoms	7.10 (6.34) n = 72	7.29 (5.44) n = 48	7.19 (6.34) n = 30	2,147	0.01	0.99
Health status	2.68 (0.84) n = 72	2.75 (0.81) n = 48	2.47 (0.86) n = 30	2,147	1.11	0.33
Health concern	5.72 (3.27) n = 69	6.00 (3.35) n = 46	6.17 (3.22) n = 30	2,142	0.22	0.80

Table 11.24. Medical Utilization by Randomization Condition

Variable	Class	Control	Video	df	F	p
Number of outpatient visits	6.00 (3.92) n = 66	5.82 (2.96) n = 45	6.57 (4.45) n = 30	2,138	0.37	0.69
Number of hospitalizations	0.42 (0.88) n = 65	0.30 (0.55) n = 44	0.28 (0.65) n = 29	2,135	0.51	0.60

Table 11.25. Initial Cognitions and Behaviors by Randomization Condition

Variable	Class	Control	Video	df	F	p
PBI	38.28 (7.69) n = 72	38.32 (8.16) n = 48	38.37 (8.05) n = 30	2,147	0.00	0.99
SPQ+	66.95 (16.08) n = 72	65.96 (16.77) n = 48	68.84 (14.33) n = 30	2,147	0.30	0.74
SPQ−	25.38 (14.39) n = 72	26.16 (13.10) n = 48	23.00 (12.26) n = 30	2,147	0.52	0.60
CES+	44.53 (9.00) n = 72	45.17 (9.01) n = 48	47.57 (6.23) n = 30	2,147	1.36	0.26
CES−	59.10 (15.15) n = 72	58.69 (13.26) n = 48	54.70 (9.15) n = 30	2,147	1.18	0.31
PAS	108.03 (14.25) n = 72	107.67 (17.29) n = 48	112.78 (12.20) n = 30	2,147	1.30	0.28
SAQ	72.11 (11.64) n = 72	72.71 (11.90) n = 48	72.80 (10.80) n = 30	2,147	2.70	0.07

Note: See Table 10.1 for a key to abbreviations.

availability of the Spanish version of the video), the three conditions were comparable across all variables of interest before the intervention.

The Presence of Ethnic Differences

Given the emphasis on recruiting and retaining an ethnically diverse sample, two questions are particularly important to consider: (1) During the screening process, did we successfully retain comparable representation of ethnic groups as originally recruited; and (2) Did the ethnic groups score comparably on the major variables of the study (family history of psychiatric disorder, outcome variables, clinical diag-

Table 11.26. Life Events and Social Desirability by Randomization Condition

Variable	Class	Control	Video	df	F	p
Life Events + Sum (0–6 months)	3.61 (4.02) n = 72	3.31 (4.05) n = 48	2.60 (3.73) n = 30	2,147	0.69	0.51
Life Events − Sum (0–6 months)	4.93 (5.71) n = 72	4.04 (5.48) n = 48	5.47 (7.86) n = 30	2,147	0.56	0.57
Life Events + Sum (7–12 months)	1.57 (2.58) n = 72	1.13 (1.91) n = 48	0.77 (1.50) n = 30	2,147	1.56	0.21
Life Events − Sum (7–12 months)	3.28 (4.99) n = 72	3.47 (4.26) n = 48	2.90 (4.13) n = 30	2,147	0.14	0.87
Crowne-Marlowe	7.50 (3.37) n = 72	7.73 (2.99) n = 48	8.33 (2.90) n = 30	2,147	0.73	0.48

noses, physical health, medical chart review, cognitive-behavioral variables, life events and social desirability), to justify the formation of a single group.

As before, ethnicity was coded as Asian/Pacific Islander, African American, Latino, Native American, and White. The actual breakdown of number of participants at initial screening and randomization are presented in Tables 11.3 and 11.12. In terms of the first question, Chi-Square analyses revealed an absence of differences in ethnic composition from first to second screening (Chi-Square = 4.84, df = 4, p = .31), second to third screening (Chi-Square = 1.47, df = 4, p = .83), and third screening to randomization (Chi-Square = 3.95, df = 4, p = .41). Thus, we have successfully retained comparable numbers of ethnic minorities at randomization as were originally recruited.

With regard to the second question, the presence of ethnic differences on major variables in the study was assessed using analyses of variance (for continuous variables) or Chi-Square tests (for categorical variables). Since the ethnicity of two participants was missing, the maximum sample size for these analyses was 148. At randomization, the groups differed on presence of a family history of psychiatric disorder (Chi-Square = 10.45, df = 4,143, p = .03). Pairwise comparisons (using alpha level = .05/10 contrasts = .005) revealed white participants to report a significantly higher prevalence rate of family history (44.44%) than Latinos (13.89%, Chi-Square = 9.23, df = 1, p = .002), and Asians (6.67%, Chi-Square = 7.25, df = 1, p = .007).

Characteristics of the Samples at Initial Screenings

In terms of the outcome variables, the ethnic groups did not differ on CES-D [F (4,143) = 2.23, p = .07], BDI [F (4,143) = .67, p = .61], quality of life [F (4,139) = 0.43, p = .79], AB+ [F (4,143) = 0.64, p = .64], and AB− [F (4,143) = 2.21, p = .07].

Turning to lifetime prevalence of major clinical disorders at randomization, no ethnic differences were found for dysthymia (Chi-Square = .72, df = 4, p = .95), bipolar disorder (Chi-Square = 1.75, df = 4, p = .78), alcohol abuse and/or dependence (Chi-Square = 1.00, df = 4, p = .91), and drug abuse and/or dependence (Chi-Square = 7.73, df = 4, p = .10). An overall difference was found in the case of major depression (Chi-Square = 10.92, df = 4, p = .03). However, no two groups were significantly different from each other.

Analysis of variance showed the number of physical symptoms reported to vary by ethnic group [F (4,143) = 3.22, p = .01]. African Americans reported significantly higher numbers of symptoms than whites (mean = 10.09 and 5.71, respectively, t = 4.38, p = .001). However, the ethnic groups did not vary in their reported health status [F (4,143) = 2.17, p = .08] and level of health concern [F (4,141) = .40, p = .81]. Ethnic differences were not found on number of hospitalizations. While the ethnic groups were found to differ marginally on number of outpatients visits made in the previous year [F (4,257) = 2.28, p = .06], pairwise comparisons showed no two groups to vary significantly.

In terms of the cognitive-behavioral variables, the five ethnic groups scored comparably on the PBI [F (4,143) = 1.90, p = .11], SPQ+ [F (4,143) = 1.06, [p = .38], CES+ [F (4,143) = 1.06, p = .38], CES− [F (4,143) = 1.86, p = .12], PAS [F (4,143) = 1.10, p = .36], and SAQ [F (4,143) = 0.67, p = .61]. However, there was an overall difference on the SPQ− [F (4,143) = 2.75, p = .03]. Pairwise comparisons showed Latinos to score significantly more pessimistic than Asians (means = 28.84 versus 17.06, t = 2.90, p = .004).

The ethnic groups did not differ in the ratings of life events. For the positive life events sum within the last six months, F (4,143) = 1.59, p = .18; and for the negative sum score during the same time period, F (4,143) = 1.50, p = .21. For the negative life events sum seven to twelve months ago, F (4,143) = 1.64, p = .16; and for the negative sum score during that time period, F (4,143) = 1.23, p = .30.

Overall differences were found on the Crowne-Marlowe [F (4,143) = 4.73, p = .001]. Whites (mean = 6.41) scored significantly less socially desirable than Asians (mean = 9.33, t = 3.32, p = .001); African Americans (mean = 8.67, t = 3.46, p = .001); and Latinos (mean = 8.21, t = 2.77, p = .006).

Given the many analyses conducted, the ethnic differences found were, by and large, unremarkable. Perhaps most noteworthy is the differential social desirability score between whites and most of the ethnic minority groups. Most likely, this finding reflects the stronger desire among whites to please the self (individual orientation) or to be "frank," as opposed to the emphasis of conforming to the group, (contextual-orientation) or to be "polite," that is more prevalent in most ethnic minority populations. This difference will be reappraised at follow-up assessments (Chapter 17), to determine if it may have biased outcome measures.

12. The Effects of Preventive Intervention on Depression

One goal of this investigation was to determine the effectiveness of our intervention in reducing depressive symptomatology and clinical episodes of depression over time. We hypothesized that those assigned to the Class condition would show a decline in depressive symptomatology and a significantly lower incidence of depression than those assigned to either the Video or Control conditions.

As noted previously, we used the CES-D (Radloff, 1977) and BDI (Beck et al., 1961) to measure level of depressive symptomatology, and the DIS (Robins et al., 1981) to assess the presence of clinical depression. Also, as stated earlier, the relationship between depressive level and presence of clinical diagnosis was less than perfect. Including measures of both allowed for a better understanding of the effect of the intervention.

Two major questions were of particular interest: (1) From preintervention to follow-up, did participants in the Class condition demonstrate a greater decline in depressive symptomatology and a lower incidence of clinical depression than the Video and Control condition participants?; and (2) Did the actual number of classes attended significantly predict to level of change in depression over time?

The need to examine both questions arose from the reality that not all participants assigned to the Class condition attended all the sessions. Thus, they could not obtain the full benefit of being in the experimental condition. In fact, there was quite a range in the number of sessions attended by the Class condition participants, as Table 12.1 shows. While half of those assigned to the Class condition attended seven or eight out of the eight class sessions, one-fifth did not attend any classes. To treat all of them as if they attended all eight sessions would be the most conservative approach (as used in responding to the first question.) However, one would also expect the number of classes attended to influence change in depression significantly.

What accounted for differential class attendance? We examined this as predicted by demographic characteristics and preintervention depressive level. Table 12.2 presents the results of a hierarchical regres-

Table 12.1. Number of Class Sessions Attended by Participants

Number of Sessions Attended	Number (Percentage) of Participants
0	15 (20.8%)
1	2 (2.8%)
2	6 (8.3%)
3	4 (5.6%)
4	4 (5.6%)
5	3 (4.2%)
6	2 (2.8%)
7	11 (15.3%)
8	25 (34.7%)
Total	72 (100%)

Table 12.2. Number of Class Sessions Attended as Predicted by Demographic Variables and Pre-CES-D Score

Variable	Standardized Beta	t	p
Step 1: Demographic Variables*			
Age	0.21	1.54	0.13
Female**	0.31	1.95	0.06
Education	0.10	0.67	0.50
Income	−0.11	−0.80	0.43
Native American**	0.14	0.98	0.33
Latino**	−0.04	−0.29	0.77
African American**	0.19	1.34	0.19
Asian/Pacific-Islander**	−0.06	−0.41	0.69
Step 2: Pre-CES-D Score***			
Age	0.20	1.52	0.13
Female**	0.26	1.71	0.09
Education	0.14	0.94	0.35
Income	−0.08	−0.56	0.58
Native American**	0.12	0.85	0.40
Latino**	−0.02	−0.12	0.91
African American**	0.20	1.40	0.17
Asian/Pacific-Islander**	−0.08	−0.55	0.58
Pre-CES-D Score	0.26	1.94	0.06

*Adjusted R-Square = 0.003, F (8,51) = 1.02, p = 0.43.

**White males make up the deleted comparison group.

***R-Square Change = 0.06, F Change = 3.74, p = 0.06, Adjusted R-Square = 0.05, F (9,50) = 1.37, p = 0.23.

sion analysis, entering demographic variables (sex, ethnicity, age, education, and income) at the first step and the pre-CES-D score at the second step. The dependent variable was the number of sessions attended. Categorical predictor variables were coded such that white males made up the comparison group, against whom the other participants were compared.

At the first step, the model was not significant, Adjusted R-Square = .003, F (8,51) = 1.02, p = .43. However, examination of the beta values showed that women were marginally likely to attend more class sessions (standardized beta = .31, p = .06). When the pre-CES-D score was entered at the second step, the Adjusted R-Square was .05, F (9,50) = 1.37, p = .23, R-Square Change = .06, F Change = .3.74, p = .06. The pre-CES-D score was marginally significant (standardized beta = .26, p = .06), that is, those with higher pre-CES-D scores were likely to attend more classes. When the relationship of sex and pre-CES-D score with the number of class sessions attended was further examined by repeating the regression analysis but deleting all demographic variables other than sex, thereby increasing the power of the analysis (improving predictor to sample size ratio), the results showed that the pre-CES-D alone was a significant predictor of the number of sessions attended (standardized beta = .32, p = .008), while sex was no longer a significant predictor (standardized beta = .001, p = .99). Adjusted R-Square for the model was .07, F (2,69) = 3.84, p = .03.

The Change in the Level of Depression by Condition over Time

Mean scores of CES-D and BDI by condition and across time are presented in Tables 12.3 and 12.4. To assess the influence of assignment condition on change in depressive level, we conducted a hierarchical regression analysis. The change in depression level (calculated as post-score minus pre-score, six-months follow-up score minus pre-score, and one-year follow-up score minus pre-score) served as the dependent variable. Negative change scores reflected decline in depressive level, and were indicative of improvement in mood. Positive change scores reflected a rise in depression, a worsening of mood.

In terms of the predictor variables, at the first step, the preintervention depressive level was entered, partialing out its contribution to the change score. At the second step, the condition of assignment was entered; the Video and Control conditions were combined and served as the comparison group, which was contrasted to the Class condition. Next, we assessed the presence of variation between the two control

Table 12.3. CES-D Score by Condition and Assessment Period

Assessment Period	Class			Control			Video		
	Mean	(SD)	n	Mean	(SD)	n	Mean	(SD)	n
Preintervention	15.57	(11.38)	72	15.77	(11.39)	48	12.67	(9.62)	30
Postintervention	12.14	(8.97)	65	14.26	(11.15)	43	12.50	(9.14)	28
Six-months follow-up	11.17	(9.43)	63	13.16	(9.38)	44	11.19	(9.87)	26
One-year follow-up	9.41	(9.48)	62	13.11	(9.90)	45	9.44	(8.16)	27

Table 12.4. BDI Score by Condition and Assessment Period

Assessment Period	Class			Control			Video		
	Mean	(SD)	n	Mean	(SD)	n	Mean	(SD)	n
Preintervention	12.58	(8.63)	72	12.23	(6.82)	48	10.16	(7.92)	30
Postintervention	8.60	(7.97)	65	9.99	(6.62)	43	9.52	(6.67)	27
Six-months follow-up	7.35	(7.37)	64	9.87	(6.80)	44	8.21	(6.07)	25
One-year follow-up	6.56	(7.85)	61	8.56	(5.71)	45	6.07	(5.26)	27

conditions, namely, the information-only Video condition and no-contact Control condition.

Since we hypothesized that the Class condition participants would demonstrate greater change in depressive level than either the Control or Video condition participants, we used a one-tailed t-test in assessing the presence of condition difference. However, we used a two-tailed test in the analysis contrasting Video and Control conditions, as no difference was hypothesized at the outset.

For all CES-D change scores calculated at post-, six-months, and one-year follow-up, pre-CES-D emerged as a significant ($p = .0001$) predictor (accounting for 38.43%, 45.41% and 47.77%, respectively, of the variance in change score at the three follow-up points). This was expected, as the pre-score was used in the construction of the change score. Those who scored higher on pre-CES-D tended to report greater change at follow-up assessments, which was likely to be reflective of the phenomenon of regression to the mean.

Beyond the contribution of the pre-CES-D score to the change scores, the condition of assignment did not make a significant contribution at post- and six-months follow-up. At one-year follow-up, participants in the Class condition scored marginally (p = .06, one-tailed test) lower (by 2.51 change points) than the other groups. Regression analyses assessing the presence of difference between the Video and Control conditions showed the two groups to not differ in change of CES-D score at any of the three follow-up points, once the contribution of the pre-CES-D score was considered.

The means and standard deviations of the BDI by condition and over time are presented in Table 12.4. To assess change in BDI by condition, we employed the same model as the one used to assess change in CES-D. Again, the preintervention BDI score made a significant contribution (p = .0001) to accounting for BDI change at all of the follow-up points (Adjusted R-Square was .28, .33, and .38 at post-, six-months, and one-year follow-up, respectively). As before, those who scored more depressed on the pre-BDI showed more improvement at follow-up. In addition, compared with others, the Class condition participants reported significantly greater decline in BDI depression levels than the others at all follow-up points. The difference in change score was 2.11 points at post- (p = .02), 2.71 points at six-months (p = .002), and 1.73 points at one-year follow-up (p = .04), supporting the hypothesis that the class intervention had a positive effect in reducing depression levels as measured by the BDI. Again, like the CES-D, BDI change scores did not vary between Control and Video conditions participants at any of the follow-up points.

Given the significant time factor found for both the CES-D and BDI, we converted the depressive scores into standardized z scores by timeline to highlight the differences across the conditions. These are presented graphically in Figures 12.1 and 12.2 for the CES-D and the BDI, respectively. In both cases, participants in the Class and Control conditions had comparable initial scores at preintervention, but at follow-up, the Class condition scored consistently below the overall mean (i.e., z was less than zero) while the Control condition participants scored consistently above it. Since the Video condition participants had a lower preintervention score, it was more difficult to compare them to the others. While the difference between the Class and Control condition participants was not necessarily statistically significant, the graphic presentation does underline the fact that on both the CES-D and BDI, the relative position of Class condition improved at post- and six-months and remained relatively steady at twelve-months follow-up.

In summary, the change in CES-D and BDI scores was predicted most convincingly by the preintervention score, with those scoring higher initially more likely to report greater decline at follow-up. In

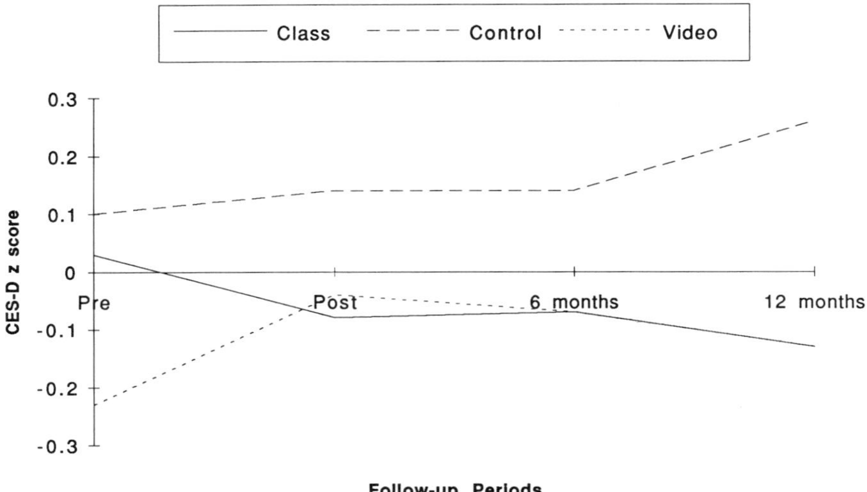

Figure 12.1. Standardized CES-D scores across follow-up periods

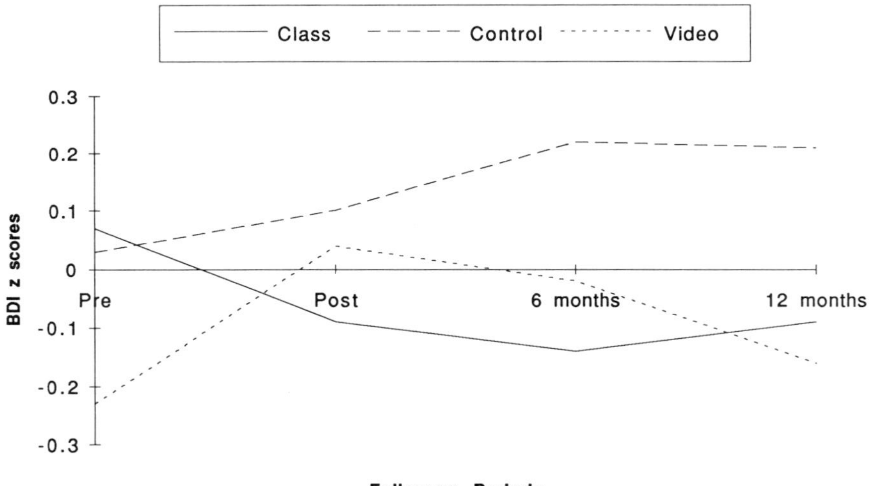

Figure 12.2. Standardized BDI scores across follow-up periods

addition, members of the Class condition reported greater reduction in BDI depressive levels than those assigned to the other conditions at all follow-up points. CES-D levels were only marginally lower at one-year follow-up. As noted in Chapter 10, the CES-D focused on the affective experience, and the BDI stressed the cognitive aspects of depression. Since altering the participant's cognitions was a major ingredient of the class intervention, the finding that Class participants generally scored less depressed on the BDI than the Video and Control condition respondents, suggested a possible differential impact on this aspect of depression.

Change in the Level of Depression over Time by the Number of Classes Attended

The analysis of the effect of sessions attended on change in depressive level included only Class condition participants. While change in depressive level was once again used as the dependent variable, the predictor variables were preintervention score, number of class sessions attended, ethnicity, and family history of psychiatric disorder. The change score was calculated by subtracting the preintervention score from each of the follow-up scores, with a smaller change score reflective of a lower follow-up depression level (it became negative if the follow-up score was smaller than the pre-score), which in turn implied improved mood level.

At the outset of the study, we hypothesized the number of class sessions attended to hold a linear relationship with change in depression level. In other words, attending more sessions would yield a greater decline in depression level. Thus, a one-tailed test was used. Ethnicity was entered to assess its potential role in accounting for variation in responsiveness to the Class intervention, as measured by depressive change score. Whites served as the comparison group. Since no ethnic differences were hypothesized, two-tailed tests were used. Finally, the potential role of having a family history of psychiatric disorders in participant's responsiveness to the class intervention was assessed. The direction of this relationship was not specifically hypothesized at the outset of the study; thus, a two-tailed test is appropriate.

In the prediction of the Class condition's CES-D change score, pre-CES-D again made a significant contribution at all follow-up points (46%, 50%, and 51% of the variance was accounted for at post-, six-months, and one-year follow-up, respectively). As before, higher scores on the pre-CES-D reported greater decline at all follow-up points. The number of sessions attended held a significantly negative relationship to change in CES-D score only at post-follow-up (b coefficient = $-.67$, $p = .02$), with those attending more sessions likely to report greater decline in CES-D score. In terms of ethnicity, African American participants reported a significantly smaller decline in depressive level than the white participants (b coefficient = 5.55, p = .01) at one-year follow-up. The presence of a family history of psychiatric disorders did not contribute to a change in CES-D.

Turning to the prediction of BDI change score, the pre-BDI score again made a significant contribution (explaining 22%, 36%, and 31% of the variance in change scores at post-, six-months, and one-year follow-up, respectively). As before, those who scored higher on the BDI at pretesting tended to demonstrate a greater decline in depressive level. The number of sessions attended held a significantly negative relationship with BDI change score at one-year follow-up (b coefficient = −.63, p = .01), with those attending more class sessions also reporting a greater decline in depressive level (again, arithmetically *smaller* change score meant *greater* change, as the score was negative.) No differences were found by ethnicity and family history of psychiatric disorders.

In summary, the previously reported relationship of preintervention depressive level and change score was found once again. In addition, as predicted, the number of sessions attended held a negative relationship with the CES-D change score at post- and with the BDI change score at one-year follow-up. Those who attended more class sessions reported lower levels of depression at follow-up assessments. However, this relationship was found to be significant only at one out of three follow-up points for each measure of depression. Compared with the finding that the condition of assignment significantly differentiates level of change on the BDI at all three follow-up points, it appeared that the total number of class sessions attended may be less important than being exposed to and learning the specific materials presented at the sessions attended.

Only for the CES-D and only at one-year follow-up did African Americans report less improvement than whites. This finding was unremarkable as it was not replicated at other follow-up points, nor with the BDI.

Having a family history of psychiatric disorder did not significantly affect change in depression level for the class participants. This suggested that familial loading (whether genetic or not) did not render one differentially unresponsive to this intervention to prevent depression.

The Incidence of Clinical Depression across Conditions

At one-year follow-up, six participants met criteria for major depression in the last year. One person met criteria for dysthymia (assigned to

Class condition). The overall incidence for major depression was 4.3 percent and 0.7 percent for dysthymia (n = 139). Of the six cases of major depression, four occurred in the Control condition (one Asian woman, one African American man, one African American woman, and one white woman), and two in the Class condition (an African American woman and a Latina). Fisher's exact test showed incidence of clinical depression not to vary by condition ($p = .38$), ethnicity ($p = .54$), or a family history of psychiatric disorders ($p = .88$).

The Incidence of Clinical Depression by the Number of Classes Attended

Of the two Class participants who met criteria for major depression at one-year follow-up, one had attended two classes and one had attended no classes. A probit analysis showed that the number of sessions attended did not significantly predict to the incidence of major depression (Chi-Square = 31.54, df = 66, $p = .99$, the regression coefficient = $-.24$, standard error = .17, $t = -.39$, failing to reach significance at $p = .05$, one-tailed test). This was not surprising, given the very small number of Class condition participants who met criteria for incidence and the limited variability in class sessions attended.

All in all, we demonstrated that a group of demographically diverse primary care patients who participated in a depression prevention course reduced their depressive levels on the BDI significantly more than a group of comparable patients from the same clinics randomly assigned to control conditions. This effect was significant even though a large proportion (37%) of the invited patients attended none or fewer than half of the eight sessions of the intervention. Considering the small number of new episodes of clinical depression, there was insufficient statistical power to test the impact of the experimental intervention on incidence.

Regarding change in depressive level, the differential results of the BDI versus the CES-D were possibly secondary to the former having a stronger relationship with the content of the class intervention than the latter. The BDI focuses more heavily on the cognitive aspect of depression, and the CES-D targets the more affective dimension. The class sessions emphasized one's greater ability to modify thoughts and behavior over affect (which was presented in the class as likely to change concomittantly with changes in cognition and behavior).

In addition, participants who attended more classes reported fewer depressive symptoms at only one out of three follow-up points. This suggested a stronger role of exposure to some unidentified parts of the experimental intervention over merely attending a greater number of sessions. Perhaps learning the general cognitive-behavioral strategy of mood management was more important than the specific methods taught at each session.

Interestingly, those with higher initial levels of depression were more likely to attend more class sessions, and to report a greater decrease in their level of depression at follow-up assessments. This pointed to the value of targeting preventive interventions to individuals who experience high levels of depression without meeting diagnostic criteria for depressive disorder. They were most likely to benefit from such an intervention.

13. The Effects of Preventive Intervention on Psychological Well-being

Besides testing the effectiveness of the experimental intervention in reducing depressive symptomatology and episodes over time, we also hoped to achieve improved psychological well-being. In other words, in addition to preventive effects, we also tested the health promotion aspects of the intervention. As discussed in the previous chapter, we hypothesized that compared with those assigned to the Video and Control conditions, members of the Class condition would experience a gain in psychological well-being from preintervention to follow-up. In addition, we predicted that those who attended more class sessions would also report greater improvement in well-being over those who attended fewer sessions.

We used two measures to assess psychological well-being, that is, the Quality of Life Scale (Flanagan, 1978) and the Affect-Balance Scale (Bradburn, 1969; Bradburn & Caplovitz, 1965). From the Quality of Life Scale, we adopted the item assessing overall life quality. From the Affect-Balance Scale, we derived the Positive Affect Score (or AB+, which was calculated from the sum of the five positive affect items) and the Negative Affect Score (or AB−, which was calculated from the sum of the negative affect items).

First, we examined the change in the quality of life experienced. Higher scores reflected a superior quality of life. The change in the quality of life was calculated by subtracting the preintervention score from the follow-up score, with higher (positive) change scores indicative of improved life quality and lower (negative) change scores reflective of a decline in life quality. A similar method was used for the AB+ and AB− scores. For AB+, since higher scores indicated better affect, higher change scores, as in the case of life quality, also reflected an improvement in mood. For AB−, since higher scores were reflective of poorer affect, higher change scores were indicative of progressive worsening of affect.

In terms of the predictor variables, we entered the preintervention score first, followed by condition of assignment, with combined Video and Control conditions serving as the comparison group against which the Class condition was contrasted. A one-tailed t-test was used, assuming that the Class condition would demonstrate greater improvement over the others. Next, the two control conditions were compared and contrasted. Here, a two-tailed test was used, as they were not expected to differ.

The Change in Psychological Well-being by Condition over Time

Tables 13.1 and 13.2 present the means and standard deviations of the three psychological well-being measures across condition and time. As expected, the preintervention score was a significant contributor (p = .0001) to the quality of life change score at all follow-up points (accounting for 31%, 27%, and 34% of the variance at post-, six-months, and one-year follow-up), as it was used to calculate the change score. Those with a higher quality of life at preintervention reported greater decline at follow-up (likely to be due to the phenomenon of regression to the mean). In addition, participants in the Class condition surpassed the other participants in their improvement in the life quality rating at all follow-up assessment points (by .32, p = .03 at post-; by .47, p = .001 at six-months; and by .40, p = .01 at one-year follow-up). The Video and Control conditions were found not to change across time periods.

Next, we compared and contrasted performance on the Affect-Balance Scale from preintervention to follow-up for the Class condition with the two control conditions. For AB+, the preintervention score held a significant relationship (p = .0001) with the change score. Indeed, those who scored higher on AB+ reported a greater decline at follow-up. The amount of variance accounted for was 31 percent at

Table 13.1. Quality of Life by Condition and Assessment Period

Assessment Period	Class			Control			Video		
	Mean	(SD)	n	Mean	(SD)	n	Mean	(SD)	n
Preintervention	3.01	(1.07)	70	3.04	(1.06)	47	3.55	(0.99)	29
Postintervention	3.48	(1.04)	64	3.12	(0.93)	43	3.48	(1.09)	27
Six-months follow-up	3.50	(1.00)	62	2.93	(1.00)	44	3.50	(0.95)	26
One-year follow-up	3.53	(1.03)	60	3.05	(0.86)	41	3.48	(1.09)	27

Note: Higher scores denote better quality of life ratings.

Table 13.2. Affect-Balance Score by Condition and Assessment Period

Assessment Period	Class			Control			Video		
	Mean	(SD)	n	Mean	(SD)	n	Mean	(SD)	n
				Positive Score					
Preintervention	3.14	(1.54)	72	2.71	(1.79)	48	3.47	(1.28)	30
Postintervention	3.62	(1.54)	65	3.43	(1.34)	44	3.64	(1.25)	28
Six-months follow-up	3.52	(1.22)	64	3.23	(1.49)	44	3.54	(1.45)	26
One-year follow-up	3.26	(1.46)	62	3.02	(1.79)	45	3.78	(1.55)	27
				Negative Score					
Preintervention	1.81	(1.73)	72	1.60	(1.71)	48	1.30	(1.39)	30
Postintervention	1.43	(1.46)	65	1.61	(1.67)	44	1.57	(1.71)	28
Six-months follow-up	1.42	(1.62)	64	1.45	(1.66)	44	1.35	(1.20)	26
One-year follow-up	1.02	(1.35)	62	1.20	(1.46)	45	1.04	(1.37)	27

Note: For a positive score, a higher number denotes a greater positive affect. For a negative score, a higher number denotes a greater negative affect.

post-, 32 percent at six-months, and 32 percent at one-year follow-up. In contrast to the life quality measure, Class condition participants did not differ significantly from the others in their change score at the three follow-up points, nor did the Video and Control conditions differ from each other.

For AB−, 21 percent, 25 percent and 44 percent of the variance in the change score at post-, six-months, and one-year follow-up, respectively, was accounted for by the pre-score ($p = .0001$), with those reporting higher AB− scores at pre- more likely to report greater improvement at follow-up. In addition, at post-follow-up, the Class condition participants reported a greater decline in AB− (i.e., by .34 points, $p = .04$) than the other participants. Again, the Video and Control conditions were found not to differ.

In summary, the Class condition participants consistently reported a greater increase in the level of life quality than the other two groups at each of the three follow-up assessment points. The three groups did not differ on change in positive affect. Also, the Class condition participants reported a greater decrease in negative affect than the other participants at post-follow-up, but no differences were found at six-months and one-year follow-up points.

As noted in Chapter 10, quality of life tapped a long-term cognitive appraisal in contrast to the short-term affective assessment captured by the Affect-Balance Scale. Our findings supported this distinction. Ultimately, we were successful in improving the Class condition participants' estimates of their life quality. They reported superior change in their life quality rating at all follow-up assessment points. Although they also reported a greater decline in negative affect, this effect was found only at the post-assessment.

The Change in Psychological Well-being by Number of Classes Attended

We assessed the presence of a relationship between the number of class sessions attended and a change in psychological well-being for the Class condition participants. The change in psychological well-being (i.e., quality of life, AB+, and AB−) served as the dependent variable, and was calculated by subtracting the preintervention score from each follow-up score. The predictor variables were the preintervention well-being score, number of sessions attended, ethnicity, and a family history of psychiatric disorder.

For the quality of life, the preintervention level (Adjusted R-Square = .20, .26, and .23, $p = .0001$ for the three follow-up points) again made a significant contribution. No other variable had an impact on the variance in the quality of life.

In the case of Affect-Balance, the pre-score was again a significant predictor of change scores at follow-up. For AB+, the amount of variances accounted for by this was 16 percent at post-, 38 percent at six-months, and 38 percent at one-year follow-up. For AB−, the amount of variance accounted for was 29 percent, 23 percent, and 47 percent, respectively. The number of class sessions attended was a significant predictor of the change score only in one instance—at post- for AB− (b coefficient = −.07, $p = .04$)—with those attending more sessions reporting a greater decline in AB−. At six-months follow-up, Latinos reported greater improvement in their positive affect score (b coefficient = .83, $p = .01$) over whites.

In summary, Class condition participants consistently reported an improvement in the quality of life over that of the Control and Video condition participants at all follow-up points. However, attending more class sessions, was not generally related to the magnitude of the change. This supported our conclusion in the previous chapter that the condition of assignment more consistently yielded differential change at outcome than did the number of sessions attended. We were less successful in modifying a respondent's affect over time. The condition of randomization and the number of sessions attended had little impact on a change of positive affect. In terms of decreasing negative affect, the Class condition surpassed the other conditions only at post-follow-up.

With regard to ethnic differences, Latinos reported a greater gain in AB+ than whites, at six-months follow-up. Since this difference was found for only one measure of psychological well-being and at only one follow-up assessment period, it should be viewed as preliminary. As in the case of depression, we did not find participants with a family history of psychiatric disorders to respond differently to the intervention from the others without such a history. This stresses the usefulness of this intervention even for those with a familial loading of psychiatric disorder.

14. The Effects of Preventive Intervention on the Use of Medical Services

Jeanne Miranda and Eliseo J. Pérez-Stable

An additional goal of this study was to determine whether a preventive intervention for depression could lower the use of primary care medical services. Nearly 40 to 60 percent of all patients visiting primary care physicians present with symptoms for which no biomedical disease is detected (Barsky, 1981; Van der Gaag & Van de Ven, 1978). The use of medical services is often related to psychiatric distress (Follette & Cummings, 1967; Mechanic, Cleary & Greenley, 1982; Myers & Weissman, 1980; Shapiro et al., 1984). In particular, depressed medical patients have more frequent outpatient clinic visits than their nondepressed counterparts (Weissman et al., 1981; Hoeper et al., 1980; Mumford et al., 1981; Hankin et al., 1982). In fact, increases in the use of medical services parallel shifts in the levels of depression (Cadoret & Widmer, 1980). Thus, we hypothesized that members of the Class condition, who would learn to maintain low levels of depression, would also use less medical services than would those assigned to the Video and Control conditions. In addition, we predicted that those who attended more class sessions would also use fewer medical services than those who attended fewer sessions.

We obtained two measures of the utilization of medical services from a review of medical records. Medical records were abstracted for twelve months preceding the administration of the DIS and twelve months following the administration of the DIS to determine the number of outpatient visits and the number of hospitalizations in each of the twelve-month periods.

We examined the hypothesis that medical service utilization would be lowered as a result of the Class condition as compared with the Video and Control conditions. Change in medical utilization was calculated by subtracting the preintervention scores from the postintervention scores for each measure of service utilization. As a result, lower numbers indicated a decreased use of outpatient visits and hospitalizations. We calculated two multiple regression equations, with the change scores serving as the dependent variables, and the preintervention scores and the condition of assignment (combined Video and Control versus Class) serving as predictor variables. The beta weight for the intervention condition reflects the impact of the intervention on the use of medical services while controlling for initial level of use of the service. A one-tailed t-test for the beta weight of condition was used, based on the hypothesis that the Class condition would produce decreases in the use of medical services.

The Change in Utilization of Medical Services as a Result of the Preventive Intervention

Table 14.1 presents the means and standard deviations of the medical utilization variables across condition and time. The results of the multiple regression analyses suggest that the intervention did not result in any change in the use of medical services. In neither case was condition of assignment a statistically significant predictor of change in medical service utilization.

Next, we calculated two multiple regression analyses to determine whether the two control conditions (Video versus Control) differed in effecting change in medical utilization. The change scores served as the dependent variables, and the preintervention scores and the condition of control assignment (Video versus Control) served as predictor variables. The beta weight for the condition was examined with a two-tailed test to determine if the change in medical utilization could be accounted for by assignment to Video versus Control condition, while controlling for the initial level of use of medical services. There were no

Table 14.1. Medical Service Utilization by Condition and Assessment Period

	Class			Control			Video		
Medical Service	Mean	(SD)	n	Mean	(SD)	n	Mean	(SD)	n
OUTPATIENT VISITS									
Preintervention	6.00	3.92	66	6.57	4.45	30	5.82	2.96	45
One-year follow-up	7.18	5.05	61	7.96	7.60	25	6.26	3.93	38
HOSPITALIZATION									
Preintervention	.41	.88	66	.33	.71	30	.29	.55	45
One-year follow-up	.20	.63	61	.16	.47	25	.34	.78	38

differences in the change in use of either medical utilization variable as a result of assignment to Video versus Control condition. Because we found no differences between Video and Control conditions in the preliminary analyses, these conditions were combined in subsequent analyses.

The Change in the Utilization of Medical Services by the Number of Classes Attended

To determine whether the number of classes attended by the Class participants was related to the change in medical service utilization, we again conducted two multiple regression analyses. The change in medical service utilization variables served as the dependent variables, again calculated by subtracting the preintervention scores from each postintervention score. The predictor variables were the preintervention medical utilization variable, number of sessions attended, and ethnicity. The beta weight for the number of sessions attended was examined to determine if class attendance was related to the change in the use of medical services after controlling for initial level of service use. The beta weight for ethnicity was evaluated to determine whether ethnicity was a significant factor in predicting change in the use of medical services after controlling for the initial level of service use and attendance at class.

The results of both multiple regression analyses showed that neither attendance nor ethnicity contributed to the change in use of outpatient visits or hospitalization from pre- to postintervention.

In summary, change in the use of medical services was related to neither assignment to the Class versus Control conditions nor class attendance. Although medical service utilization does appear to be related to psychiatric distress, this intervention aimed at preventing depressive symptomatology did not appear to lower the use of medical services.

Predictors of the Utilization of Medical Services

Given the negative findings regarding the intervention effects on the utilization of medical services, we examined other variables in the Depression Prevention Research Project data that might be related to a higher utilization of medical services (Miranda et al., 1991). Previous studies linking psychiatric distress to medical utilization have failed to provide a conceptual model that predicts which patients are likely to present somatized complaints to physicians and under what circumstances these visits are likely to occur. We examined Mechanic's (1972) attribution theory of somatization to predict outpatient medical visits to primary care clinics. Mechanic proposed that bodily symptoms resulting from stress are the basis of somatization. Specifically, these symptoms may be attributed to either psychological or physical causes. Somatizers, because of background characteristics and early learning, are particularly likely to attribute these symptoms to physical causes and, therefore, seek treatment from physicians for them. Accordingly, we predicted that somatizers who mistake the symptoms of stress for organic problems would use outpatient services primarily for psychosocial reasons. Thus, they would seek outpatient medical services inappropriately following stressful life events.

Our results (Miranda et al., 1991) supported Mechanic's model. Multiple regression analysis revealed that patients who were somatizers, according to abridged criteria developed by Escobar and others (Escobar et al., 1987, 1989), had a greater number of medical visits as stressful life events increased than did nonsomatizers. In addition, our results suggest that a psychiatric disorder may be related to the utilization of medical services only because of its relationship to somatization and stress. Specifically, somatization was highly related to depression and phobias, whereas diagnosable psychiatric disorders per se did not contribute to medical service utilization.

These results offer interesting implications for reducing the use of medical services by patients with medical complaints that are not serious. Specifically, preventive interventions might best focus on coping with stress, and somatizers might benefit most from such interventions. Some patients might be helped to decrease their stress by altering environmental stressors, such as work or social situations. Case managers may be used for short-term interventions to help somatizing medical patients alter stressful environments. Others might benefit from structured treatments that have been shown to reduce stress, such as cognitive behavioral techniques (Hollon & Najavits, 1988), assertiveness training (Linehan, Goldfried & Goldfried, 1979), or stress inoculation training (Meichenbaum, 1975).

15. The Mediating Effects of Change in Cognitions and Behaviors on Depression and Psychological Well-being

In Chapters 12 and 13, we examined the direct effect of the Class intervention on outcome (i.e., depression and psychological well-being). Another question of interest is the mechanism of change. The level of depression and psychological well-being in our studies was expected to change with the modification of cognitions and behaviors, the target of the class intervention. Did the participants in the Class condition report significantly more change in their cognitions and behaviors in the predicted direction than the others at follow-up assessments? If so, did this change affect outcome, that is, depressive level and psychological well-being? Given the small number of new episodes of clinical depression at one-year follow-up, incidence was not further examined. Also, as no differences between Control and Video condition participants were hypothesized at the outset, these two groups were also not further contrasted. Instead, we focused on the presence of variation between the Class participants versus all others.

First, we examined the hypothesis that compared with the combined Control and Video condition participants, those in the Class condition experienced a greater change in cognitions and behaviors from preintervention to follow-up assessments. More specifically, they became less irrational, more optimistic, generated more positive but fewer negative thoughts, engaged in more pleasant activities and social interactions. Next, we assessed the change in outcome (depression and psychological well-being) due to change in cognitions and behaviors. Finally, we examined the concurrent change of these two; that is, the indirect impact of condition on outcome as mediated by cognitions and behaviors. The model utilized may be described as follows:

The Effects of Change in Cognitions and Behaviors

$$\frac{\text{Change in Outcome}}{\text{Change in Condition}} = \frac{\text{Change in CB}}{\text{Change in Condition}} \times \frac{\text{Change in Outcome}}{\text{Change in CB}}$$

To test the first term on the right-hand side of the equation, that is, whether change in cognitions and behaviors (CB) may be attributed to randomization condition, the following regression model was specified. As before, the difference between the follow-up and the preintervention scores (i.e., the pre-score subtracted from the follow-up score) served as the dependent cognitive or behavioral variable. Its preintervention score was entered first, followed by the condition of assignment. The two control conditions served as the comparison group against which the Class condition was contrasted. A one-tailed test was used for this comparison.

For the second term on the right-hand side of the equation, that is, whether a change in depression and other outcome variables was mediated by a change in cognitions and behaviors, the dependent variable was the change at outcome (again, the pre-score was subtracted from the follow-up score). The predictor variables consisted of the preintervention level of the outcome score; condition (again, we contrasted Class versus Others); the preintervention cognitive or behavioral score; and the cognitive or behavioral score at the follow-up assessment period corresponding to that of the outcome. For instance, if the outcome variable of interest was the post-pre-score differential, the fourth term of the equation included all cognitive-behavioral variables measured at post-follow-up.

The three measures used to assess cognition were the Personal Beliefs Inventory (PBI, Muñoz, 1977), the Subjective Probability Questionnaire (SPQ, Muñoz, 1977) and the Cognitive Events Schedule (CES, Muñoz, 1977). To assess behavior, the Pleasant Activities Scale (PAS, MacPhillamy & Lewinsohn, 1971), and the Social Activities Questionnaire (SAQ, Youngren, 1978; Youngren et al., 1975; Zeiss et al., 1979) were used. As noted earlier, an improvement on these measures was demonstrated by a decrease on the PBI, increase on SP+, decrease on SP−, increase on CES+, decrease on CES−, increase on PAS, and increase on SAQ.

Change in Cognitions and Behaviors by Condition over Time

We examined change in these variables across conditions at the three follow-up points. The means and standard deviations of all cognitive-behavioral variables by condition over time are presented in Tables 15.1 through 15.5.

The regression analyses comparing Class versus other participants regarding differences in cognitive-behavioral variables over time included the preintervention score and condition. The results showed the preintervention score emerged as a significant predictor for all variables at all follow-up points. In addition, compared with the others at postintervention, the Class condition participants reported a signifi-

Table 15.1. Personal Beliefs Inventory (PBI) Score by Condition and Assessment Period

Assessment Period	Class			Control			Video		
	Mean	(SD)	n	Mean	(SD)	n	Mean	(SD)	n
Preintervention	38.28	(7.69)	72	38.22	(8.16)	48	38.37	(8.05)	30
Postintervention	36.82	(8.37)	66	36.32	(8.13)	44	37.92	(8.54)	28
Six-months follow-up	36.03	(8.70)	64	36.16	(8.72)	44	38.59	(7.82)	26
One-year follow-up	35.79	(8.04)	61	36.89	(8.31)	45	36.56	(9.61)	27

Table 15.2. Subjective Probability Questionnaire (SPQ) Score by Condition and Assessment Period

Assessment Period	Class			Control			Video		
	Mean	(SD)	n	Mean	(SD)	n	Mean	(SD)	n
				SPQ Positive					
Preintervention	66.95	(16.08)	72	65.95	(16.77)	48	68.84	(14.33)	30
Postintervention	68.89	(13.83)	66	63.90	(21.45)	44	69.08	(16.68)	28
Six-months follow-up	67.88	(15.76)	64	63.00	(18.46)	44	70.38	(16.62)	26
One-year follow-up	64.83	(18.85)	61	64.34	(17.75)	45	71.29	(16.43)	27
				SPQ Negative					
Preintervention	25.38	(14.39)	72	26.16	(13.10)	48	23.00	(12.26)	30
Postintervention	25.17	(12.13)	66	25.35	(12.01)	44	29.19	(16.49)	28
Six-months follow-up	23.75	(12.58)	64	25.30	(12.59)	44	27.90	(17.06)	26
One-year follow-up	19.80	(13.47)	61	24.18	(13.02)	45	21.71	(12.05)	27

Table 15.3. Cognitive Events Schedule (CES) Score by Condition and Assessment Period

Assessment Period	Class			Control			Video		
	Mean	(SD)	n	Mean	(SD)	n	Mean	(SD)	n
				CES Positive					
Preintervention	44.53	(9.00)	72	45.17	(9.01)	48	47.57	(6.23)	30
Postintervention	45.91	(9.71)	66	45.50	(9.68)	44	46.96	(6.79)	26
Six-months follow-up	45.36	(8.87)	64	42.52	(8.71)	44	46.15	(7.07)	26
One-year follow-up	43.58	(10.04)	62	43.30	(9.46)	44	47.19	(7.97)	27
				CES Negative					
Preintervention	59.10	(15.15)	72	58.69	(13.26)	48	54.70	(9.15)	30
Postintervention	55.12	(10.49)	66	57.86	(9.41)	44	56.88	(9.52)	26
Six-months follow-up	55.09	(10.28)	64	55.00	(10.36)	44	56.88	(11.32)	26
One-year follow-up	53.39	(11.26)	62	54.41	(10.14)	44	54.33	(10.53)	27

Table 15.4. Pleasant Activities Schedule (PAS) Score by Condition and Assessment Period

Assessment Period	Class			Control			Video		
	Mean	(SD)	n	Mean	(SD)	n	Mean	(SD)	n
Preintervention	108.03	(14.25)	72	107.67	(17.29)	48	112.78	(12.20)	30
Postintervention	111.98	(15.85)	66	105.07	(16.41)	43	113.70	(12.58)	28
Six-months follow-up	111.95	(14.42)	64	102.75	(15.03)	44	110.03	(14.50)	26
One-year follow-up	108.37	(17.35)	62	104.71	(17.55)	44	110.07	(12.67)	27

cantly greater decline in negative cognitions (b coefficient = −2.82, p = .03), and a greater increase in pleasant (b coefficient = 4.42, p = .01), and social activities (b coefficient = 3.53, p = .02). At six-months follow-up, the Class condition participants reported a significantly greater increase in positive thoughts (b coefficient = 2.62, p = .01) and pleasant activities (b coefficient = 7.84, p = .0001). At one-year follow-up, they reported a marginally greater decline in SP− (b coefficient = −3.31, p = .06) than the others. Except for SP+ and PBI, the Class

Table 15.5. Social Activities Questionnaire (SAQ) Score by Condition and Assessment Period

Assessment Period	Class			Control			Video		
	Mean	(SD)	n	Mean	(SD)	n	Mean	(SD)	n
Preintervention	72.12	(11.64)	72	72.71	(11.90)	48	77.80	(10.80)	30
Postintervention	75.78	(13.69)	65	73.10	(14.04)	44	77.41	(11.21)	27
Six-months follow-up	73.32	(11.59)	64	72.15	(11.79)	44	76.27	(10.84)	26
One-year follow-up	72.12	(12.82)	62	70.79	(10.57)	44	77.35	(13.16)	27

condition reported significantly greater change on all cognitive-behavioral variables at one or more of the three follow-up assessments. The change was always in the predicted direction. Thus, comparatively, Class condition participants became less pessimistic, had more positive (self-rewarding) and fewer negative (self-punishing) thoughts, and engaged in more pleasant and social activities at one or more follow-up assessment periods.

Change in Outcome by Change in Cognitions and Behaviors

We examined whether change in outcome was mediated by cognitive-behavioral variables at the corresponding follow-up assessment period. The equation utilized change in outcome (follow-up minus preintervention CES-D, BDI, quality of life, positive Affect-Balance and negative Affect-Balance scores) at the three follow-up assessment periods as the dependent variable. The predictor variables included preintervention outcome score, condition (Class versus Other), preintervention cognitive-behavioral scores, and the follow-up cognitive-behavioral scores (the follow-up score used was matched to that of the outcome being studied in terms of timeline.) We examined the contribution of the follow-up cognitive-behavioral scores after the contribution of the other three sets of variables had been accounted for. A one-tailed test was used. The results are presented by outcome measure in Tables 15.6 to 15.10.

A greater decline in CES-D depressive level (indicated by higher negative change scores) was significantly predicted by increasing positive (CES+) and decreasing negative (CES−) thoughts at post-follow-

Table 15.6. CES-D Change Score as Predicted by Cognitive-Behavioral Scores at the Corresponding Follow-up Assessment Period

	Post Change Score		Six-Months Change Score		One-Year Change Score	
Variable	b coefficient	p*	b coefficient	p*	b coefficient	p*
PBI	−0.03	0.39	−0.15	0.03	−0.07	0.22
SPQ+	−0.06	0.13	0.01	0.39	−0.01	0.43
SPQ−	0.05	0.18	0.05	0.18	0.10	0.04
CES+	−0.21	0.04	0.01	0.49	−0.05	0.31
CES−	0.38	0.001	0.53	0.001	0.40	0.001
PAS	0.02	0.39	−0.28	0.001	−0.21	0.002
SAQ	−0.02	0.39	0.08	0.17	−0.05	0.29

Note: See Table 10.1 for a key to abbreviations.
*One-tailed test used.

Table 15.7. BDI Change Score as Predicted by Cognitive-Behavioral Scores at the Corresponding Follow-up Assessment Period

	Post Change Score		Six-Months Change Score		One-Year Change Score	
Variable	b coefficient	p*	b coefficient	p*	b coefficient	p*
PBI	0.02	0.34	−0.06	0.14	−0.05	0.18
SPQ+	−0.01	0.47	−0.05	0.07	−0.05	0.05
SPQ−	0.07	0.03	0.02	0.26	−0.01	0.35
CES+	−0.05	0.27	0.01	0.43	−0.01	0.44
CES−	0.24	0.001	0.25	0.001	0.31	0.001
PAS	−0.07	0.10	−0.06	0.14	−0.12	0.004
SAQ	0.01	0.46	−0.03	0.32	0.02	0.36

Note: See Table 10.1 for a key to abbreviations.
*One-tailed test used.

up; by increasing irrational beliefs (PBI), decreasing negative thoughts (CES−), and increasing pleasant activities (PAS) at six-months follow-up; and by decreasing pessimistic tendencies (SPQ−) and negative thoughts (CES−), and increasing pleasant activities (PAS) at one-year follow-up. All of the findings were in the predicted direction, except for the PBI. We shall examine this outcome later in the chapter.

In the case of the BDI, improved depressive level (also indicated by

Table 15.8. Quality of Life Change Score as Predicted by Cognitive-Behavioral Scores at the Corresponding Follow-up Assessment Period

	Post Change Score		Six-Months Change Score		One-Year Change Score	
Variable	b coefficient	p*	b coefficient	p*	b coefficient	p*
PBI	0.01	0.11	0.02	0.001	0.01	0.34
SPQ+	0.02	0.01	0.01	0.002	0.02	0.002
SPQ−	−0.01	0.09	−0.01	0.04	−0.01	0.20
CES+	0.01	0.36	0.01	0.25	0.01	0.27
CES−	−0.03	0.002	−0.02	0.01	−0.03	0.001
PAS	0.01	0.10	0.01	0.08	0.01	0.15
SAQ	0.01	0.47	−0.01	0.11	0.01	0.12

Note: See Table 10.1 for a key to abbreviations.
*One-tailed test used.

Table 15.9. Positive Affect Balance Change Score as Predicted by Cognitive-Behavioral Scores at the Corresponding Follow-up Assessment Period

	Post Change Score		Six-Months Change Score		One-Year Change Score	
Variable	b coefficient	p*	b coefficient	p*	b coefficient	p*
PBI	−0.01	0.39	0.01	0.48	0.03	0.04
SPQ+	0.01	0.24	0.01	0.12	−0.01	0.26
SPQ−	−0.01	0.40	−0.01	0.31	−0.02	0.01
CES+	0.03	0.07	0.01	0.18	0.03	0.05
CES−	−0.02	0.06	−0.03	0.01	−0.02	0.04
PAS	0.01	0.36	0.02	0.08	0.03	0.01
SAQ	0.01	0.34	0.01	0.26	0.01	0.26

Note: See Table 10.1 for a key to abbreviations.
*One-tailed test used.

higher negative change scores) was mediated by decreasing pessimism (SPQ−), and negative thoughts (CES−) at post-follow-up; decreasing negative thoughts (CES−) at six-months follow-up; and increasing optimism (SPQ+), decreasing negative thoughts (CES−), and increasing pleasant activities at one-year follow-up. All findings were in the direction predicted.

Table 15.10. Negative Affect Balance Change Score as Predicted by Cognitive-Behavioral Scores at the Corresponding Follow-up Assessment Period

	Post Change Score		Six-Months Change Score		One-Year Change Score	
Variable	b coefficient	p*	b coefficient	p*	b coefficient	p*
PBI	−0.01	0.20	−0.02	0.04	−0.02	0.13
SPQ+	−0.01	0.06	−0.01	0.45	−0.01	0.44
SPQ−	0.01	0.16	0.03	0.001	0.01	0.08
CES+	−0.04	0.02	−0.01	0.25	0.01	0.39
CES−	0.04	0.001	0.04	0.005	0.04	0.001
PAS	0.01	0.17	−0.01	0.29	−0.01	0.12
SAQ	0.01	0.28	−0.01	0.24	−0.02	0.10

Note: See Table 10.1 for a key to abbreviations.
*One-tailed test used.

Improved quality of life (indicated by higher positive change scores) was predicted by increasing optimism (SPQ+), and decreasing negative thoughts (CES−) at post-follow-up; increasing irrational beliefs (PBI), increasing optimism (SPQ+), decreasing pessimism (SPQ−) and negative thoughts (CES−) at six-months follow-up; and increasing optimism (SPQ+), and decreasing negative thoughts (CES−) at one-year follow-up. Again, contrary to expectation, an increase in PBI was related to improved life quality.

Increased positive affect (indicated by higher change scores) was significantly predicted by decreasing negative thoughts (CES−) at post; by decreasing negative thoughts (CES−) at six-months follow-up; and increasing irrational beliefs (PBI), decreasing pessimism (SPQ−), increasing positive thoughts (CES+), decreasing negative thoughts (CES−), and increasing pleasant activities (PAS) at one-year follow-up.

Finally, a decline in negative affect (indicated by a higher negative change score) was predicted by increasing positive thoughts (CES+), decreasing negative thoughts (CES−), and, marginally, by increasing optimism (SPQ+) at post-follow-up; by increasing irrational beliefs (PBI), decreasing pessimism (SPQ−) and decreasing negative thoughts (CES−) at six-months follow-up; and decreasing negative thoughts (CES−) at one-year follow-up. Again, contrary to expectation, increase in PBI predicted to improved outcome.

In summary, after condition and preintervention outcome and cognitive-behavioral scores had been accounted for, all cognitive-behavioral variables at follow-up, other than social activities, significantly predicted to change in outcome at one or more follow-up assessment periods. Most noticeably, decreasing negative thoughts (or the number of self-punishing ideas) consistently mediated improvement on all five outcome variables and across all follow-up assessment periods. Contrary to expectation, increasing PBI resulted in improved outcome. PBI items were originally conceptualized as "irrational," thereby leading to depression. However, agreement with at least some of the items might be indicative of acknowledgment of real constraints (e.g., "persons living in slum conditions are almost certain to feel depressed and miserable"). In that case, higher scores on the PBI reflected a more realistic view of the less-than-perfect world, and, subsequently, not holding oneself *entirely* accountable for this state of affairs. The finding that PBI levels did not vary by condition at follow-up also suggested that the level of "irrational beliefs" held by the Class condition participants might have been adaptive rather than maladaptive, and thus resistant to change.

The Mediating Effects of Change in Cognitions and Behaviors on Outcome

We used the findings obtained in the two previous sections—change in cognitions and behaviors given change in condition, and change in outcome given change in cognitions and behaviors—to assess the presence of their joint relationship. To obtain the estimates of the desired b coefficient for this—change in outcome/change in condition—we calculated the product of the beta weights for the expression "change in cognition and behavior/change in condition" and "change in outcome/change in cognition and behavior." The variance for this product was calculated using the formula given by Chiang (1968): (variance of the first term × variance of the second term) + (variance of the first term × the squared term of the second b coefficient) + (variance of the second term × the squared term of the first b coefficient). We then calculated the t-statistic (i.e., b coefficient for the joint relationship divided by the square-root of the joint variance), which showed the indirect effect of change in cognitive-behavioral variables by condition on outcome.

The results indicated that at post-follow-up, on the average, every additional unit of decrease in negative though score (CES−) led to a 1.06 unit decrease in CES-D change level ($t = -1.75$), a .68 unit decrease in BDI level ($t = -1.73$), a .08 unit increase in quality of life ($t = 1.56$), and a .11 unit decrease in AB− ($t = -1.58$) for the Class condition participants. While the relationship was significant at the .05 level (using a one-tailed test) for CES-D and BDI change scores, it was marginally significant for quality of life and AB−. In addition, at six-months follow-up, every additional unit of increase in pleasant activities (PAS) led to a 2.16 unit decrease in CES-D change level in the Class condition ($t = -2.76$, $p = .01$).

The findings were in the direction predicted. The persistent role of the Class condition's decreasing negative thoughts mediating outcome at postintervention assessments was quite impressive. In fact, out of the 105 joint relationships assessed, the probability that this variable would have significantly predicted four out of the five outcome change scores by chance was only .000005; and the probability that it would have emerged to be significant for two of the five outcome change scores by chance was .005. The finding that a reduction in negative thoughts mediated improved outcome for the Class condition only at postintervention assessments suggested its influence to wane over time, and pointed to the potential utility of booster sessions to reinforce its usefulness.

We also found increased pleasant activities in the Class condition to mediate greater decline in CES-D depressive level at six-months follow-up. Interestingly, it did not emerge as significant at postintervention. Although the Class condition participants reported a significantly greater improvement on PAS than the others, PAS did not significantly predict to change in CES-D at postintervention. This may be the result of a delayed mediating effect of increasing pleasant activities or of a statistical artifact, that is, related to the problem of multicollinearity between negative thoughts and pleasant activities, and their competing for the same variance at postintervention assessment.

In the previous two chapters, we reported numerous instances of differential change in outcome by condition. Compared with the findings reported in this chapter, the intervention apparently had a greater direct effect and a smaller indirect effect on outcome through change on cognitions and behaviors. However, the postulated indirect effect was present and was most notable in the case of the role of negative thoughts at postintervention assessment. The usefulness of the other techniques taught in the class requires further analysis in future studies. In addition to increasing the sample size (and power), future depression prevention investigations should also consider incorporating booster sessions to ensure longer-lasting effects.

16. The Mediating Effects of Change in Life Events on Depression and Psychological Well-being

The experimental intervention was intended to improve the mood and psychological well-being of participants assigned to the class through a modification of their cognitions and behaviors. A potential secondary effect of this intervention was greater control over life events. The role of life events in mediating mood and well-being is stressed throughout the literature on this subject. While we did not address life events in our class intervention directly, once learned, the cognitive-behavioral techniques could have in turn increased the occurrence of positive and decreased the occurrence of negative life events. In addition, this might have mediated change in outcome. We review these issues in this chapter.

The model utilized in this chapter is similar to the one presented in the previous chapter, and may be described as:

$$\frac{\text{Change in Outcome}}{\text{Change in Condition}} = \frac{\text{Change in LE}}{\text{Change in Condition}} \times \frac{\text{Change in Outcome}}{\text{Change in LE}}$$

The first term on the right-hand side of the equation was assessed as follows. The pre-score subtracted from the follow-up score served as the dependent life events (LE) score. In terms of predictor variables, the preintervention score was entered first, followed by the condition of assignment (Class was contrasted to Others). For the second term on the right-hand side of the equation, the dependent variable was the change at outcome (again, the pre-score was subtracted from the follow-up score.) The predictor variables included the preintervention level of the outcome score, the condition of assignment (again, contrasting Class versus Others), the preintervention life events score, and the life events score at the follow-up session corresponding to that of the outcome. For example, in the case where the outcome variable of interest was the six-months follow-up change score, the fourth term of the equation included all life events variables measured at the six-months follow-up.

The Life Experiences Survey was administered only at six-months and one-year follow-up. As previously discussed, four scores were derived, positive and negative life sum in the last six months, and positive and negative life sum seven months to a year ago. Life events reported for the seven to twelve months before the six-months follow-up assessment were likely to have occurred primarily before or during the experimental intervention, and thus were not of interest here. Life events reported for the previous seven to twelve months at one-year follow-up were likely to overlap with those reported for the previous six months at the six-months follow-up, and were also not examined. We retained the life events scores reported to have occurred within the previous six months. At six-months follow-up, this period coincided with the first six months of the study; at one-year follow-up, this coincided with the seventh to twelfth months of the study year.

The timing of the follow-up assessment was determined by the initial DIS administration date (i.e., six months or one year after that date). Thus, the six-month period before the six-months follow-up assessment had a potential time range from preintervention to four months after the intervention, depending on the date of the initial DIS administration. The six months before the one-year follow-up covered the period of two to nine months after the intervention. Thus, if life events changed primarily subsequent to the intervention, the larger effect should be evident at one-year follow-up.

Change in Life Events by Condition over Time

Table 16.1 shows the means and standard deviations of the positive and negative life event scores by condition over time.

Regression analyses were conducted to assess the contribution of the preintervention life events score and condition of assignment (Class versus Others) on the change in life events sum scores at follow-up. The pre-score was found to be significantly predictive of both the positive and negative life events change score at six-months (accounting for 12% and 42% of the variance, respectively) and one-year follow-up (accounting for 26% and 52% of the variance, respectively). In the case of the positive life events, those with initially lower scores reported greater improvement; while in the case of the negative life events, those with initially higher scores reported significantly greater decline at follow-up. When the condition of assignment was entered, compared with other participants, the Class condition participants were

Table 16.1. Life Events Score by Condition and Assessment Period

Assessment Period	Class			Control			Video		
	Mean	(SD)	n	Mean	(SD)	n	Mean	(SD)	n
	Positive Sum in the Previous Six Months								
Preintervention	3.61	(4.02)	72	3.31	(4.05)	48	2.60	(3.73)	30
Six-months follow-up	3.57	(6.07)	61	2.25	(3.20)	44	2.68	(4.07)	25
One-year follow-up	3.26	(4.62)	62	2.64	(3.27)	44	2.93	(3.97)	27
	Negative Sum in the Previous Six Months								
Preintervention	4.93	(5.71)	72	4.04	(5.48)	48	5.47	(7.86)	30
Six-months follow-up	3.51	(4.36)	61	2.61	(3.18)	44	5.24	(9.72)	25
One-year follow-up	2.76	(3.13)	62	4.32	(5.18)	44	3.37	(5.86)	27

found to report a marginally greater decline in negative life events at one-year follow-up (b coefficient = −1.18, p = .06, one-tailed test).

Although the experimental intervention did not include explicit methods to influence life events, the results revealed a greater decline in negative life events experienced for the Class condition during the six months before the one-year follow-up. This is equivalent to roughly two to nine months after the end of the intervention. Although the finding reached only marginal statistical significance (p = .06), it did suggest that the targeted changes in cognitions, behaviors, and mood levels may have reduced the probability of negative life events. Perhaps greater control over one's thoughts and actions translates into what we term "the healthy management of reality" (see Chapter 24). This may be a specific example of reciprocal determinism: even in generally stressful environments, adaptive changes in the organism's subjective responses may change modifiable aspects of the objective environment for the better. Additional studies are needed to clarify the role of preventive interventions in modifying life events.

Change in Outcome by Change in Life Events

We assessed whether change in outcome was mediated by life events scores at the corresponding follow-up assessment periods. The equation utilized change in outcome (follow-up minus preintervention CES-D, BDI, quality of life, positive Affect-Balance and negative

Affect-Balance scores) at six-months and one-year follow-ups as the dependent variable. The predictor variables included the preintervention outcome score, the condition of assignment (Class versus Other), the preintervention life events scores, and the follow-up life events scores, which were matched with outcome by follow-up assessment period. We were interested in the contribution of the follow-up life event scores after the contribution of the other three sets of variables had been accounted for. A one-tailed test was used.

A greater decline in CES-D depression level (indicated by higher negative change scores) was significantly predicted by a decrease in both positive and negative life events at six-months follow-up; and by an increase in positive life events and a decrease in negative life events at one-year follow-up (Table 16.2). A greater decline in BDI level was not related to life events at six-months follow-up, but was significantly predicted by a decrease in negative life events at one-year follow-up (Table 16.3). The finding that a decline in positive life events mediated a decline in CES-D depressive level at six-months follow-up was contrary to expectation.

Table 16.2. Change in CES-D as Mediated by Life Event Scores at the Corresponding Follow-up Assessment Period

	Six-Months Change Score		One-Year Change Score	
Variable	b coefficient	p*	b coefficient	p*
Positive Life Events	.33	.03	−.43	.02
Negative Life Events	.43	.01	.79	.0001

*One-tailed test used.

Table 16.3. Change in BDI as Mediated by Life Event Scores at the Corresponding Follow-up Assessment Period

	Six-Months Change Score		One-Year Change Score	
Variable	b coefficient	p*	b coefficient	p*
Positive Life Events	.10	.20	−.20	.07
Negative Life Events	.07	.24	.40	.001

*One-tailed test used.

An improvement in the quality of life (indicated by higher change scores) was not related to life events at six-months follow-up, but was significantly predicted by an increase in positive life events and marginally significantly predicted by a decrease in negative life events at one-year follow-up (Table 16.4). Improved positive affect (indicated by higher change scores) was mediated by an increase in positive life events at six-months follow-up, and by an increase in positive and a decrease in negative life events at one-year follow-up (Table 16.5). Finally, a decline in negative affect (indicated by higher negative change scores) was not related to life events at six-months follow-up, but was significantly predicted by a decline in negative life events at one-year follow-up (Table 16.6).

In summary, after the contribution of the condition of assignment, preintervention outcome, and life event scores had been accounted for, positive and negative life events significantly predicted to some or all of the outcome measures at six-months and one-year follow-ups. This supported the role played by life events in depressive level and psychological well-being, which had been identified in the previous literature.

Table 16.4. Change in Quality of Life as Mediated by Life Event Scores at the Corresponding Follow-up Assessment Period

	Six-Months Change Score		One-Year Change Score	
Variable	b coefficient	p*	b coefficient	p*
Positive Life Events	−.02	.07	.06	.01
Negative Life Events	.01	.33	−.04	.06

*One-tailed test used.

Table 16.5. Change in Positive Affect Balance Score as Mediated by Life Event Scores at the Corresponding Follow-up Assessment Period

	Six-Months Change Score		One-Year Change Score	
Variable	b coefficient	p*	b coefficient	p*
Positive Life Events	.07	.001	.11	.001
Negative Life Events	−.02	.22	−.06	.01

*One-tailed test used.

Table 16.6. Change in Negative Affect Balance Score as Mediated by Life Event Scores at the Corresponding Follow-up Assessment Period

	Six-Months Change Score		One-Year Change Score	
Variable	b coefficient	p*	b coefficient	p*
Positive Life Events	.03	.11	−.04	.11
Negative Life Events	.03	.11	.06	.01

*One-tailed test used.

The contribution of life events was more pronounced at one-year follow-up. In contrast, the findings at six-months follow-up were less striking, likely to be due to the fact that the period assessed by the six-months follow-up life events measure included a preintervention period for some class participants.

The Mediating Effects of Change in Life Events on Outcome

We used the findings presented in the previous two sections, change in life events/change in condition, and change in outcome/change in life events to assess the presence of their joint relationship. The estimate of the b coefficient was the product of the beta weights of these two expressions, and the variance term was calculated using Chiang's (1968) formula (presented in the previous chapter). The t-statistic was calculated from these two terms; and a one-tailed test was used to test its significance. No joint relationship was found to be statistically significant. At one-year follow-up, change in negative life events marginally mediated greater decline in CES-D and BDI (b coefficient = −.93, t = −1.48, and b coefficient = −.47, t = −1.40, respectively) for the Class condition participants.

In summary, we found some support for the differential change in life events by condition, and change in outcome by life events after completion of the intervention (i.e., the months assessed by the one-year follow-up life events measure). However, the joint relationship did not quite reach statistical significance. Still, the results were promising. We did not deliberately intend to modify life events, but found it to be a secondary benefit of the intervention. Clearly, the modifiability of life events merits attention in future depression prevention intervention studies.

17. Measurement Issues

Like any study involving self-report data, the validity of the data may be questioned. One potential source of bias is the respondent's tendency toward social desirability. This problem pervades research involving depression, because the measurement of depression is dependent on self-reporting. In this investigation, our particular concern was whether increased contact with the research team (that is, being assigned to the Class condition and attending more class sessions) significantly increased the social desirability of the participant so that it became confounded with class attendance. Another problem that may bias the findings in an outcome study is that of nonrandom missing data at follow-up periods. In this chapter, we address these two problems.

Change in Social Desirability over Time by Condition and Number of Class Sessions Attended

We used the Crowne-Marlowe Social Desirability Scale (Crowne & Marlowe, 1960) to assess the motivation of social desirability. As noted in Chapter 11, the three conditions did not vary on social desirability at the outset of the study. Table 17.1 shows the means and standard deviations of the Crowne-Marlowe scale over time and condition.

Of special interest was whether, compared with others, Class condition participants scored in a more socially desirable direction at follow-up points because of their repeated contact with research staff. This was assessed using regression analysis. The dependent variable was the change in social desirability from preintervention to the various follow-up points. The predictor variables included preintervention social desirability level and the condition of assignment. First, the Class participants were compared with all others; next, the Video participants were compared with the Control participants to assess if coming to watch the tape alone might have resulted in a change in social desirability. Since no difference was hypothesized at the outset, a two-tailed test was used.

As expected, the preintervention social desirability score significantly predicted the change in social desirability at all follow-up points

Table 17.1. Crowne-Marlowe Score by Condition and Assessment Period

Assessment Period	Class			Control			Video		
	Mean	(SD)	n	Mean	(SD)	n	Mean	(SD)	n
Preintervention	7.50	(3.37)	72	7.73	(2.99)	48	8.33	(2.90)	30
Postintervention	8.07	(3.24)	66	8.25	(3.31)	44	7.59	(3.24)	28
Six-months follow-up	7.95	(3.32)	64	7.90	(3.63)	44	8.02	(3.91)	26
One-year follow-up	7.81	(3.41)	62	8.16	(3.27)	44	8.56	(3.29)	27

(accounting for 12%, 4%, and 10% of the variance), with those scoring higher at preintervention more likely to demonstrate greater decline at follow-up. However, at follow-up assessments, social desirability in the Class condition did not vary significantly from that of the two control conditions. On the other hand, Video condition participants reported a significantly greater decline in social desirability than the Control condition participants at postintervention assessments (b coefficient = −1.21, p = .03, using a two-tailed test).

Another approach was used to assess the change in social desirability secondary to increased contact. For the Class participants, the change in social desirability was regressed onto preintervention score, number of sessions attended, and ethnicity. Again, while the preintervention social desirability score significantly predicted to change at follow-up (accounting for 16%, 7%, and 17% of the variance at the three assessment periods), increased contact (i.e., attending more sessions) did not. Only at one-year follow-up did Latinos score significantly more socially desirable than whites (b coefficient = 1.79, p = .01.) By and large, social desirability did not appear to pose a significant threat to the validity of the results.

Missing Data at Outcome

Another problem that may have compromised the validity of the findings was that of missing data at outcome, especially if there were differential rates of nonresponse across conditions. Table 17.2 presents the number of respondents who missed follow-up sessions by randomization condition. At each follow-up, approximately 10 percent of the participants could not be reached for the assessment. A Chi-Square analysis was conducted to assess differences in percent-

Table 17.2. Number of Participants Missing Follow-up Assessments by Randomization Condition

	Class	Control	Video	Total
Total number randomized	72	48	30	150
Number (%) missing at Assessments				
Postintervention	6 (8.33%)	4 (8.33%)	2 (6.67%)	12 (8.00%)
Six-months	8 (11.11%)	4 (8.33%)	4 (13.34%)	16 (10.67%)
One-year	10 (13.89%)	3 (6.25%)	3 (10.00%)	16 (10.67%)

age of participation across randomization conditions for each assessment period. The findings indicated the proportion of participants missing follow-up assessments did not vary significantly by condition (at post-intervention, Chi-Square = .09, df = 2, p = .96; at six-months follow-up, Chi-Square = .51, df = 2, p = .77; and at one-year follow-up, Chi-Square = 1.78, df = 2, p = .41).

All analyses reported here utilized listwise deletion. Next, probit analyses were conducted to assess the presence of differences between those who did and did not miss (dependent variable) each of the three follow-up assessments. Independent variables entered into the equation included age, sex, ethnicity, education, marital status, employment status, initial health concern and health status, and randomization condition. For categorical variables, male, unmarried, unemployed, white Class condition participants made up the deleted comparison group. Altogether, these variables did not significantly differentiate participation at follow-up assessments, as Tables 17.3 to 17.5 show.

At postintervention assessment, Chi-Square = 89.92, df = 112, p = .94; at six-months follow-up, Chi-Square = 75.25, df = 112, p = .99, and at one-year follow up, Chi-Square = 98.77, df = 112, p = .81. However, examination of the individual regression coefficients and standard errors revealed a significant contribution of initial health in predicting to follow-up assessment attendance. There was a greater likelihood of missing the six-months follow-up if one was more concerned about health (t = 2.03, p = .05), and a greater likelihood of missing the one-year follow-up if one reported poorer health status (t = 2.22, p = .05) at the initial screening. This suggested missing a follow-up assessment session was likely to be related to the participant's initial health; participants with poorer health were more likely to miss the follow-up assessment. In fact, in several cases, participants had died by the time we tried to contact them for follow-up. This was

Table 17.3. Probit Analysis Assessing Missing Status at Postintervention Assessment

Variable	Regression Coefficient	Standard Error	t
Age	0.02	0.02	0.93
Education	0.02	0.06	0.25
Health concern	0.11	0.08	1.37
Health status	−0.08	0.27	−0.28
Female*	−0.25	0.41	−0.60
Never married*	−0.33	0.62	−0.53
Formerly married*	−0.16	0.46	−0.35
Employed*	−0.09	0.50	−0.18
Asian/Pacific Islander*	−0.50	0.69	−0.72
African American*	−2.93	4.52	−0.65
Latino*	−3.03	10.63	−0.29
Native American*	−0.86	0.88	−0.98
Control condition*	−0.22	0.47	−0.46
Video condition*	−0.04	0.53	−0.08

Note: Intercept = 2.90, Standard Error = 1.62, Pearson Goodness-of-Fit Chi-Square = 89.92, DF = 112, p = 0.94.

*For categorical variables, male, married, unemployed, white, Class condition participants make up the deleted comparison group.

Table 17.4. Probit Analysis Assessing Missing Status at Six-Months Follow-up Assessment

Variable	Regression Coefficient	Standard Error	t
Age	−0.01	0.02	−0.85
Education	0.04	0.07	0.62
Health concern	0.16	0.08	2.03
Health status	−0.28	0.26	−1.06
Female*	0.61	0.40	1.51
Never married*	−3.04	2.76	−1.10
Formerly married*	0.22	0.42	0.51
Employed*	−0.14	0.45	−0.31
Asian/Pacific Islander*	−0.30	0.75	−0.40
African American*	−2.74	2.86	−0.96
Latino*	−0.63	1.06	−0.59
Native American*	−0.35	0.87	−0.39
Control condition*	−0.43	0.45	−0.96
Video condition*	−0.21	0.51	−0.40

Note: Intercept = 4.24, Standard Error = 1.62, Pearson Goodness-of-Fit Chi-Square = 75.25, DF = 112, p = 0.997.

*For categorical variables, male, married, unemployed, white, Class condition participants make up the deleted comparison group.

Table 17.5. Probit Analysis Assessing Missing Status at One-Year Follow-up Assessment

Variable	Regression Coefficient	Standard Error	t
Age	−0.02	0.02	−1.49
Education	0.08	0.06	1.44
Health concern	0.04	0.06	0.65
Health status	0.63	0.29	2.22
Female*	−0.69	0.40	−1.72
Never married*	−0.70	0.52	−1.35
Formerly married*	−0.02	0.39	−0.06
Employed*	−0.30	0.42	−0.73
Asian/Pacific Islander*	−0.01	0.69	−0.01
African American*	−0.03	0.76	−0.03
Latino*	−2.69	8.44	−0.32
Native American*	−0.81	0.86	−0.94
Control condition*	−0.52	0.40	−1.30
Video condition*	−0.57	0.51	−1.13

Note: Intercept = 3.15, Standard Error = 1.41, Pearson Goodness-of-Fit Chi-Square = 98.77, DF = 112, p = 0.81.

*For categorical variables, male, married, unemployed, white, Class condition participants make up the deleted comparison group.

related to the chronicity and severity of many of the participants' medical illnesses. However, given the small number of participants who missed follow-up assessments, this was not a major threat to the validity of the data reported here. Thus, neither social desirability nor differentially missing follow-up assessment sessions appeared to play a strong role in potentially biasing our findings.

18. Implementation Issues

Most often, research reports restrict themselves to the theoretical model, the study method, and the results. These are, of course, necessary in any scientific report. However, at times we almost forget that testing the model, implementing the method, and obtaining valid data are also dependent on the cooperation of the people who generate the data. These individuals include the study participants and the people who are in a position to give or deny access to the sample pool. Without their assistance, even a well-conceptualized study will falter.

As researchers, we rarely allow the reader a behind-the-scenes-look at the very real constraints placed on us. As we stated at the outset, one goal of this book is to provide the interested reader with a realistic (and we hope, encouraging) understanding of what such a study entails. The importance of doing so was emphasized in a previous work of the first author, entitled *Social and Psychological Research in Community Settings* (Muñoz, Snowden, Kelly & Associates, 1982).

In this chapter, we describe how we dealt with the constraints we faced in carrying out the study. In particular, we describe two essential phases of the study, the recruitment phase and the implementation of the class intervention.

Face-to-Face Recruitment

Because the DPRP was focused on multi-ethnic medical patients, the first task of the study implementation was gaining access to these patients. This required the cooperation of the medical staff who ran the clinic where the potential participants were seeking medical services. The assistance that was *essential* included allowing the researcher access to the patient charts (to determine eligibility to participate) and to the patient himself/herself (to conduct the initial interview). In addition, the assistance that was *desired* included encouraging the patient to participate, alerting the researcher when a patient was available for interview, and perhaps, when possible, allowing the researcher to complete the interview even when the physician or nurse may be ready to examine the patient.

Thus, before we had the opportunity to encourage a patient to participate in the study, we first had to convince the clinic staff of (1) the importance of the investigation; (2) its potential benefit to both the staff and the patient (i.e., the staff would be given reports on the findings of the study, thereby learning about the prevalence of depression and level of symptomatology experienced by their patients; and the patients, if assigned to the Class condition, might benefit from it); (3) our not requiring additional work from the already overburdened staff; and (4) our causing only minimal interference with the clinic's routine.

The introduction of the DPRP and its research team to the medical clinic staff was facilitated by a person who was a member of both groups, an insider to both. The primary person who served as the initial liaison between the study and the clinics was the physician on the DPRP team, Eliseo J. Pérez-Stable. Dr. Pérez-Stable had been a fellow in the SFGH General Medical Clinic since a year prior to the study, and was well-acquainted with the staff. During the course of the study, he became a faculty member at the UCSF Division of General Internal Medicine. Thus, at both the SFGH and UCSF clinics, he was viewed as an insider. This was important because the research team was consequently less likely to be seen as a group of outsiders "intruding upon" a clinic. Rather, the group was endorsed by someone who was already trusted. If the scientific merit of the study and its potential benefits had not been sufficient, the DPRP was tolerated as a project belonging to a member of the clinic staff.

Dr. Pérez-Stable's intimate understanding of the structure and workings of the clinics, and his ability to identify the key personnel who would be able to facilitate or hinder the recruitment were invaluable. The fact that he was well-liked by the clinic staff was also quite apparent and an important asset to the success of the recruitment.

The official endorsement of the clinic directors was fairly easy to obtain. At SFGH-GMC and UCSF, the directors were already colleagues of Dr. Pérez-Stable. In fact, the SFGH-GMC director willingly endorsed and supported the project when we approached a second primary care clinic at SFGH, the Family Practice Clinic. The administrator at that clinic was particularly delighted with the Spanish-speaking component of the study, given that the demographic composition of the clinic population included approximately 50 percent Latinos.

While the clinic directors' cooperation was necessary, it was insufficient to ensure successful collaboration between the research team and a service-oriented clinical team. To facilitate a dialogue, Dr. Pérez-Stable introduced the Principal Investigator (Muñoz) and the Project Coordinator (Ying) to the clinic staff. All three met with the entire clinic staff, including clinic clerks, faculty physicians, nurses, licensed vocational nurses, and residents, and discussed the design of the study, and, perhaps more important, the specific practical aspects of the recruitment. The actual procedure for recruitment was developed and continually modified with input from the clinic staff.

Thus, with the advice of the clinic staff, we obtained the list of patients with appointments and reviewed their charts a day before the appointment to identify those who met inclusionary criteria (e.g., no more than 69 years old, had a chart open for at least six months). This prevented the research staff from hovering over the charts when nurses, physicians, and licensed vocational nurses needed to access the chart on the day of the appointment. They would have surely resented another pair of hands competing for the chart at that time. We discovered that the best time to approach a patient on the day of the appointment was when the licensed vocational nurses had checked them in but before the nurse had talked with them. This was when the patients were likely to be waiting the longest. The waiting between seeing the nurse and being examined by the physician was less predictable, and was used only if the patient could not be approached prior to this point.

Clearly, the assistance of the licensed vocational nurses and nurses was especially important. Some of the nursing staff alerted the recruiter when they had completed their work with a patient. Some nurses also encouraged patients to participate in the study. These interventions were welcome but not expected. We did not encounter active animosity or resistance to the study. Nurses who were less enthusiastic simply ignored the recruiters and did not go out of their way to assist. No one actively tried to interfere with the recruitment effort. Perhaps this spoke to the success of our preparation prior to entering the clinics for recruitment, and maintaining a cordial relationship with the clinic staff throughout the recruitment process.

It was stated earlier that Dr. Pérez-Stable served as the primary liaison person between the study and the clinics. Formally, this was true throughout the study. Questions about the study from the medical staff were directed to Dr. Pérez-Stable. Difficulties that arose during the recruitment, if they involved clinic staff or clinic routine, were handled primarily by him as well. However, over time, it is perhaps more accurate to say that the real day-to-day liaison people were the frontline recruiters. Their role was especially important.

Most of the recruiters were undergraduate psychology majors from the University of California at Berkeley. They were carefully selected and interviewed by the Project Coordinator (Ying) to assess interest in the project, interpersonal sensitivity, dependability, and ability to work independently.

Given the patient population, we were particularly interested in recruiting ethnic minority interviewers. While we were successful in the case of Latinos and Asians, we were unfortunately not able to bring on any African-American recruiters (none applied). This might have been partly due to the absence of African-American investigators on the research team. Given the large number of African-American patients in the clinics from which we recruited, we ought to have more actively recruited African-American students, and included at least one African-American investigator on our research team. Our focus on providing linguistically appropriate services increased our emphasis on Spanish- and Chinese-speaking staff. (A Chinese-speaking intervention was also pilot-tested with a community sample and is not reported here because its population was not composed of medical patients.) This, in addition to the fact that three of the investigators were Latino and the Project Coordinator was Chinese, added to this bias. Having ethnic minority researchers is not enough. As much as possible, explicit attention to the ethnic composition of the research team in relation to that of the population with whom one is working is necessary.

The importance of recruiter-patient match was most visible for the Spanish-speaking group. A similarity in ethnic background and language spoken facilitated rapport between the recruiter and the potential participant. As reported elsewhere (Muñoz et al., 1987), of those approached in person, the acceptance rate of first screening interview was 46.4 percent for the Spanish-speaking group as compared with 24.3 percent for the English-speaking group.

The recruiters had the task of joining an existing clinic structure, and creating a niche where previously there was none. They were informed about the terrain they were about to enter and the key people they needed to work with. They were not members of the clinic staff but had to be accepted (or at least tolerated). If they were successful, they received much assistance from the clinic staff in accessing the patients. Otherwise, they found that after many hours in the clinic, they had recruited few participants.

While all recruiters were given training on the clinic setting, how to conduct the recruitment, how to approach the staff and the patients (and much of the training occurred on site, with the Project Coordinator working side by side with the recruiters), there was clearly variation in how recruiters handled the challenge. Some recruiters were more timid by nature, and too readily accepted patient hesitation as meaning "no." Others were too aggressive, recruiting many patients who later refused to continue. In these cases, modification in style was encouraged. The most successful recruiters were those who were sensitive to the demands of the setting and able to respond to them with flexibility. They developed a rapport with the staff, and correctly distinguished those patients who were amenable to persuasion and likely to continue in the screening process.

Trying to "catch" patients in between licensed vocational nurses, nurses, and physicians in a busy clinic was a stressful experience for all involved. At weekly recruiter meetings, the Project Coordinator discussed methods of successful recruitment, and answered questions about how to handle various situations. For example, with only a few questions remaining, could a recruiter ask the physician to wait? The answer was yes, but only if the physician was amenable to it. If a staff person wanted to use a corner that had been delegated for study screening, did the recruiter have to surrender the space? The reply was, if in the middle of an interview, try to negotiate with the staff member; otherwise, find another space.

Over time, morale became a problem for some recruiters. Partly, this was due to the feeling that they were in the front line doing the most difficult job of recruitment, while others (mostly graduate students) could remain and administer second and third screenings in the comfort of project offices. In response to this, the Project Coordinator returned to the clinics to recruit participants. This significantly improved morale ("If you are willing to do that, it really must be important"). In retrospect, it would have been better if the Project Coordinator simply continued to recruit after teaching the recruiters "the ropes," conveying the message that recruitment was essential for the success of the study. This also points to the importance of investigators being intimately and actively involved in all phases of a research project. While it is not possible for an investigator to do everything, delegating may be misunderstood as abdicating responsibility or devaluing the task's importance, and holds its dangers. Thus, for example, the Principal Investigator (Muñoz) took part in the Spanish-speaking recruitment, the administration of the DIS, and the teaching of some of the classes.

The Implementation of the Class Intervention

The success of the implementation of any intervention may be analyzed from many different perspectives. Most importantly, of course, is the question of whether the participants understood, accepted, and integrated the materials, resulting in changes in how they thought and behaved in their lives. While earlier chapters address the question of precisely how well the DPRP Class intervention accomplished this, here we limit our discussion to other facets of the intervention. These include: (1) ensuring that we taught everything we intended to cover; (2) increasing the likelihood that the participants would accept and benefit from the intervention; and (3) ascertaining the participants' reaction to the intervention during its implementation.

Ensuring the Comparable Coverage of Materials across Classes

Since the Class intervention was administered in English and Spanish, and taught by several instructors, the issue of comparable presentation for participants assigned to different classes arose. Several methods were employed to ensure this. First, the intervention protocol (see Appendix A) included instructor notes and class outlines (which were distributed to the participants at each class and mailed to those who missed that particular session). The outlines specified the major points to be covered. The instructors studied these notes and outlines before each class to familiarize themselves with (or review) the content of that week's lecture. The instructors' task was to cover all the points discussed in each class outline.

Each instructor's success was assessed by research assistants and more advanced clinicians (in most cases, the first author). All classes were observed by research assistants who provided feedback to the instructor regarding adequacy of coverage of the materials in the class outline. In addition, all instructors observed the first author teaching the eight-week course in the language the instructor later taught the course. Thus, the psychologist who taught the Spanish-speaking course (Ana Alvarez) had observed the first author teach it in Spanish first. All instructors were observed by either the first or second author for at least one eight-week run of the course. The mutual observations and feedback helped all teachers to standardize the coverage of the materials.

Ensuring the Acceptability of the Intervention

To promote the likelihood that the participants would benefit from the intervention, a number of techniques were utilized throughout the course by all instructors. They became integral parts of the intervention. As noted previously in the presentation of class content, the course began with a rationale of the intervention. This was echoed at each class session with a discussion about the relationship between mood, behavior and cognition, and how mood may be altered through the latter two. This was reinforced as the fundamental principle on which the intervention was built. Throughout the eight weeks, the instructor explained why the techniques could be helpful. Ultimately, the emphasis on the rationale of the program was intended to empower the participants with knowledge about themselves, their environment, and their ability to influence both.

In addition to explaining concepts and techniques, we encouraged discussion from the class participants. This provided the opportunity for the participants to "try on the idea for size," to pose clarifying questions, and for the instructor to assess if the ideas were correctly understood.

To gain mastery over the ideas and techniques, practice was emphasized throughout the course. We discussed the importance of taking "book learning" outside of the classroom. Ideas needed to be tested for their validity. It was important to find applications to real life. Participants were asked to complete certain assignments or homework. For example, the participants would keep track of their daily mood and observe its variation with presence of positive and negative thoughts, or engagement in pleasant or social activities. At the following class, homework exercises and the consequences of doing them were discussed. Those who successfully completed the homework were encouraged to reward themselves. Those who did not complete the homework, usually because of other demands or forgetfulness, were encouraged to discuss their difficulties. The instructor invited other members of the class to brainstorm with these participants to help them tackle their conflicts.

Rarely did a participant fail to understand the nature of the assignment. Adequate time was always allotted to explain the assignment before ending each class session. Some participants found certain techniques to work better than others in improving their mood. This was not regarded as a problem. Instead, we presented the techniques like a menu in a restaurant, expecting the participants to have different tastes and preferences. We hoped that at least some of the techniques would be palatable to them. In fact, this appeared to be the case.

In addition to explanation, discussion, practice, we also tried to increase the acceptability of the intervention by incorporating our knowledge of the participants in our discussion of the concepts and use of examples. We were aware that low income status in many cases did limit access to available resources, and reduced control. We felt, however, that given those limitations, it was still possible to increase the probability of experiencing positive mood. For instance, in discussing pleasant activities, we emphasized that it was not necessary to have a lot of money to have a good time. One group exercise encouraged participants to generate a list of enjoyable activities in the surrounding community that were either free or cost little money.

In illustrating various concepts, we also tried to employ examples that would be relevant to this population. Since all participants were medical patients, the power of the mind in managing physical disabilities secondary to illness was a favorite example. The instructor would not dispute the reality of the physical discomfort and pain (this was always acknowledged), but tried to encourage a view that could be described as "given these limitations, what can I still do to improve my life or mood?"

Often, participants themselves would give examples that reflected their ethnic origins, beliefs, or their current life situation. For some African-American participants, integrating church teachings and our techniques seemed to be especially helpful. For immigrant Asian and Latino participants, using the techniques to address their feelings of loss of family and friends, and the stresses they were encountering while adjusting to this society was common. Since all instructors were either Asian or Latino immigrants, they often shared personal immigration experiences, conveying a sense of empathy and understanding, and illustrating how the techniques were helpful to them. Again, as noted earlier, it would have been beneficial to also have African American instructors. Of course, it was not possible for the instructor to offer the most appropriate example for each participant. However, encouraging the participants to share examples allowed for the participants to integrate the techniques into their lives in a meaningful manner.

Ascertaining the Participant Receptivity of the Intervention

Immediate feedback regarding the participant receptivity of the classes was accomplished by noting their reaction at the end of each class. Participants rated the session on a continuum of boring to interesting, confusing to clear, practical to impractical, as improving or worsening their mood, and whether they intended to practice the techniques taught. Across all classes and participants, 95.20 percent of the participants rated the class as interesting or very interesting, 87.09 percent found the presentation clear or very clear; 95.96 percent rated the ideas discussed as practical or very practical; 93.33 percent stated the class made them feel better or much better; and 98.10 percent planned to try the techniques presented. These evaluations provide an indication of the receptivity of the participants to the ideas and techniques covered. In addition, they also facilitated the discussion that was held after each class, attended by the instructor, research assistant and observing psychologist. These professionals would review the evaluations and discuss how the session went, focusing on areas that might benefit from improvement.

Finally, it is important to state explicitly the dual purposes of the intervention, namely, to allow the researchers to test its usefulness, and to help real human beings. We played the dual role of researcher and teacher/clinician. In the former role, we were in the asking role, that is, we wanted data from the participants to test our hypotheses. In the latter, we were in the giving role, that is, we had something to offer them. Generally, this did not pose a conflict. For instance, collecting data on participant mood and thought held a research function, but monitoring participants' practice of the techniques being taught (viewed as the mechanism necessary for improvement of mood at follow-up) also had real pedagogical value. It allowed the participants to experience the helpfulness of the technique, and contributed to improving their mood.

The success in the implementation of the study depended on our building and maintaining collaborative relationships with the participants. Research projects are often interventions. They have the potential of changing peoples' lives, whether or not this is part of the stated purpose. While we deliberately set out to change the lives of the participants (at least those in the Class condition), in the process, we, the researchers, have learned more about the plight of suffering from serious, chronic medical illness. At the same time, we have also come away with renewed respect and admiration for the human will to live, and to live well.

Part IV

The Implications of Research on Preventive Interventions

19. Screening and Outreach

The goal of mental health services is to reduce the prevalence (that is, the total number of cases) of mental disorders. This can best be accomplished by a combination of treating existing cases of the disorders successfully and preventing new cases from developing. The former is treatment; the latter is prevention. At present, the mental health system relies entirely on treatment approaches. Let's examine whether treatment approaches to reducing prevalence are feasible using demographic and epidemiologic data to estimate the extent of major depression in one subgroup of the U.S. population: Spanish-speaking Hispanics.

How Many Adult U.S. Hispanics Suffer from Major Depression?

To answer this question, we need estimates of the number of U.S. Hispanics, and of the rates of depression, as found in epidemiologic studies. Considering that Hispanics belong to several major national and cultural groups, epidemiological rates for each of the major groups will need to be estimated.

Hispanic adult population figures were obtained from *The Hispanic Population in the United States: March 1991* (U.S. Bureau of the Census, 1991). Out of a total of 21,437,000 Hispanics in the United States, 65 percent (approximately 14 million) are 18 years old or older, 50.2 percent are male, 62.6 percent are estimated to be of Mexican origin, 11.1 percent Puerto Rican, 4.9 percent Cuban, 13.8 percent Central and South American, and 7.6 percent other Hispanic (U.S. Bureau of the Census, 1991). Moscicki and colleagues (Moscicki et al., 1987) provide six-month prevalence rates for major depression: Mexicans, 1.0 for males, 3.6 for females; Puerto Ricans, 3.4 for males, 7.4 for females; Cuban Americans, 1.4 for males, 2.9 for females. Estimates for Central and South Americans and others are unavailable, and thus will be conservatively made by using the Cuban rates. Rates for residents of Puerto Rico are based on reports by Canino and colleagues (Canino et al., 1987) and are 2.4 percent for males and 3.3 percent for females. Table 19.1 presents the results of these estimates.

It appears, from U.S. official figures, that, if one included Puerto Rico, over 100,000 Hispanic men and approximately 300,000 Hispanic women meet criteria for major depressive episodes during any six-month period.

How Many Persons with Major Depression Need Spanish-speaking Services?

The number of Hispanics whose primary language is Spanish varies across groups and geographical regions. The proportion of Mexican Americans who completed the UCLA ECA interview in Spanish was 47 percent (Burnam et al., 1987). In San Francisco, community studies of Latinos have reported that from 70 to 83 percent (Lang et al., 1982) of respondents chose to complete interviews in Spanish. Assuming that 60 percent of adult Hispanics in the United States mainland are primarily Spanish-speaking, and thus would need mental health services in Spanish, and using the figure of 361,044 total depressed Hispanics (not including those in Puerto Rico; see Table 19.1), we can estimate that well over 200,000 adult Hispanics require treatment for depression in Spanish in any six-month period in the United States.

Table 19.1. Number of Adult Hispanics in the United States and Puerto Rico Meeting Criteria for Major Depressive Disorder (MDD) during a Six-Month Period

All Hispanics (100%) (18 years and older)	Males	MDD	Females	MDD	Total MDD
Mexican Origin	4,301,592	43,016	4,099,954	147,598	190,614
Puerto Rican	713,192	24,249	794,614	58,801	83,050
Cuban	442,885	6,200	430,655	12,489	18,689
Central & South American	970,652	13,589	1,038,979	30,130	43,719
Other Hispanic	563,633	7,891	588,991	17,081	24,972
Total Depressed (in the 50 States)		94,945		266,099	361,044
In Puerto Rico (17 to 64 years old)	851,000	20,400	941,000	31,000	51,400

Note: See text for sources.

How Many Spanish-speaking Therapists Are There in the United States?

Figures for psychologists were available from the National Science Foundation (1988, p. 27). The good news is that between 1977 and 1987, the proportion of employed doctoral-level psychologists who identify themselves as Hispanic doubled. The bad news is that the actual figures were 0.9 percent in 1977 (300 out of 33,700 psychologists nationwide) and 1.8 percent in 1987 (1,000 out of 56,400 nationwide). Since 37 percent of psychologists are in the clinical area and another 15 percent in counseling (National Science Foundation, 1988, p. 133), we can estimate that 370 are clinical psychologists, and 150 are counseling psychologists, for a total of 520 in the mental health services.

The assumption that all 520 are Spanish-speaking will now be made, to account for the fact that figures for other therapists, such as social workers and psychiatrists, were not available to the authors, and that some non-Hispanic therapists speak Spanish. (Otherwise, using the earlier 60% figure of Spanish-speaking persons within the Hispanic community, we would have arrived at 312 as our figure.)

How Many Spanish-speaking Persons with Major Depression Could Be Treated by the Estimated 520 Spanish-speaking Therapists?

The newer brief psychological treatments for major depression require 20 one-hour sessions. In six months (26 weeks) at 40 hours of patient contact per week (for a total of 1040 hours), a professional could provide treatment for 52 patients. Leaving some time for vacations and other absences, 500 psychologists seeing 50 patients each could treat 25,000 depressed patients in six months. This would leave 175,000 untreated Spanish-speaking cases of major depression.

Note that the above estimates assume that the Spanish-speaking therapists would treat only adults with major depression. No children or adolescents would be seen, nor patients with other disorders.

How Effective Would Prevention Efforts Have to Be in Order to Be Comparable to Treatment Efforts?

Focusing for the moment only on the 200,000 cases of major depression estimated to occur in any six-month period in Spanish-speaking persons, we find that a reduction in incidence of as little as one-eighth (12.5 percent) would match the 25,000 cases that could be treated by all available Spanish-speaking U.S. therapists.

How large is a reduction of one-eighth, in terms of incidence? For illustrative purposes, let's set one-year incidence for major depression at 4 percent (it is actually somewhat less than that). One-eighth of 4 percent is 0.5 percent. Thus, a one-eighth reduction would result in an incidence of 3.5 percent. Clearly, even a small prevention effect can have consequences easily rivaling that of treatment, even assuming treatment were 100 percent effective.

How Effective Are Current Treatments for Depression?

The most carefully conducted studies of the effect of treatments for depression are randomized controlled trials. It is very likely that such trials provide an overestimate of efficacy. Even with this positive bias, results are far from satisfactory.

The sources of positive bias in treatment outcome studies are many. Therapists are carefully selected, systematically trained, and continuously supervised. It would be rare for this type of careful selection and overseeing of treatment to occur in either public or private clinical services. In addition, the research team is likely to be motivated to obtain good results, which are intended to be made public. Most therapists outside of research contexts do not keep accurate records of overall effectiveness, and they generally do not disclose such data, even if kept. For these reasons, it is likely that therapists in research studies would perform at the upper range of potential effectiveness.

Patients, too, are carefully selected. To begin with, only 20 percent of those who meet criteria for major depression seek treatment (Shapiro et al., 1984). A small percentage of those seeking treatment are likely to choose to enter research studies. The effects of this selection factor is unknown, but is likely to produce bias in favor of motivated patients. From the researcher's side, there is further selection: only about 10 percent of those who inquire about clinical trials are even scheduled for evaluation (Bellack, Hersen & Himmelhoch, 1981), and about 36 to 45 percent of those evaluated are accepted into the trial (Elkin et al., 1989; Murphy et al., 1984; Rush et al., 1977). Often, the studies have several exclusion criteria, including physical illness, illiteracy, ability to speak English, and so on. In addition, of course, patients having trouble keeping appointments eliminate themselves by never completing the evaluation phase. By the time the preliminaries are over, the study sample is likely to be motivated, compliant, relatively well-functioning, probably well-educated, and with sufficient resources to afford repeated travel to the clinical site and with enough control over personal time to attend sessions. These characteristics are likely to give the treatments being tested a higher likelihood of showing good effects than if they were implemented with a representative sample of the general public, or with persons who use public sector clinics (Organista, Muñoz & González, 1991).

How positive are the effects shown?

Dropout rates from treatment are considerable. Attrition usually produces dropout rates between 20 and 52 percent (DiMascio et al., 1979; Simons et al., 1984). In the National Institute of Mental Health Collaborative Study (Elkin et al., 1989), out of 250 randomized patients, 11 dropped out before treatment started, and another 77 during treatment, for a total of 88 (35%). The proportion of patients recovered ranged from 36 to 56 percent for all who entered treatment, and from 51 to 70 percent for all who completed at least 15 weeks of treatment. Sustained improvement is poor, even for those who recover. In the Murphy and Simons study (Murphy et al., 1984; Simons et al., 1986) out of 95 patients randomized, 25 (26%) dropped out; of 70 completers, 44 (63%) responded to treatment; of 44 who responded, 28 (64%) did *not* relapse at one year. Thus, of 95 randomized (after careful screening), only 28 (29%) were remitted at a one-year follow-up.

In addition to the low utilization and less than satisfactory effectiveness of treatment, there are some drawbacks and risks to entering treatment. There is the stigma of becoming a "mental patient," which is particularly salient in Hispanic populations, but which has in fact been known to have serious effects on individual careers. Perhaps the most celebrated of these in recent times was the almost forced withdrawal of Senator Eagleton from a presidential race when it was disclosed he had received treatment for depression. Other risks involved in certain treatments range from minor side effects to the potential use of antidepressants to commit suicide.

We can conclude, then, that treatment for depression has several limitations and some risks. Even if the 25,000 Spanish-speaking persons with major depression to whom mental health professionals could offer treatment were treated, only about two-thirds of them would complete treatment, up to about two-thirds of those completing treatment would respond well, and less than a third (approximately 8,000 of the 25,000) would be well one year later. To match this level of performance, prevention programs would have to reduce incidence rates only by $^1/_{25}$ (8,000 well cases at one year divided by the original 200,000 Spanish-speaking cases). Reductions greater than this would have a markedly greater impact than all available treatment services. Considered another way, given that all currently available therapists would produce only 8,000 well cases after one year, if prevention programs were to reduce incidence in Spanish-speaking populations by 20 percent (40,000 cases), this would be the equivalent of providing five times as many Spanish-speaking therapists as are estimated to be currently available. Seen from this perspective, it seems logical to develop effective prevention methods that can reach large segments of the population.

Can Major Depression Be Prevented in Hispanic Peoples?

Proper studies to assess the prevention of depression among Hispanics would involve intervention trials with Spanish-speaking populations. Professionals able to design these interventions and the studies to test preventive effects are in short supply. Spanish-speaking professionals with these skills are even more rare. Ideally, graduate programs should provide this training.

But even assuming that such studies have taken place, and that they have supported our prediction that when depression symptom levels can be reliably reduced, incidence decreases. Would this be sufficient? If professionals are engaged in the direct provision of preventive services, and especially if these services are delivered to small groups of individuals, the impact on incidence would be minimal. We would have the same problems of having limited numbers of professionals, and thus, minimal impact on the population as a whole.

To make prevention feasible, a combination of effective interventions and delivery strategies that can reach the people who need them the most is needed. Utilization rates for mental health services are extremely low for all ethnic groups, but are even worse for Hispanics. Data from the Epidemiological Catchment Area Los Angeles site (Hough et al., 1987) are probably the most accurate estimate of utilization *by diagnosed persons.* It shows that among those with a diagnosable mental disorder, only 22 percent of non-Hispanic whites sought care from mental health providers, compared with 11 percent of Mexican-Americans. It is important that comprehensive mental health services not be delivered only to easily available populations. Methods of service delivery must be developed that will reach those most at risk, even if it means creating services that can be used at their convenience and in their own homes. Chapter 22 presents a framework for evaluating the cost and efficacy of these kinds of service.

Screening and Outreach

The Need to Develop Innovative Methods

To address the problem of depression in Hispanics, interventions that go beyond treatment by professionals must be developed and evaluated. Specifically, a focus on prevention, and on the development and implementation of adjuncts to expand mental health service delivery is crucial.

It is particularly important that technological advances in mental health be made available to the Spanish-speaking population from the outset. Professionals serving this population should not keep on playing "catch-up" in this area, as in all others. To suggest that Hispanics can not respond to the most advanced methods of intervention is condescending. Concerted efforts are needed to adapt technology to their life-styles, as well as campaigns to expose them to the technology so they have a chance to learn how to use it. *Culturally and linguistically appropriate computer applications* must be a high priority for community-oriented practitioners who have dedicated themselves to working with minorities. For example, with the use of analog-to-digital "speech boards," computers could be used to routinely screen primary care patients for depression by having the computer present the screening questions verbally, and programming the computer to accept the person's verbal responses (Starkweather & Muñoz, 1989; González, Muñoz & Starkweather, 1991). This method would be particularly helpful because medical staff are usually too busy to add another screening procedure to their protocol. It would be essential for monolingual Spanish-speaking patients in clinics where there are few or no Spanish-speaking providers. The results of the screening procedure could be printed out and made available to the primary care provider. Even if he or she could not intervene, at least the condition would have been identified, and the process of locating appropriate help would begin. Interventions such as those developed in the computerized or bibliotherapeutic projects described in Chapter 22 could be made available to patients with mild and moderate cases of depression.

The introduction of new services is always problematic. Prevention is no exception. Preventive interventions are most likely to be accepted if combined with treatment services. Consider the following scenario:

Combined prevention and treatment services in a primary care clinic. Each primary care clinic serving Hispanics should routinely provide screening and triage for major depression. Such screening could be done with paper-and-pencil self-report depression scales, such as the Center for Epidemiological Studies–Depression Scale (CES-D) (Radloff, 1977), or the Beck Depression Inventory (BDI) (Beck et al., 1961), or with computerized versions of such scales, as described above.

The screening system would identify three groups:

1. "Depressed," or those with high enough depression scores to be likely to meet clinical criteria for depression, and thus in need of professional evaluation. (It would be possible to set up a computerized system that automatically checks for the presence or absence of symptoms for major depressive episode, melancholia, or suicidality, if a person scores above a certain point on the screening scale. Final diagnosis and disposition would still require a personal interview, however.)
2. "High risk," that is, unlikely to meet criteria for clinical depression currently, but having enough risk factors to recommend preventive intervention. Risk factors might include a personal history of depression, family history, high symptom level, and a high number of stressful life events.
3. "Low risk," that is, neither currently depressed, nor having high-risk factors. No intervention is needed for this group once the screening procedure has been validated.

Once screening has taken place, triage would occur. Patients in the "depressed" category would be seen by a mental health professional, diagnosed, and referred to emergency services (if acutely suicidal, psychotic, or unable to care for self), outpatient treatment (if patient agrees), antidepressant treatment by the primary care provider (if the patient refuses to see a specialist). If the patient has mild to moderate levels of depression and is not suicidal, he or she would be assigned to any of the "adjuncts" discussed in Chapter 22: a paraprofessional instructor on mood management, a volunteer support person, a mutual aid (self-help) group, audio or video materials on mood management, self-administered computerized treatment, or printed self-help manuals.

Patients in the "high-risk" category would also be given information about courses in mood management, support groups, audio or video materials, computerized preventive self-change programs, and printed depression prevention programs.

The development and evaluation of such interventions will require professionals to be trained in a number of areas (Muñoz, in press): high-risk factor research, outreach methods to attract and intervene with populations at risk (rather than merely with available populations), the development of interventions, computer applications, evaluation research, and the development of comprehensive programs across mental health, primary care, occupational, economic, and educational settings. To serve many Hispanics, such professionals will need to also be bilingual and bicultural.

A Parting Thought-Problem

Currently, most cases of depression are not being detected, even by primary care professionals. Even so, the mental health treatment system, especially in the public sector, is unable to meet the demand. Long waiting lists are very common. What will we do with all the cases that the screening process described above will uncover? (*Hint:* Deciding *not* to find the cases is not an acceptable solution.)

20. The Prevention of Depression in Primary Health Care

ELISEO J. PÉREZ-STABLE

JEANNE MIRANDA

Primary health care providers are uniquely positioned to contribute to the prevention of depression. The feasibility of a clinical or public health intervention leading to the primary prevention of depression has not been studied, but there are some general guidelines that clinicians may consider applying in their practice. If subgroups of primary care patients who are at greater risk for clinical depression can be identified, clinicians may be able to target these persons for a preventive intervention. This chapter focuses on the factors that may prove helpful in predicting patients at higher risk, and how to accomplish this task in a busy clinical practice. Patients who have had an episode of major depression in the past or who are currently treated but asymptomatic are at greater risk of recurrent episodes and should be the target of specific preventive measures.

Depression in Primary Care Settings: The Magnitude of the Problem

Depression is a common clinical problem of major public health importance. Morbidity can be measured not only by the pain and suffering of patients and loved ones but also by the high costs of health services utilization, adverse effects of pharmacologic therapy, and time lost from employment. Mortality from major depression is mostly secondary to suicide, which in 1984 accounted for 30,904 deaths and was the fifth leading cause of years of potential life lost (YPLL) before age 65 (Centers for Disease Control, 1987). Recognition of clinical depression by clinicians and appropriate treatment or referral are essential in reducing morbidity and mortality from depression (Murphy, 1975).

Most people with psychological problems are managed by primary care physicians rather than mental health care professionals. Furthermore, approximately 50 percent of patients in primary care settings have psychosocial rather than biomedical reasons for their visits (Stoeckle, Zola & Davidson, 1964). The prevalence of depression in persons seen in primary care clinics is higher than in the general population, although rates vary according to setting, diagnostic criteria, and method of detection. Six studies using structured interviews with research or clinical diagnostic criteria to define depression in medical outpatients have reported rates of 5.8 percent (Hoeper et al., 1979), 9.7 percent (Schulberg et al., 1985), 22.3 percent (Jones et al., 1987), 10.3 percent (Von Korff et al., 1987), 10.0 percent (Barrett, Barrett, Oxman & Gerber, 1988), and 26 percent (Pérez-Stable, Miranda, Muñoz & Ying, 1990). This compares with rates of a lifetime major depressive episode in the general population of 3.7 to 6.7 percent in three U.S. cities (Robins et al., 1984). Studies using self-report symptom scales have found significant depressive symptomatology in 12 to 55 percent of patients studied (Katon, 1987; Katon, Berg, Robins & Risse, 1986; Linn & Yager, 1980; Linn & Yager, 1984; Moore, Silimperi & Bobula, 1978; Nielsen & Williams, 1980; Pérez-Stable et al., 1990; Rosenthal et al., 1987; Rucker, Frye & Cygan, 1986; Schulberg et al., 1985).

The Recognition of Depression in Primary Care

Primary care practitioners fail to recognize depression in up to 50 percent of outpatients with this condition (Jones et al., 1987; Katon, 1987; Katon et al., 1986; Linn & Yager, 1980; Linn & Yager, 1984; Moore et al., 1978; Nielsen & Williams, 1980; Rosenthal et al., 1987; Rucker et al., 1986; Schulberg, McClelland & Gooding, 1987; Thompson, Stoudemire, Mitchell & Grant, 1983; Von Korff et al., 1987; Zung, Magill, Moore & George, 1983). The Medical Outcomes Study found that only 45.9 to 51.2 percent of depressed patients who visited medical clinicians had their depression detected at the time of the visit (Wells et al., 1989). This compared with 78.2 to 86.9 percent recognition of depressed patients who visited a mental health specialist (Wells et al., 1989). Those patients with health care financed by prepayment were significantly less likely to have their depression detected or treated by a physician during the visit (Wells et al., 1989). A study from a university-based group practice and a county hospital clinic in San Francisco found that of 70 depressed patients who had been diagnosed using the Diagnostic Interview Schedule, only 25 (35.7%) were recognized by their physician over the preceding year (Pérez-Stable et al., 1990). However, misdiagnosis also occurred because 36 of 185 (19.5%) nondepressed patients were characterized as depressed by their physician (Pérez-Stable et al., 1990). The observations that depression is underrecognized and misdiagnosed by primary care physicians are supported by the fact that many patients in these settings are prescribed psychotropic medications without a diagnosis of a mental disorder. Although antidepressants are useful in the management of chronic pain, most of these prescriptions are for benzodiazepines, presumably for insomnia or anxiety. There is reason to suspect that many patients with depression are inappropriately prescribed benzodiazepines by primary care physicians.

Depressed patients in medical settings may focus on the somatic complaints accompanying the affective disorder, which may lead to unnecessary tests and medications, occasional iatrogenic morbidity, and a high rate of dissatisfaction in both patient and physician (Katon, 1987). About one-third of depressed patients in a primary care setting may deny having a depressed mood. In addition, clinical presentation may be dominated by somatic complaints such as headache, nausea, fatigue, insomnia, anorexia and unexplained pain. Generally, somatization of depressive symptoms is more frequent in ethnic minorities and in persons of less privileged socioeconomic background and with fewer years of formal education.

It is especially important that primary care physicians recognize and treat depression appropriately because only 20 percent of persons with depression are treated by mental health care professionals (Link & Dohrenwend, 1980). Depression is so common in medical outpatients that primary care physicians should conduct a focused interview applying diagnostic criteria of major depression in any patient suspected of the diagnosis. This approach is consistent with the medical model using specific criteria to define a disease. In addition to the presence of dysphoric mood the mnemonic A SAD FACE (Appetite, Sleep, Agitation, Death, Failure, Anhedonia, Concentration, Energy) may help clinicians remember the DSM-III-R criteria for diagnosing major depression (see Chapter 2 for details of the diagnostic criteria).

Clinicians detect and manage depression better in younger persons than among the elderly (German et al., 1987). Special attention to the criteria that define clinical depression in the context of chronic diseases and with the possibility of dementia as part of the differential diagnosis need to be considered. The so-called diagnosis of pseudodementia (depression masquerading as dementia) is a difficult one to make, even for the skilled geriatrician. The response of "I don't know" to orientation questions as opposed to guesses is an easily remembered clue to the presence of depression. Extensive cognitive function tests by specialized units are relatively expensive and of unproven benefit. Occasionally, a therapeutic trial of antidepressant pharmacotherapy is warranted in managing this clinical challenge in elderly persons.

Identifying Persons at Higher Risk for Depression

Epidemiological studies in the United States have found that the overall prevalence of major depression is about two times higher for women (4.9 to 8.7%) than for men (2.3 to 4.4%) (Robins et al., 1984). Additional risk factors for depression include less privileged socioeconomic status, a past history or a family history of affective disorders (carrying a twofold to threefold lifetime risk), and a "formerly married" status (especially if divorced or separated). Weissman also identified younger age (defined as persons born after World War II) as a risk factor (Weissman, 1987). Multiple logistic analyses of data from a longitudinal study of risk factors in an urban community in Alameda County showed additional risk factors independently associated with significant depressive symptoms: physical disability, poor perceived health, job loss, and social isolation (Kaplan, Roberts, Camacho & Coyne, 1987). The epidemiologic data provide some insight in helping a clinician formulate a demographic profile of patients at higher risk for depression.

Recent epidemiologic and clinical studies have reported a significant association between current cigarette smoking and depression. A population-based survey of Latinos in San Francisco found that current cigarette smokers have 1.7 times greater risk of significant depressive symptoms when compared with nonsmokers (Pérez-Stable, Marín, Marín & Katz, 1990). National data from the Health and Nutrition Examination Survey Epidemiologic Follow-up Study reported that 10 percent of smokers with significant depressive symptoms compared with 17 percent of those without significant symptoms were able to quit after nine years of follow-up (Anda et al., 1990). The association between smoking and depression is further supported by a longitudinal study of adolescents (Kandel & Davies, 1986) and clinical studies that reported high relapse rate among smokers attempting to quit who had a history of major depression (Glassman et al., 1988). In the primary care setting, these observations imply that current smokers should be considered at higher risk of clinical depression and that special attention should be given to depressive symptoms in smokers who are trying to quit.

The use of over 200 different medications has been associated with depression, although most are isolated case reports. Oral contraceptives were reported to cause depression in up to 5 percent of women, but this is considerably less common with low estrogen preparations. Medications to lower blood pressure are commonly prescribed by adult primary care physicians, and some antihypertensives that have been reported to cause depression include reserpine, alphamethyl-DOPA, and clonidine. None of the four major categories (diuretics, beta-blockers, converting enzyme inhibitors, and calcium channel blockers) of recommended medications for first-line pharmacotherapy of hypertension has been shown to cause depression conclusively. Psychotropic drugs including major tranquilizers, benzodiazepines, and narcotic analgesics can also be associated with and actually trigger depression. These medications, especially the latter two, are often prescribed in adult outpatients. Other frequently used medications in primary health care that have been associated with significant depressive symptoms in a small number of patients taking them are cimetidine (used for peptic ulcers and related disorders), digoxin (for cardiac problems), nonsteroidal anti-inflammatories (for arthritis or pain), and corticosteroids (used to treat a wide variety of clinical problems).

In depressed patients, the clinician should consider changing medications that may be associated with depression. For example, lipophilic beta-blockers such as propranolol or metoprolol have a greater penetration into the brain and may be more likely to cause depressive symptoms. These can be replaced with lipophobic beta-blockers such as atenelol or nadolol. A trial without a possible depression-causing medication should show results in two to four weeks. Anti-anxiety agents are sometimes used as adjunctive therapy of specific symptoms, but are not indicated as the sole treatment of depression.

Depressive symptoms may be the initial manifestation of a wide spectrum of metabolic or neurological conditions. Endocrine disorders most likely to present as depression are hypothyroidism (Gold, Pottash & Extein, 1981), hyperparathyroidism, and Cushing disease (hypercortisolism). Cerebritis from systemic lupus erythematosis and other autoimmune disorders may present as depression, but other manifestations are usually evident. Pancreatic cancer has been associated with depression, and other malignancies may initially present with systemic symptoms suggestive of depression. A fifteen-year follow-up of a nationally representative sample found no significant increased risk for cancer incidence or mortality associated with the level of depressive symptoms after adjusting for age, sex, and other possible confounders (Zonderman, Costa & McCrae, 1989). The causal connection between depressive symptoms and cancer is thus questioned, and depressed patients should not be screened more intensively for cancer than otherwise recommended.

Persons who survive a major disease episode may have an increased risk of major depression. A report from New York of 283 patients with myocardial infarction found that 45 percent met criteria for dysthymia or major depression at the time of diagnosis (Schleifer et al., 1989). After three to four months, 171 patients were reinterviewed, and 33 percent were still depressed (Schleifer et al., 1989). Depression did not correlate with the severity of cardiac disease but was associated with the severity of noncardiac medical illness. Although studies of depression rates following other major disease episodes are lacking, patients who survive a major stroke present a particularly challenging group because of the resulting physical disability.

Screening Instruments

Physicians and other primary care providers can integrate screening measures for depression to be systematically applied to all patients in an ambulatory practice. A short self-administered symptom scale can be added to a questionnaire distributed before a scheduled "new patient" appointment without interfering in a clinical practice. Demographic and other factors (women, formerly married status, poor, less educated, current smokers) to identify persons at higher risk for depression can lead to targeted periodic rescreening for depression. Patients with chronic debilitating disorders, who have survived a major medical event, or who are treated with specific medications may also be at increased risk of depression. Screening in these patients is likely to facilitate the diagnosis. The U.S. Preventive Task Force published recommendations for screening, and their statement on depression follows. "The performance of routine screening tests for depression in asymptomatic persons is not recommended. Clinicians should maintain an especially high index of suspicion for depressive symptoms in those persons at increased risk for depression" (U.S. Preventive Services Task Force, 1989).

Several published depression scales are sensitive for identifying depressed persons, but most have low specificity and thus result in a positive predictive value of no more than 50 percent (Coulehan, Schulberg & Block, 1989; Pérez-Stable et al., 1990). Thus, screening instruments are best used to alert a physician that further clinical evaluation, such as a directed interview, is necessary. Treatment should not be initiated on the basis of results from screening instruments alone. Targeting depression screening to persons considered at high risk may further facilitate detection. Three easily administered screening measures are presented below.

The Center for Epidemiologic Studies–Depression Scale (CES-D) is a twenty-item self-administered scale that takes one to five minutes to complete (Radloff, 1977). The CES-D has a sensitivity for detecting major depression or dysthymia between 80 and 95 percent when a cutoff of 16 points or greater is used (Coulehan et al., 1989). This scale was developed for epidemiologic field studies, and the average scores of the general population are 8 to 10 points (Radloff, 1977). Women and blacks on average have higher CES-D scores compared with men and whites.

The Beck Depression Inventory (BDI) is a twenty-one item self-administered measure developed for clinical use in psychiatry. The BDI has been found to be from 86 to nearly 100 percent sensitive for detecting depression when a cutoff of 11 or more is used (Coulehan et al., 1989; Pérez-Stable et al., 1990). The BDI takes ten minutes to complete and includes a suicide item. It has been used frequently as an outcome measure in clinical studies evaluating antidepressant pharmacotherapy.

The Medical Outcomes Study depression scale is an eight-item self-report measure developed to screen for depression in a clinical setting (Burnam, Wells, Leake & Landsverk, 1988). The scale uses six items from the CES-D and adds two items that contain diagnostically relevant durations of depressed mood.

Preventing Depression: Guidelines for Primary Care Physicians

The recommended guidelines for preventing depression are founded in cognitive behavioral theory. Primary care physicians may be able to help patients without depending on a prescription by adopting a modification of the approach used by psychotherapists. Physicians should not underestimate the importance of their role in supportive counseling.

Physicians can increase the frequency and duration of contact, through follow-up visits or by telephone, with patients who may be at increased risk of depression. The support and interest of the physician may be very useful ingredients in the management of the problem. Telephone contact may also help to increase social support, and these patients need to be encouraged to increase their daily social contact. Physicians can also assist patients in improving their interpersonal skills by setting up role-playing in hypothetical situations. Dwelling on obsessive negative thoughts plagues depressed patients and usually represents overgeneralizations or exaggerations. Thus, patients at risk for depression should be taught how to substitute a realistic thought for an unduly pessimistic one, to reduce unnecessary thinking that leads to depressive mood, and to use constructive thinking.

Behavioral prescriptions to increase positive or pleasant activities after determining what the patient usually enjoys is an essential aspect of management. One study randomized forty-three depressed patients to a training program in aerobic exercise or control program in occupational therapy (Martinsen, Medhus & Sandvik, 1985). The patients in the exercise program had a significantly lower level of depressive symptoms compared with the control group at nine weeks of follow-up (Martinsen et al., 1985). Thus, by prescribing regular exercise, depressive symptoms may be decreased. The likelihood that such a decrease may prevent clinical episodes is high, though it has not yet been tested adequately. It would also be helpful if physicians and other health care professionals could teach basic relaxation techniques to be used when patients are confronting depressive symptoms. There are also self-help books written for nonprofessionals (but useful for physicians to read as well) that can be recommended to motivated patients who are susceptible to getting depressed (Burns, 1980; Ellis & Harper, 1975; Lewinsohn, Muñoz, Youngren & Zeiss, 1986).

Antidepressant Pharmacotherapy

Pharmacologic therapy of major depression is effective in 70 to 80 percent of persons who meet diagnostic criteria. Some clinical improvement in depressed patients is expected one week after a full therapeutic dose of an antidepressant, but beneficial response may be delayed for three to four weeks. Pharmacologic therapy is usually recommended for at least six months in most patients. There is increasing evidence that continuation of therapy at a reduced dose for an additional six months after resolution of symptoms will prevent relapse. Many patients with milder episodes of depression will do well with shorter courses of pharmacotherapy. Some symptoms, such as insomnia, respond fairly quickly to pharmacotherapy, and can lead to an increased sense of hope, which can then be used to encourage a focus on the thoughts and activities to manage mood. There is some evidence that learning these self-control methods results in a reduction in relapse rates when compared with the use of pharmacotherapy. The natural history of a major depressive episode is usually limited to six months' duration. However, relapse rates may be as high as 60 percent in the ensuing year and is greater in untreated patients.

Summary

Because most persons with psychological problems present to a medical setting, physicians in primary care practice need to be skilled at recognizing and treating depressive disorders. Depression is a common diagnosis in medical outpatients that may present with somatic complaints and lead to extensive evaluations. Simple self-administered screening instruments may be used to alert physicians that a patient has significant depressive symptoms. Cognitive behavioral concepts can be applied to the practical management of mood in primary care settings. This approach may promote prevention of depression in high-risk persons. Appropriate treatment of persons with major depression will decrease the likelihood of a relapse in the ensuing two years.

21. Ethical Issues

Three broad types of ethical issues are raised by preventive interventions:

1. claiming the effects of preventive interventions to be positive (or negative) in contradiction to available evidence;
2. ignoring possible negative side effects from preventive interventions;
3. identifying societal responsibilities once preventive interventions have been found to be effective.

Preventive Effects and the Available Evidence

The clearest case of ethical issues in prevention involves falsely promising preventive effects for an intervention that has not been tested or that, if tested, has been found to be clearly ineffective (or, worse, actually harmful) in terms of preventing the target disorder. Some elements that must be taken into account in this instance involve the current societal norms regarding the level of evidence generally required to offer services to the public. For example, not all treatments for mental disorders have been tested in randomized controlled trials. Even for those that have been so tested, the populations on which they have been studied are often not representative in terms of ethnicity, gender, or educational, economic, and health status. Thus, for many cases, there is a lack of evidence that directly addresses the likelihood of the effectiveness of particular treatments. Often, then, the level of evidence required to show that a particular treatment was properly chosen for a particular case is the prevailing community standard, that is, whether the treatment offered would have been among those routinely considered by other practitioners. Preventive interventions suffer from two disadvantages within these norms: first, there are very few controlled trials of preventive interventions for most mental health problems, and second, since there are few prevention practitioners, the concept of a "community standard" for prevention would be hard to crystallize. Often, there is no such standard.

Advocates of prevention point out that prevention programs should not be held to a higher standard than treatment programs. This suggests that reasonable standards for programs that are intended to be preventive would include professional judgment that such interventions are likely to be beneficial to the consumer.

The opposite side of the coin is often neglected, that is, declaring that psychological disorders are not preventable or that specific preventive interventions are not effective. For example, an NIMH publication in 1984 (Lobel & Hirschfeld, 1984) asserted that depressive episodes cannot be prevented. In fact, studies testing this assertion had not yet been conducted. Technically, of course, although one positive study would make the claim false, no matter how many negative studies are conducted, one could never prove that depression is not preventable, but only that all attempts to date have failed. Thus, the only negative statement regarding the prevention of depression that can ever be strictly true would be that "to date, no intervention has been shown to prevent depressive disorders." The issue here involves taking away hope prematurely, and perhaps reducing the motivation of individuals to attempt changes in their lives that would reduce their chances of developing depression or other disorders. At another level, it involves precluding financial and other societal support for efforts that might yield significant benefits.

Once there are interventions that actually reduce the incidence of depression, statements that falsely label such interventions ineffective can also have the effect of keeping a helpful intervention away from people who need it. The problem, of course, is that since prevention projects are expected to have effects on the probability that someone will develop a disorder, it is almost assured that some people will become depressed even if they practice the intervention to the fullest. In this sense, critics could accuse the intervention of not being effective. (The same can be said of treatment approaches, of course. Since there are no panaceas, every treatment will have a failure rate.)

Negative Effects

The more potent an intervention, the more likely it is to have effects beyond those intended. In the case of preventions focused on depression, a major negative effect might be having individuals pay excessive amounts of attention to their mood states and perhaps bring on higher levels of demoralization (or at least discontent) than if they had been left alone.

Negative effects can also occur in relation to aspects besides the disorder itself. For example, changes in ideology or religious beliefs might ensue once people begin to question the effects of their thinking on their lives. Depending on whether one supports the original belief or the new one, effects such as these could be viewed as positive or negative.

Chains of effects may also be triggered by interventions. For example, an intervention that encourages persons to change their current partners if these partners are causing them stress might result in increasing numbers of children raised in single-parent families. If this is a risk factor for other problems, then the intervention could have unintended negative consequences.

The implication of these issues is that both intended and unintended effects should be monitored when preventive interventions are evaluated. The final decision, as in most cases of social policy, will involve a cost-benefit analysis. Few, if any, interventions are entirely benign.

Let us examine one particularly controversial issue that has been thrust into the public forum by the recent advances in genetic research. Attempts to identify the gene or genes that are linked to depressive disorders have raised several issues. The identification of such a gene could lead to at least three types of preventive intervention:

1. prenatal screening and the abortion of affected fetuses;
2. genetic counseling and advice to affected potential parents not to have children. If the technology ever progresses sufficiently, one can imagine the identification of sperm or eggs that contain the gene or genes, to prevent the conception of new affected individuals, and still permitting affected individuals to have children without the "depression gene;"
3. the identification of individuals who have genes linked to depression, and interventions for those individuals designed to reduce the probability of depressive episodes.

Type 1 can be conceptualized as destroying the affected individual; type 2 as preventing the existence of affected individuals; and type 3 as preventing the disorder in affected individuals. Each of these applications of genetic knowledge raises several dilemmas.

Perhaps the most clear-cut issue is the identification and abortion of affected fetuses. Naturally, for those who view abortion as categorically unethical, there is no dilemma. Such an intervention is inherently unethical. But even for those who would consider abortion to be an ethical choice under certain circumstances, there is a major underlying problem: is the elimination of fetuses carrying the depression gene "prevention," or is it the most blatant instance of "blaming the victim"? What is being prevented through abortion? If the answer were to be "depressive disorders" or "depressive episodes," it would clearly smack of the often-criticized practice of "treating the illness rather than treating the patient." (One of the reviewers of this book responded to this section as follows: "I think that too much is made of the negative effects of possible interventions. In the case of depression, it is highly unlikely that preventive intervention #1 (prenatal screening and abortion of affected fetuses) will ever be used because depressive illness doesn't warrant such a drastic intervention." We agree that depressive illness does not call for such intervention. However, judgments regarding what warrants such intervention vary widely. For example, there are reports that female fetuses are selectively aborted in Asian countries with easy access to amniocentesis (*Time*, 1990). Yet, most people in the United States would probably agree that being female "doesn't warrant such a drastic intervention." It is important for the field to consider how the knowledge that is developed might be used, even if such uses are contrary to the intent of the developers.)

The second instance, the prevention of the conception of affected individuals, is somewhat less controversial. Such a practice does not directly affect human organisms carrying their complete genetic code. Persons who consider "tampering with nature" to be unethical in itself might be expected to raise objections to such procedures. But several other issues are involved.

First, is depression severe enough to warrant such a strategy? Who decides this? How would such a decision be made? Also, we must consider the effect on the lives of potential parents, who would either choose to remain childless or would live with the fear that their children might become afflicted with the disorder.

Finally, if the technology ever progresses to the point that sperm and eggs can be screened before conception, the issue would not longer affect potential parents, since they could still have (unaffected) children. However, society would be affected by the eventual lack of individuals who have the gene or genes in question. Since it is most likely that any gene or combination of genes influences a variety of human characteristics, society would eventually lose the positive traits also linked to these hypothetical "depression genes."

The third type of genetic intervention, early identification and interventions to prevent the occurrence of depressive episodes (that is, interventions designed to prevent the expression of the pathological aspects of the gene or to prevent the genotype from becoming the feared phenotype), brings up the impact on the affected individuals of being identified as at risk, "different" from the rest of society, and feeling the need to be protected from the impending disorder. The potential to be shunned by others, to be rejected as a marital partner, and to be passed over for occupational or leadership roles because of genetic makeup are realistic issues that require much thought. (If the genetic "defect" could be permanently "fixed," similar issues to those raised in the type 2 strategy earlier would be raised.)

The Ethical Issues Raised by Effective Interventions

Once effective methods of preventive intervention have been identified, and once adequate identification of high-risk groups has been achieved, several ethical issues arise.

The combination of high and low accuracy in identifying high-risk groups and high and low levels of preventive effects results in at least four possibilities:

— highly accurate identification of risk and high levels of preventive effects. In this case, the argument for identifying those at risk and offering them intervention is the strongest. Would mass screening campaigns be reasonable in this case? Questions then arise regarding the effect of informing at-risk persons of their risk level when it is very high, and of the level of outreach required by public health personnel when the risk is so high. Would there be a tendency to use persuasion bordering on the coercive to ensure high levels of compliance with the intervention?

Looking at this issue from the opposite viewpoint, would it be ethical to limit preventive services to volunteers? What if certain segments of the population underutilize preventive services? Let's say that a certain ethnic or gender group totally avoids using the preventive intervention. Is there justification for making a special effort to reach such a group? How far should such efforts go?

— highly accurate identification of risk and low levels of preventive effects. Here, the case for the identification of persons at risk becomes problematic, especially if the likelihood of reducing risk is low. The issues in this case involve frightening high-risk persons without offering them reasonable hope for altering their risk. Mass screening campaigns would not be justified in this case. Emphasis on voluntary participation in the intervention would be warranted.

— low accuracy in identifying high-risk groups and high levels of preventive effects. If our screening methodology falsely attributed high-risk status to many persons with low risk, and failed to identify many of those with true high-risk status (that is, if the screening procedure had low specificity and low sensitivity), many of those identified would not experience depressive episodes, even if no intervention were offered, and many not identified would have no access to the intervention. If the preventive intervention were very effective, one ought to consider community-wide interventions rather than identifying individuals. Emphasis would be placed on increasing awareness as well as the likelihood that those hearing about an intervention would implement it.

— low accuracy in identifying high-risk groups, and low levels of preventive effects. This condition demands further research. Such screening and intervention programs can be justified only if they are extremely inexpensive or if they are evaluated in such a way as to yield information to increase the accuracy and effectiveness of future screening or prevention.

We contend that research on preventive intervention, especially research focused on depression, must be pursued actively. However, this strong stand is taken with full recognition that advocates of prevention must consider the ethical implications of their programs. Because preventive projects will generally involve outreach or the implementation of interventions with populations that did not seek such services, there is a greater responsibility for us to examine the potential unintended effects of these interventions.

22. Measuring Cost

The argument for prevention is often accompanied by a claim that the costs of health care will be reduced if preventive programs are instituted. While this may be a side benefit of prevention, it is important to remind ourselves that a reduction in economic costs is not necessarily the best justification for pursuing preventive interventions. A reduction in human suffering, dysfunction, and societal disintegration can well be worth an increase in health care costs. Nevertheless, the issue of cost must be considered in an analysis of prevention. After all, policymakers must allocate the resources for preventive efforts, and must weigh the benefits of allocating these resources to preventive programs over others.

How to Determine Cost

Comparing the costs of two alternative approaches to health care is quite a complex process. In addition to the direct costs of each of the approaches, there are the objective long-term consequences of each, plus the subjective value of two other kinds of costs: the costs incurred by the recipient to take part in the intervention and the short- and long-term sequelae as experienced by the recipient.

In a provocative monograph on this topic titled *Is Prevention Better Than Cure?*, Russell (1986) reviewed data on the comparative cost of addressing the problem of measles via treatment versus preventive vaccinations. Between 1963 and 1968, the cost of treating measles cases in the United States would have totaled $174 million if preventive interventions had not been instituted. The cost of vaccinations for those years was $108 million. However, since not all children were vaccinated, and since not all vaccinations produced immunity, there were still measles cases that had to be treated even with the immunization program. The costs of treatment were approximately $97 million. Thus, the actual difference between prevention and treatment was $205 million versus $174 million, or a $31 million *greater* cost for prevention. Thus far, the ledger favors treatment as less costly. In addition to direct intervention services, however, one needs to add expenditures for institutional care for those persons retarded by measles: nearly $500 million without vaccinations versus $299 million when vaccination is instituted. When this difference of $201 million in favor of prevention is taken into account, the overall cost differential is $170 million dollars in favor of the preventive approach (Russell, 1986, p. 32).

Moreover, health effects show that instituting a vaccination policy resulted in 973 fewer deaths, 3244 fewer cases of retardation caused by measles, 58,380 fewer patients hospitalized, and nearly 34 million fewer days lost from school or work. These data help to balance the total effect of a preventive program. In addition, we can consider the consequences for the relatives of the retarded or deceased victims of measles, as well as the psychological cost of hospitalization and the lost wages or reduced productivity in school due to absences. Other costs that might have been included in an analysis would be side effects and possible negative health effects of the vaccination. Truly, even in a fairly straightforward case such as a simple immunization procedure, issues of cost can easily become convoluted.

Russell (1986) also examined screening for and treatment of hypertension (which clearly adds to medical expenditures), and changes in life-style. In relation to preventive interventions that require behavior change, she pointed out that "two aspects of any preventive measure can be evaluated—the cost-effectiveness of the measure itself as a way to improve health, and the cost-effectiveness of ways to persuade people to adopt the measure" (p. 82). Addressing an issue that we have made in the chapter on ethical issues, she reminded us that "prevention puts more people at risk, earlier, than does acute care and it is correspondingly more important to be sure that the magnitude of that risk lies within reasonable bounds" (p. 107).

Table 22.1 follows Russell's balance-sheet method (Russell, 1986, pp. 102–3) for organizing the results of a cost analysis. It is important to note that the costs of evaluating preventive interventions can be much higher that the interventions themselves, given the large sample sizes needed and the longitudinal nature of prevention outcome studies. Researchers reporting cost of interventions must differentiate between the intervention costs and the research costs. Implementation of interventions found to be effective may be several times less expensive than the cost of the randomized trials that evaluated the interventions.

Table 22.1. Table Shell Showing Items in a Cost-Effectiveness Evaluation of Depression Prevention Programs (Balance-Sheet Method of Presentation)

Health Effect	In Natural Units	In Years of Healthy Life Gained
Number of suicides prevented		
Years of life saved		
Cases of disability prevented*		
Cases of substance abuse prevented		
Cases of child neglect prevented		
Cases of divorce prevented		
Cases of job failure prevented		
Cases of school dropout prevented		
Cases of high-risk behavior prevented		
Driving under the influence		
Sex without contraception		
Unsafe sex		
Violent interactions		
Fewer side effects, if any		
Cost		**In Dollars**
Costs incurred in prevention program		
Program implementation costs		
Expenses related to preparing information		
Staff costs		
Space costs		
Materials		
Cost incurred by participants		
Time involved in attending program		
Expenses related to increasing activities		
Expenses related to social activities		
Time involved in reading materials, doing monitoring, other tasks		
Costs incurred in persuading people to join a prevention program		
Mass media costs		
Educational materials		
Advertisement		
Legislative activity		

*See Wells et al. (1989) study for variables.

The Implications of Research on Preventive Interventions

Expanding Mental Health Services Beyond the Professional Office: A Framework for Cost Analysis

Table 22.2 presents a grid in which the columns represent three chronologically ordered services that ideally ought to be part of a complete mental health care system: prevention, treatment, and maintenance (see Chapter 1). The rows represent six possible means of service delivery: professionals, paraprofessionals, partner-companions, peer clients, paraphernalia, and print. They have been given alliterative names as a mnemonic device (Christensen, Miller & Muñoz, 1978). At present, most resources are devoted to one of the resulting eighteen cells: treatment by professionals. Attention must be given to the development and evaluation of service delivery methods that involve the other seventeen cells (Christensen, Miller & Muñoz, 1978; Muñoz, 1980, 1982).

Prevention refers to interventions for persons who do not meet criteria for clinical disorders, but who are at risk for developing such disorders. The intent of preventive interventions is to reduce the incidence of the disorders. *Treatment* refers to interventions administered to persons who already meet criteria for the disorder. These interventions are designed to cure the disorder or to stop its progression to more severe levels. Early case finding (usually termed "secondary prevention") actually fits into the treatment realm. Treatment interventions aim at reducing prevalence by terminating clinical episodes. However,

Table 22.2. A Framework for Research: Expanding Mental Health Services

	Prevention	Treatment	Maintenance
Professionals			
Paraprofessionals			
Partner-companions			
Peer clients			
Paraphernalia			
Print			

there are disorders that are chronic or cyclical in nature. In these cases, continuing care is required. *Maintenance* refers to such care, in which the aim is to reduce the level of dysfunction, to provide support for the patient, and perhaps to prevent acute exacerbations of the condition. Maintenance services do not reduce prevalence (in fact, they may actually increase prevalence for disorders that would generally end in early death of the victim). When effective, they do reduce disability in those affected, however.

The five additional service delivery methods need some description: *Paraprofessionals* are here defined as persons with specialized training in the administration of specific interventions, but who do not have a degree and license that permits them to engage in independent mental health practice. They are, however, paid for their work. Such persons might have a bachelor's degree in psychology, for example, and have training in teaching deep muscular relaxation procedures to primary care patients about to undergo anxiety-producing procedures.

Partner-companions would be volunteers who share knowledge gained through their past life experiences with people who are currently facing similar experiences. For example, these might be immigrants who have been in the United States for ten or more years, who meet with groups of recent immigrants to provide information, support, and advice on how one copes with this stressful time. Partner-companions are clearly in a helping role.

Peer-clients are persons in mutual help groups. All participants in services of this nature would be considered to be "in the same boat." The source of preventive or therapeutic effect comes from sharing experiences with others in the same situation. For example, a support group for Hispanic freshmen at a university would fall under this category. There are several successful examples of this level of intervention, such as Alcoholics Anonymous. The self-help group movement is, in fact, quite large (Riessman, 1986).

Paraphernalia refers to equipment, gadgets, the mass media, and other adjuncts by which information, individualized programs of self-change, and interactive training methods can be administered. A television program focused on ways to reduce depression level is one example. Computer applications to prevention and treatment are a still-untapped source of individualized interventions that will gradually come into their own. It is important that such technological advances by adapted to non-English-speaking populations, to illiterates, and to persons who are unable to attend services away from home (for example, because they provide child care to grandchildren).

Print refers to the written word, illustrated manuals, and other sources of information and guidance. Such materials are widely available for English-speaking persons, and they need to be developed for others (Muñoz, 1980). More importantly, materials designed to have preventive effects in the mental health area should be carefully prepared and evaluated.

The ideas underlying the proposed framework and the implications included in its format are many (Christensen, Miller & Muñoz, 1978). First, adjuncts are more plentiful and less costly than professionals. In addition, adjuncts can maintain greater contact with clients in their natural environments. This is especially true for paraphernalia and print, which can be used at the individual's convenience.

Professionals (especially Spanish-speaking and other bilingual professionals, of whom there are still so few) should devote significant time to supervision, program development, training, diagnosis, and evaluative research, and not just to direct services.

Evaluation is essential at all levels of the proposed framework: It must not be assumed that any level is effective for any problem and any population. Intervention applied using one level will not necessarily be effective when applied at another level of the framework. It is possible that some levels lower in the framework will be more effective and certainly more efficient than higher levels. For example, mass media approaches, even if proportionately less powerful than direct personal services, might have more impact on the population, given the greater number of persons who are affected by it. A television intervention that produces a 2 percent reduction in incidence for an audience within which are found 100,000 people at 100 percent risk has more numerical impact (2,000 episodes prevented) than a group intervention with 50 percent reduction in incidence that is only available to 200 people at the same level of risk (100 cases prevented).

A lower level adjunct (i.e., a less expensive one) can be used as a minimal standard against which to evaluate interventions higher in the framework.

Since each level may be useful for different segments of the population, many more persons will be served by the more plentiful and less expensive adjuncts. The more difficult cases will still need to be seen by well-trained professionals.

Functions that will gain importance for the professional include developing and providing the adjuncts, matching clients and services, and evaluating the effectiveness of the adjuncts.

Measuring Cost

The Feasibility of Adjuncts and Their Measurable Effects

Most mental health studies focus on the effect of professional interventions on the treatment of disorders. However, some research projects have published findings relevant to the proposed framework.

Paraprofessionals. The Hispanic social network prevention intervention study recruited natural caregivers in a Mexican community and trained them in the delivery of cognitive-behavioral methods to prevent depression (Vega et al., 1987). The process of training and the delivery of the intervention were successful. Those with low depression scores prior to the intervention showed comparatively lower scores after the intervention if assigned to the experimental conditions.

Rappaport and colleagues (Rappaport, Seidman & Davidson, 1979) reported on the successful use of college students as companions for juveniles on legal probation. The students were trained to provide social learning-oriented behavioral contracting and advocacy skills. The number and seriousness of police contacts were markedly reduced for the experimental group compared with a randomly assigned control group.

Partner-companions. Although we are not aware of studies actually showing measurable mental health effects, there are several ongoing programs that routinely use this level of intervention. The Big Brother and Big Sister programs pair responsible adults with children in high-risk situations. The popularity of the program shows that the idea is definitely feasible. An evaluation of effect would be interesting, perhaps using waiting lists as controls. Widow-to-widow programs have also been put into practice, in which newly-bereaved women are contacted by others who have undergone the experience of losing their husbands, and who can offer ongoing support (Silverman & Murrow, 1976). We do not know if such programs are available for the Spanish-speaking.

Peer-clients. Alcoholics Anonymous is considered an important resource among professionals working with alcoholics. As with most types of treatment approaches, it requires acceptance of its underlying philosophy, namely the twelve-step process, and thus is not appropriate for everyone. However, the great number of mutual support AA groups across the nation speak well for the feasibility of the idea. There is also a large self-help movement (Riessman, 1986), which suggests that substantial segments of the population are willing to participate in such groups. Active participation in self-help groups has been reported to have positive effects on mental health variables (Lieberman & Borman, 1981; Vachon et al., 1980).

Paraphernalia. Television messages have been shown to have measurable effects on psychological variables. Behavior and mood showed intended changes in a randomly selected sample of San Francisco residents who had seen a series of spots on how to manage one's mood (Muñoz et al., 1982). Alcohol consumption was reduced through television advertising in Australia for respondents who had been sensitized to the ads with a letter (Barber, Bradshaw & Walsh, 1989).

Computer-administered cognitive-behavioral treatment produced significantly greater decline in depressive symptoms than a waiting-list condition, and no differences from therapist-administered cognitive-behavior therapy (Selmi et al., 1990). Encouraging results have also been found with a computerized smoking cessation program (Burling et al., 1989).

Print. Scogin, Jamison and Gochneaur (1989) provided mildly and moderately depressed older adults with cognitive or behavioral bibliotherapy or delayed treatment. Both active treatments showed significant decreases in symptoms compared with the delayed condition, and no differences from each other. Gains were maintained at six-month (Scogin, Jamison & Gochneaur, 1989) and two-year follow-ups (Scogin, Jamison & Davis, 1990).

Cost analysis can be pursued using this framework along a number of dimensions. Within each row, the relative cost of devoting all resources to treatment can be compared with the allocation of partial resources to prevention and maintenance services. Similarly, within each column, the relative cost of using more expensive service provision methods can be compared, taking into account accessibility and outreach factors, as described earlier. Finally, combinations of approaches could also be compared; for example, the allocation of resources to mass media approaches for prevention purposes and the use of professionals for treatment, as was done in Chapter 19 for Spanish-speaking depressed adults.

The intent of such a line of research would not be to find the perfect combination of approaches and level of intervention. It is very likely that societal changes, including technological advances, will continually change the parameters of cost-effectiveness. However, this framework can provide a systematic way to move beyond a single approach to mental health problems, namely, treatment by professionals. And the framework also provides a way to include cost issues into the decision-making process.

23. Future Steps toward the Prevention of Depression

The most important element in advancing the quest for effective methods to prevent depression will be commitment on the part of key individuals in the mental health fields. Resources must be allocated to three main areas: training (Muñoz, 1991, in press), improvement in the delivery and efficacy of interventions, and applying depression prevention methods to conditions or disorders that are exacerbated by depression.

Training

A number of conceptual, methodological, and technological areas could be useful in training scientists and practitioners to contribute to the depression prevention enterprise. This section provides a brief listing of these areas, their possible application to the depression prevention field, and the current limitations of each of the areas. Key references are included throughout to assist the interested reader with entry into each of the often self-contained literatures. This section will remind readers why modern prevention research requires multidisciplinary teams. No practitioner or researcher can expect to have in-depth knowledge in all these areas.

The Concept of Convergence

Picture the field of depression as a large, primarily unexplored geographical region, with each area of study an outpost of human dwellings. Clearly, there are clusters of areas that are showing great advances, but that are not necessarily connected to even their closest neighbors. For example, the advances in identification of possible genetic markers for mood disorders in certain pedigrees have not been translated into the biochemical factors that produce depressive symptoms. With few exceptions, theories about depression are limited to psychological factors, social factors, or biological factors, but do not encompass all these factors at once. The field of depression prevention (and the field of depression in general) is in great need of precisely this kind of communication system (metaphorical roads, telecommunication links) between the communities of scholars and practitioners that dot the landscape. We need to use our understanding of depression from each of our perspectives to converge upon areas that are currently unexplored border regions.

Theories of Depression

A number of important attempts to integrate aspects of depressive phenomena have been published recently. For example, Lewinsohn et al. (1985) listed several of the factors that theories of depression should address, and then present a complex framework that includes variables related to reinforcement, interpersonal interactions, cognitions, and biochemical states. Ehlers, Frank, and Kupfer (1988) offered an intriguing way of understanding how dysregulation of biological rhythms might be triggered by the occurrence of life events that disrupt what they call social "zeitgebers" (i.e., persons or events that "give timing to" or punctuate one's daily routines). Their work addresses some of the need for convergence, in this case between the life events literature and the biological literature. Still, theories about depression have not advanced significantly since the publication of Akiskal and McKinney's (1973) attempt to provide a unified hypothesis.

In an update to their hypothesis, they (Whybrow, Akiskal & McKinney, 1984, Chapter 9) describe affective illness as a final common path to adaptive failure. Heredity and temperament, developmental and characterological parameters, precipitating stressors (such as life events and biological insults), and modulating parameters (such as age, sex, and endocrine status) are presumed to affect neurochemistry and neurophysiological arousal, which in turn can produce (and be affected by) limbic-diencephalic dysfunction, which produces (and is affected by) the affective syndromes.

Scientists and practitioners interested in prevention need to become aware of these theories (and the empirical information on which they are based). Even more importantly, however, they must recognize that the specific ways in which these elements are hypothesized to exert their influences are not sufficiently detailed. The underlying question becomes one of deciding how much detail is needed in which area to be able to intervene in a preventive fashion. At some point, this becomes an empirical question. If specific interventions produce reliable preventive effects, this information can itself serve to shape more detailed theories.

The Measurement of Depression

Depression is a construct, not a physical entity. As described in Chapter 2, the word refers to a mood, a symptom, a syndrome, or a disorder (Clayton, 1987). And there are likely to be many depressions, rather than one. Wender and Klein (1981, pp. 42–43) suggest that there are at least three major states to which the word is applied: demoralization, nonvital or neurotic depression, and vital or physiological depression, in which the ability to experience the pleasure of a usually satisfying consummation is lost. Boyd and Weissman (1982), in their review of the epidemiology of depression, chose to discuss three types: depressive symptoms independent of a specific diagnosis, bipolar disorder defined by one or more manic episodes, and "non-bipolar depressions."

It is perhaps best to conceptualize the depressions as "latent variables" (see Breckenridge, 1987, pp. 239–43), that is, hypothetical constructs that cannot be directly observed, but that are measured through multiple indicators, such as scores on self-report scales, diagnostic criteria, observed behaviors, and, in some cases, biological markers.

At present, the two most widely accepted methods to measure depression are symptom scales and diagnostic procedures. The major vexing problem with these methods is how to construe their lack of agreement. For example, Gershon et al. (1982) pointed out that there may be no "true" rate of diagnosable affective disorders. Existing rates are a function of the procedures and criteria used and the culture of the population being sampled. Given no final criterion for either the measure of level of depression symptoms or the presence of a diagnosable disorder, one is left with having to decide somewhat arbitrarily which of these methods of measuring depression will be used for the particular study one is conducting. This is clearly an area in which further progress (or at least some consensus) is badly needed. For further issues in the measurement of depression, see Marsella, Hirschfeld, and Katz (1987). For a review and discussion of current issues related to diagnosis and assessment see McReynolds (1989), Millon and Klerman (1986), and Frances, Widiger, and Pincus (1989).

The Epidemiology of Depression

Given the focus of prevention research on rates of disorder in populations, some familiarity with the epidemiological literature is essential

(Fletcher, Fletcher & Wagner, 1988; Hulley & Cummings, 1988). Psychiatric epidemiology has been greatly influenced in the past decade by the NIMH Epidemiological Catchment Area Project (Eaton & Kessler, 1985; Robins & Regier, 1991). The relationship of psychiatric epidemiology to prevention has also been addressed (Hough et al., 1986; Roberts, 1987).

Some basic definitions and their implications are found in Bloom (1977):

> The *prevalence* (number of cases at a specified moment in time) of any disease is a function of two independent variables—*incidence* and *duration. Incidence* refers to the number of new cases diagnosed during any specified time period, and *duration* refers to the time between the initial diagnosis and the termination of the disease, either by recovery or by death. The greater the incidence *or* the greater the duration, the higher the prevalence. To put it another way, two diseases may have the same prevalence, but one (such as the common cold) may have a very high incidence and low duration, while the other (such as diabetes) may have a low incidence but a high duration. As you can see, primary prevention programs serve to reduce prevalence by reducing incidence, while secondary and tertiary prevention programs serve to reduce prevalence by reducing duration. (P. 75)

Other epidemiological terms that are of use to prevention researchers and practitioners are those related to risk. Gruenberg (1981) defined four types of risk:

Individual risk is obtained by determining the proportion of persons within a defined category (for example, age or sex) who have a certain disorder. The probability of contracting the disorder for an individual who fits this category is assumed to be equal to the proportion of persons within the category who have the disorder in question.

Contingency risk is the increased risk that a person with a history of a risk factor has of contracting a disorder. For example, one could set up a contingency risk table for those with or without early parental loss and determine the proportion within each group who become clinically depressed. From these proportions, one could determine the increase in the probability of developing depression given early parental loss.

Relative risk measures how strongly a risk factor affects incidence rates. It is the incidence of a disorder in a group exposed to a risk factor divided by the incidence of the same disorder in a nonexposed group. This estimate allows for methods to examine the total risk resulting from clusters of individual risk factors.

Attributable risk is the proportion of cases attributable to a specific risk factor. For example, if inadequate levels of pleasant activities are related to depression, what proportion of depressed cases would be prevented if one could increase a population's activity to adequate levels? These rates are best measured in preventive trials.

The first three types of risk can serve to identify the population to be targeted by a prevention program, as well as contribute to the evaluation of theories of depression. The fourth category of risk is the most relevant to prevention trials, in terms of serving to identify modifiable risk factors. It is also the category that can provide the strictest tests for etiological theories of depression.

Biological Aspects of Depression

Biological approaches to psychiatry have provided the field with an exciting and challenging influx of theory, methods, and applications for both practice and research (Andreasen, 1984; Wender & Klein, 1981; Whybrow et al., 1984). An interesting review of the biochemical manifestations of depression and their relation to stress has been published (Gold, Goodwin & Chrousos, 1988). Depue and Iacono (1989) reviewed the neurobehavioral aspects of affective disorders from a psychological perspective.

The role of brain on mood and behavior is being discussed from a number of perspectives. Four current topics in aspects of brain function are parallelism in cortical information processing, plasticity in both development and adulthood, the richness and complexity of cortical pharmacology, and the search for cortical circuits and mechanisms (Wise, 1989). The issue of plasticity of the brain suggests the possibility of particular periods in human development when physical or emotional injury has a greater impact on placing someone at high risk for depression from then on. Recent initiatives for the mapping of the brain (Roberts, 1991) have obvious implications for research on mood regulation. The conceptualization of the brain itself as a gland, rather than only as a computer-like network of neural circuits, has been suggested in a provocative book by Bergland (1985). His recounting of the major theories of mind throughout history and the major errors accepted as fact by the best scientists of times past is very humbling. As health science educators like to say: "We know that half of what we teach our students is wrong. We just do not know which half."

Convergence between biological and anatomical brain variables in depression is the subject of speculation. For example,

> Among depressed individuals ventricular enlargement is associated with positive psychotic symptoms. . . . Additionally, hypercortisolism may be a major factor in producing ventricular enlargement in patients with affective disorder. This suggests a potential for reversibility, which remains to be investigated. (Coffman, 1989, pp. 47–8)

The range of plasticity of the human organism both in terms of increased sensitization to stress, as well as the possibility of reversibility is an unresolved issue. The concept of "kindling" and its possible relation to depressive states is intriguing. Post, Rubinow, and Ballenger (1984) reviewed several models based on animal experimental work that may have relevance for the course of affective disorders in humans. Kindling refers to the eventual development of motor seizures in response to repeated electrical or chemical stimulation of the brain with levels of stimulation originally insufficient to produce overt behavioral effects. Neural excitability may increase even without motor seizures. Behavioral sensitization refers to increasing effects on behavior of low doses of psychomotor stimulants and dopamine agonist agents.

Post et al. (1984) suggested that phenomena similar to kindling or behavioral sensitization may be at work in the observed increase in recurrences of affective episodes and the gradually more rapid and apparently autonomous onset of episodes. Perhaps the human organism is altered in terms of neuronal (or hormonal) excitability by the occurrence of single episodes. In addition, conditioned psychological, physiological, and neurotransmitter responses caused by such episodes may increase the probability of affective dysfunction in the future. If processes such as kindling are involved in depression, preventive approaches that reduce the probability of first onset, or even prevent early recurrences of depressive episodes, may reduce the likelihood of severe recurrent depressions. This model provides a very interesting rationale for interventions focused on subclinical depressions.

Although the knowledge explosion in biological approaches to depression is impressive, numerous vexing questions remain unsolved (see Chapter 3). Nevertheless, the state of the science offers several indications that biological mechanisms play a major role in the development of depressive states. Pharmacological interventions that are intended to increase available biogenic amines at the synapse produce therapeutic effects in depression. Depression has been associated with a number of pathologies in hormonal regulatory systems (Sachar, 1982). But there are presently no good biological markers for identifying persons at high risk for depression. Most such markers appear to be state-dependent, disappearing once the depressive episode lifts. Explicit attempts to delineate the preventive implications of this line of research could be very influential. The inclusion of biologically trained researchers in prevention research teams thus seems wise.

The Genetics of Depression

The more severe forms of depression have long been known to run in families. Although *familial* is not synomymous with *genetic*, twin and adoption studies have yielded evidence supporting the genetic hypothesis. This has been particularly true for bipolar disorder, in which monozygotic twins tend to have significantly higher concordance rates than dyzygotic twins (Mendlewicz, 1988).

As we recounted in Chapter 3, the continuing search for the gene or genes that cause depression or manic depression has yielded several contradictory findings and no solid results as of 1992.

There are several implications of these findings. First, although there is considerable evidence to indicate that genetic factors are involved in bipolar illness, the specific genes connected to this disorder have not yet been identified, and genetic linkage findings may be less robust than originally anticipated. Since unipolar depression is often found in families with large bipolar loadings, the likelihood that these two forms of depression are related is high. At the same time, the evidence that unipolar depression by itself is inheritable is less strong. Also, "milder disorders such as DSM-III dysthymia or RDC minor depression may not be heritable" (Goldin & Gershon, 1988, p. 165). Therefore, it is very likely that for the milder end of the continuum, the heterogeneity of genetic influences on mood and behavior will make genetic approaches to prevention impractical.

Even for the severe forms of the disorder, opinion is mixed regarding implications for prevention. Mendlewicz (1988, p. 209) suggested that the clearest indication for using caution is in the case of two persons with bipolar disorder having children, in which he set the risk that the child may have the disorder as high as 70 percent. With only one parent affected, he states, the risk is low, but not negligible (around 15%). Gershon (1983), on the other hand, reminded us that "twin and family studies strongly suggest that some persons with the genetic tendency to mood disorder will be phenotypically well" (p. 451). He went on to say:

> In light of current knowledge, the possibilities for prevention are limited. We know that families of patients with bipolar illness have greatly increased risk for affective and related disorders compared with the rest of the population, but we cannot identify individuals at risk before the onset of illness. Nor can we identify any environmental manipulation, including genetic counseling, that would reduce the risk. (P. 454)
>
> . . . Since only 15% of the bipolar patients seen by the author and his group at NIMH have a bipolar parent, even from the most hardheaded primary prevention viewpoint such advice [not having children] is not necessary. (P. 456)

Even in Egeland's original report, maximum penetrance (i.e., expression of the disorder given that the gene is present) was estimated at 63 percent (Egeland et al., 1987, p. 785). Thus, it is likely that many individuals carrying the predisposing gene or genes will not develop the disorder. Can penetrance be modified by natural or planned environmental interventions?

The work of McGuffin and Katz (1986a, 1986b) addressed this question in a balanced manner. The authors discussed a number of concepts, including methods by which to estimate the relative contributions of genetics and environment in the occurrence of mental disorders. They suggested that for bipolar illness, genetic contributions are consistent and compelling, but that for "neurotic" patterns of depression, although also familial, the effect of genes appears to be small and nonspecific, perhaps because environmental effects also contribute heavily. Using a "liability-threshold" model, in which it is assumed that a variable termed "liability to develop the disorder" is continuously distributed within the population but that only those individuals whose liability exceeds a certain threshold manifest the disorder, they concluded:

> Most of the heterogeneity which is seen in affective disorders can be accounted for by the quantitative differences based on liability threshold models rather than discrete qualitative factors. Thus BP [bipolar] and UP [unipolar] disorder can be considered as "narrow" and "broad" versions of essentially that same condition occupying the same continuum of liability. . . . Thus, we should probably think of more genetic and less genetic (or of more biological and less biological) forms of affective illness than of a genetic versus non-genetic typology. (P. 47)

The role of genetics in depression research is becoming more pronounced. The concepts and vocabulary connected to this area are sometimes esoteric. Nevertheless, the depression prevention enterprise cannot ignore this very productive field. Students of prevention would benefit from some background in genetics to better understand the potential and the limits of genetic approaches to prevention.

On "Causal Decoupling"

Professionals and those in training who are serious about depression prevention research and practice may wonder how much they need to know before they can actually intervene and evaluate their interventions. Do we have to wait until brain function is fully understood? Do we need to wait until major advances in the cognitive sciences shed light on the difference between thinking and believing, and the exact interaction between behaviors and mood?

The concept of "causal decoupling" (Pagels, 1988, pp. 222–25) is helpful here: "Although genetics is supported by a material structure—DNA—and ultimately governed by the laws of chemistry, once we know the rules of genetic combination we can 'forget' the detailed laws of chemistry. Genetics becomes 'causally decoupled' from the laws of chemistry" (p. 222).

Similarly, although psychology is supported by a biological structure—the human body—and is ultimately governed by the laws of biology, chemistry, and physics, once we know the rules of psychological functioning, we can "forget" the detailed laws of biology. Psychological interventions become "causally decoupled" from the laws of the physical sciences. Thus, when applying cognitive and behavioral approaches to mood management, the specific biological changes that these methods produce do not have to be known by the therapist to produce change. Nevertheless, there are at least two reasons why being familiar with biological and other factors is important. First, these factors may have a role in setting a level of risk for the individual which, if it can be known, can influence decisions regarding the intensity with which such individuals ought to be sought and offered preventive interventions. Second, as researchers, understanding the relationship among these different levels of analysis can add to our knowledge of human functioning and help to target such factors more efficiently.

Improving Interventions

Interventions focused on individual change require further study to determine which are the most powerful. At least three elements of change must be examined when a particular change is targeted: (1) How much change is there in the target variable (for example, specific thoughts or behaviors)? (2) How much change is there in depression level? and (3) How strong is the relationship between change in the target variable and change in depression level?

The first element of change relates to the ease with which a particular skill can be taught. (Note that this may vary according to the characteristics of the instructor, the target group, and the interaction between them.) Even if a particular preventive strategy were to be theoretically very effective, if it is difficult to teach (either because it is unacceptable to many people or inherently complex), its potential effect will not be realized. A concept that is less powerful but simpler to grasp may be more effective with more people. For example, some of the more sophisticated rational analyses of cognitive therapy and rational emotive therapy can be lost in persons with little education, while the concept of positive thinking espoused by Norman Vincent Peale (1952) appears to be readily grasped by most people. Philosophical sophistication may not always be the highest priority in community-wide prevention efforts. Still, it is important not to take the elitist view that "the masses" can be given only simplistic solutions. Part of the task, as we see it, is to increase the pedagogical power for conveying mood management strategies. Even supposedly difficult concepts can be presented so that they are understandable to most individuals. It may be that the complexity is not in the ideas, but in the way they have been presented to date. There is, after all, more than a bit of pride involved in talking in ways that others cannot understand, be it professional jargon, the obscure allusions of the highly educated, or street slang. The task for prevention practitioners is to convey the message well. The task of prevention researchers is to be able to detect change in these target variables when they occur.

The second element, change in depression levels, is more straightforward. Given an intervention of any type, are depression levels in the participants less than in control groups? Interventions with greater relative reductions in depression levels across time are preferred to those with little or no relative advantage, of course. If the interventions do not make theoretical sense, that fact alone would make them particularly interesting: new theories would need to be constructed to make sense of the empirical findings.

The third element is particularly crucial to our understanding of depression. It is logically possible that the targeted variables are measurably changed, and that depression levels are more reduced in the intervention condition, but that there is little detectable relationship between the two. (For example, those who change the most in thoughts or behaviors are not necessarily those who show the greatest effect on depression levels.) This pattern of findings can again led to rethinking the mechanisms that we believe affect the experience of depression (and suggest the next intervention and research question).

Interventions focused on community change must be developed and tested. With new findings reinforcing the relationship between low socioeconomic status and risk for psychiatric disorders (Bruce, Takeuchi & Leaf, 1991), it is ethically questionable to neglect examining this relationship (and how to modify it) within a scientific context.

Several controversies arise when this area is examined. For example, in Chapter 1, we described (and critiqued) the argument that community change is outside the realm of mental health practice. However, assuming one were to agree that, if community conditions affect mental dysfunctions, mental health professionals ought to address such conditions in their work, arguments can still be made regarding the effect of such interventions. For example, the senior author has had discussions with colleagues in the prevention field regarding whether depression prevention efforts focused on helping unemployed persons find work can effect a net reduction in incidence in the community. They argue that, for the participants to obtain jobs, some other members of the community must become unemployed. They hold that given a fixed number of jobs, interventions such as these only reshuffle who is unemployed. Increasing the number of jobs, they suggest, is a function of the economy, and, they say, the economy is beyond the mental health bailiwick. The argument has some merit, although one is at a loss as to what the implication ought to be: should we not help the poor to get more resources because the only thing we would be doing is reshuffling who is poor?

At a meeting of a San Francisco grass roots organization, the senior author had the inspiring experience of sitting in the audience with several delegations of residents of housing projects, some of whom had been psychiatric patients at San Francisco General Hospital. At this meeting, they were working to improve the conditions of their environment, as active members of the community, rather than as "mental patients." The sense of taking control over their neighborhoods, poor and crime-ridden as they are known to be, must have had some preventive effect on demoralization. The motto of the group is "Don't Agonize: Organize!" The effect of such interventions on depressive symptoms would be worth studying.

Applying Depression Prevention Methods to Conditions or Disorders That Are Exacerbated by Depression

Efforts at preventing depression may reach a wider audience if they are applied to problems such as drug abuse, behaviors that place a person at high risk for infection with the human immunodeficiency virus (HIV) and AIDS, school dropout, or criminal behavior. Clinical experience indicates that depression or feelings of demoralization are probably involved in substantial numbers of people affected by these problems. Someone who has an already bleak vision of the future due to depression is less likely to want to protect that future. Experiences that temporarily distract one from feelings of depression, such as drug use, sex, and physical danger, may become reinforcing. Suicidal tendencies may also be involved in such behavior. And reduced motivation keeps the affected individual from breaking free of these self-destructive patterns. If depression prevention methods reduced the likelihood of any of these public epidemics, they would contribute greatly to the general welfare.

In response to the growing evidence that persons with a history of depression or with high levels of depression are at greater risk for starting to smoke, less likely to quit, and more likely to relapse (Anda et al., 1990; Glassman et al., 1990), Hall, Muñoz, and Reus (1991) conducted a randomized trial. Smokers joining a smoking cessation program at the University of California, San Francisco, Habit Abatement Clinic were randomly assigned to either the clinic's standard smoking cessation group or a smoking cessation group that included the depression prevention methods developed for the Depression Prevention Research Project. Both groups received nicotine gum as part of the treatment. All participants were administered a structured diagnostic interview to determine whether they met criteria for a history of major depression. (Those meeting criteria for major depression at the time of the study were screened out.)

Follow-up data at 26 weeks after the group ended indicated no difference in abstinence rates for those without a history of major depression: 38 percent were abstinent in the standard smoking cessation condition and 34 percent in the smoking cessation plus depression prevention condition. These rates are comparable to earlier Habit Abatement Clinic groups, and better than community smoking cessation rates. For comparison purposes, a recent study comparing a transdermal nicotine patch versus placebo found a 24 percent abstinence rate with the patch, and 5 percent abstinence rate with the placebo at 26 weeks (Tønnesen et al., 1991). For those with a history of major depression, the abstinence rates were 12 percent for the standard condition, and 50 percent for the condition that included depression prevention training. These encouraging findings suggest applications for depression prevention methods for other drug addictions.

González et al. (1991) attempted to apply methods from the Depression Prevention Course with Spanish-speaking intravenous drug users in a methadone maintenance program. Many of the patients in the program are already HIV-positive due to high-risk behaviors such as needle sharing and unprotected sex. In this pilot study, eleven Latino patients were recruited, of whom six attended the six-week, two-hour per week course on how to maintain a healthy mood ("Curso para Mantener un Estado de Animo Saludable"; Muñoz, González & Pérez-Arce, 1991). Depression level for this sample was very high at initial assessment: a mean of 26.1 on the Center for Epidemiological Studies–Depression Scale. Pre-to-post course mean scores for the five nonattenders were 22.8 and 22.4. The six attenders had a mean score of 28.8

at pre- and 20.3 at post-testing, which reached statistical significance, even with the small sample size. Four of the attenders were HIV-positive. Their scores were 33.8 at pre- and 24.8 at post-testing. We find these results to be encouraging. It appears that even with persons in severe life circumstances, the methods developed in the Depression Prevention Course can have an immediate effect on lowering depression symptoms. Further work is required to determine the duration of the effect, and the impact of the effect on staying "clean" (that is, off drugs), and on avoiding high-risk behaviors.

Similar applications to other areas could prove productive. Funding for projects that cut across areas is becoming more available. Depression prevention researchers and practitioners are likely to find collaboration across areas intellectually exciting, beneficial to individuals who would not generally participate in depression prevention efforts per se, and conducive to the advancement of the prevention field.

Part V

Personal Reflections on the Preventive Intervention Enterprise

24. Philosophical Issues

Several concepts underlie much of our work on the prevention of depression. This chapter will elaborate those concepts. Obviously, one could approach prevention from various perspectives. Ours is just one of many.

Unnecessary Suffering

The quest for prevention assumes that aspects of human suffering can be avoided. The term we have found helpful in describing this idea is "unnecessary suffering." To describe this concept, we begin with the acknowledgment that pain is an inevitable part of human life. Illness, injury, the death of loved ones, and other events that are the direct consequence of being biological beings cannot be totally eradicated. In fact, pain can have survival value if it focuses our attention on needed action to protect our body or our emotional health. Examples include the pain caused by heat, which motivates us to move our hand out of reach of hot objects, or the pain caused by interpersonal discord, which frequently motivates us to maintain cordial relationships with others.

Suffering, however, can be exacerbated by our reactions to these "natural" events. For example, labeling ourselves as "careless" or "stupid" when we injure ourselves can add emotional pain to the pain of the injury. Believing that it is a sign of strength not to back down in an argument can lead to increased pain for ourselves and those with whom we interact. Even if we are rewarded by this type of behavior in the short run, say, by getting our way, in the long run we may become estranged from people who may have been a source of comfort and support. We label this type of added pain or suffering "unnecessary suffering." We propose to reduce this type of occurrence. This concept has been neatly characterized with the phrase: "Pain is inevitable; suffering is optional" (Goodman, 1990, p. 41).

Some elements of "inevitable" pain may be susceptible to reduction. For example, the amount of pain felt in reaction to the death of a loved one can be greatly modified by cultural norms regarding mourning, by philosophical or religious perspectives toward death, by the availability of support from relatives and friends, and by having made arrangements for continued access to economic and other practical resources that the deceased provided for the survivors.

The extent to which the sorrow over death could be ameliorated remains an open question subject to empirical test. Whether such sorrow *ought* to be ameliorated is a separate issue. The amount of importance that ought to be given to the ending of an individual's life, the significance of felt pain as a measure of one's love for that person, and the possible beneficial aspects of mourning rituals (what some refer to as "working through" the loss a loved one) are all areas of controversy, which go beyond the mere practicality of reducing emotional suffering.

We conclude, then, that there are two elements to human pain and suffering: an unavoidable element and an optional one. The boundary between avoiding "unnecessary suffering" and facing the reality of the human dilemma, however, is subject to controversy. Nevertheless, given the immensity of unnecessary suffering, we have plenty to do to help others cope with those areas in which there is little controversy. Clearly, one such area is the reduction of depression, in its clinical and nonclinical aspects.

The Healthy Management of Reality

In our work with depression, we have found it useful to present the achievement of a "healthy management of reality" as a positive goal, balancing the more "negative" objective of forestalling depression. We explain that one of the elements of depression is a feeling of being overwhelmed by the burdens of our situation. To bring this sense of helplessness and hopelessness under control, we offer some insight into human nature and provide practical ways to cope, beginning with the following ideas:

Human beings, as finite beings in an infinite universe, are at constant risk for becoming overwhelmed. After all, there is no conceivable way in which we can understand or control our world completely. To lead a healthy life, human beings need to learn how to attend to selected aspects of their reality. By limiting our scope of thought and action, we can manage our survival needs as well as reach an optimal level of enjoying our potential. By actively carving out of this infinite universe a finite portion, we can encompass it in our finite mind and address it with the resources of our finite organism.

One way to delineate segments of the universe into digestible chunks is to conceptualize and name them. In our work with depression, we divide reality into two parts: internal and external. *Internal reality* refers to the aspects of reality found inside our mind. Thus, *internal reality* refers to subjective, or mental reality. The elements of this part of reality include our thoughts, beliefs, attitudes, knowledge, experience, values, and so on. *External reality* refers to aspects of reality that are observable and measurable, and that can be verified by others. Thus, *external reality* refers to objective, or material reality. The elements of this part of reality include facts about our physical body, our environment, the economic and social resources available to us (such as money, property, friends), substances we ingest, the historical and geographical aspects of our condition, and so on.

Our cognitive-behavioral methods are designed to increase the level of control over internal and external reality. In terms of methods, the cognitive techniques are most relevant to internal factors, and the behavioral techniques to external factors. Thus, we teach how to identify specific thoughts that produce a positive mood or a negative mood, and how to measure the effect of one's physical and social environment on one's mood. Then, attempts can be made to change the thoughts or to expose oneself more to constructive environments and less to destructive ones. Again, concepts are helpful in showing a direction for change. For example, we talk about the potential and the actual environment, and describe how two people living in the same city (and with the same level of income) can place themselves in settings within that city which will lead to health or to demoralization. The potential environment is similar for both. The actual environment is very different for each.

By "management" of reality we refer to gaining a greater degree of influence over our life and our world. The word *control*, which we have used in earlier writings (Lewinsohn et al., 1986; Miller & Muñoz, 1982), has for many people a connotation of absolute or total control, which we never intended. The word *manage* conveys somewhat more clearly the elements of adaptation and reciprocal influence that are exerted by the individual and the environment.

The word *healthy* refers to the notion that there is a range within which managing one's reality is beneficial, but that either too little or too much influence over reality can have untoward effects. This concept is similar to the idea of the "therapeutic window" in pharmacotherapy, which refers to the fact that the level of medication for specific disorders must be above a basic threshold to be effective but below another threshold to avoid negative effects. You can have "too much of a good thing."

We believe that the concept of "the healthy management of reality" has great potential for not only health promotion and disease prevention in individuals, but also for the well-being of communities and societies. The human ability to mold our mental and physical environment consciously and systematically, great as it already is, is probably only beginning its development. Its full potential is still to be studied.

The Probabilistic Nature of Preventive Thinking

At both the individual and the aggregate level, a probabilistic construction of reality is advisable. The specific strategies people use to deal with their situations increase or decrease the chances of achieving a healthy mood: they do not guarantee either a good or a bad outcome. Similarly, preventive interventions in communities affect the incidence and prevalence of several conditions. Few interventions, even if administered to all members of a community, can be expected to produce complete eradication of mental disorders.

This view of life goes against some human tendencies: the desire for certainty, the desire for a world in which those who perform good actions are rewarded and those who engage in immoral or unhealthy behavior are punished. On the other hand, if we recognize that the infinity of the universe, of which we spoke earlier in the chapter, applies as well to an infinity of alternative outcomes, we will adapt better. More importantly, learning to influence probabilities to some extent can be a source of comfort and optimism. It can increase feelings of self-efficacy and decrease the helplessness and hopelessness that often are the hallmarks of depression.

Are There Limits to Prevention?

In *Mirage of Health* (1959), Rene Dubos made the argument that as we attempt to reduce prevalence of one disorder, another will increase in prevalence. This suggests that there may be a kind of homeostasis in terms of the level of health to which we can aspire. This also implies that we need to make decisions regarding which combination of disorders we are willing to live with, rather than how to reduce the level of disorders across the board.

In a similar vein, Kaplan pointed out that "at least five studies have reported that dietary changes reduce the incidence of deaths due to heart disease. However, in each of these studies, there was an unexpected finding for total deaths; mortality averaged over all causes was not affected by the experimental dietary interventions. Reductions in deaths due to heart disease are associated with increases in deaths from other causes, in most cases cancer" (Kaplan, 1985, p. 570). "It is somewhat unsatisfactory to leave life expectancy unaffected while influencing only the reason listed on a death certificate" (Kaplan, 1985, p. 572).

This is an intriguing notion, touching on the realist's argument that there is no Utopia, no state of perfection that human beings can hope to reach. Kaplan's points suggest that it is incumbent on prevention practitioners and researchers to maintain data on more than just their target disorder or condition. An ecological perspective is essential for preventively oriented professionals.

Yet, it is entirely too premature to restrain our efforts to prevent depression and other mental health problems. The scientific study of prevention of psychological problems has barely begun. We are far from reaching the asymptote that separates our universe from Utopia. Though perfection is unattainable, it can be an eminently useful guiding star.

25. Recommendations

For Policymakers

Policymakers are the most likely people to decide if prevention will ever be widely practiced.

We should support both practice and research. Each realm informs the other. Thus, policymakers in charge of research should allocate some of their funds for preventive intervention research, some of which should clearly be earmarked for research on depression prevention. Policymakers overseeing services should also insist that some proportion of their work focus on prevention.

There is great controversy regarding the extent of depression prevention efforts, and if they should be limited to the prevention of clinical episodes. It is our opinion that a reduction in high levels of depressive symptoms, as measured by self-report scales such as the Beck Depression Inventory or the CES-D, is a reasonable goal to strive for. The justification for reducing levels of depression can be found in terms of reducing dysfunction at home and at work, reducing the likelihood of substance abuse and high-risk behaviors, and reducing the likelihood of parental neglect or abuse of children. Successful increases in healthy mood can also be expected to affect personal striving for improved educational and economic status, thus affecting the overall quality of life in our communities, particularly those communities that are currently overrepresented in lower income strata. At a straight humanitarian level, of course, a reduction in demoralization will prevent much suffering and desperation, including the "quiet" type, which is usually ignored. Finally, a reduction in depression levels can be logically expected to result in a reduction in clinical cases, since fewer people would be going over the threshold into a full-blown clinical depression.

In both practice and research settings, individuals who are committed to prevention should be encouraged to pursue their goals. At this stage, the field needs a few champions for the cause of prevention who will be willing to spend the vast amounts of energy required to develop, implement, and test interventions. It is most likely that no stunning advances in documenting a reduction in incidence will be made for some time. The segment of the field working in the reduction of incidence is most likely to progress gradually, and change will be evident only in the long term. Thus, relentless persistence will be the most important factor.

For Practitioners of Preventive Interventions

Try out your ideas. Check to see if your methods have the expected effect.

Seek prevention support groups to keep the flame alive.

Attempt to document and publish your efforts, even if they are not in a traditional research format. Prevention practitioners must develop a type of article analogous to the clinical "case study" that describes the methods and the outcomes of preventive interventions.

Seek alliances with consumers. People who have felt the benefits of prevention programs are most likely to help keep such programs going. Those who have felt the pain of severe depression in themselves or their relatives, such as members of the National Alliance for the Mentally Ill, have generally responded well to the ideas presented in this book: they know first-hand what it is we intend to prevent, and they realize how much suffering would be avoided if we developed these techniques sufficiently (Muñoz, 1991b). Be sure to include all segments of the population. Do not preach just to the converted. Allot some proportion of your efforts to the hard-to-reach. Do not forget the large segments of the population who do not speak English: they are the most likely to need these services.

Try to keep an open mind regarding both the theoretical basis for your approaches and the method of delivery. Consider developing methods that could be implemented via adjuncts such as those in the "Professionals, Paraprofessionals, Partners, Peers, Paraphernalia, and Print" model described in Chapter 22.

For Researchers

Prevention viewpoints can inform the research enterprise. They push the investigator beyond the remotely etiological and the immediately palliative into issues of attributable risk: How much impact will altering modifiable risk factors have on the emergence of the disorder?

There is a great need to evaluate prevention ideas. If nothing else, allying oneself with a practitioner who is serious about evaluating the effect of his or her programs would be a major contribution to this field.

The potential for working with populations that usually do not interact with clinical researchers also increases the scope of one's study. The theories and the studies that stem from this broader view are more likely to include important components in the phenomena we are investigating.

For Students

Prevention is still a young field. There is room to make major contributions, partly because there are so few serious investigators and practitioners in the area.

On the other hand, prevention is a risky area. Financial support for practice and research is precarious. There is no question that emergency-focused services are likely to be funded even when money is scarce. Prevention outcome studies do not lend themselves easily to quick publication of several research articles: the need to follow people for long periods of time makes this type of study problematic for someone who needs to make tenure soon. In addition, professional identities are easier to form when we are engaged in recognized roles. When one is a therapist and treats a person, and the person gets better, both the patient and the therapist feel that good work was accomplished, and the improvement is generally noticeable. When one is engaged in prevention, it is often unclear whether there were actually fewer cases of the problem as a result of the intervention. Even if this is shown unequivocally, one still cannot tell *which* persons avoided a period of pain and dysfunction. Thus, practitioners dedicated to prevention are less likely to have grateful consumers and need to obtain gratification from internal sources, from supportive colleagues, and from the process of intervention itself.

At an intellectual level, however, prevention offers tremendous gratification. The opportunity to address an important issue, to understand it enough to develop an intervention, and to test whether the intervention had the desired effect is a challenging task. Depression as the target is a fascinating problem. Biological, psychological, social, cultural, economic, historical, environmental, philosophical, and spiritual issues are involved in a full understanding of depression. Thus, there is room for persons who are interested in any of these factors, or in a combination of them.

For the Public

If you are already depressed and the level of depression you are experiencing is interfering with your life or activities, seek treatment.

If you have had a period of severe depression in the past, consider learning some of the methods used to manage one's mood, including the ideas described in this book (see Chapters 7 and 24, and Appendix A).

Practitioners and researchers often take too long in sharing effective interventions with the public. In the area of depression prevention, however, a number of resources are available and, to the best of our knowledge, do not have negative side effects. There are many books describing the effect of psychological variables on mood (e.g., Burns, 1980; Ellis & Harper, 1975; Lewinsohn, Muñoz, Youngren & Zeiss, 1986).

Self-help books have been around for a long time, of course, and although academics often look down on them, one must ask why they are so popular. The systematic application of common sense to life is not limited to academicians, professionals, or researchers. Thus, there is no reason to discount the beneficial effects of such works. At some level, one needs to try different methods to live the life one wants to live. And one does not need to wait until research studies give unequivocal results. (This rarely happens, anyway.)

So, go ahead and try methods to forestall the depression that you may encounter. Share your findings with others, including, if you are so inclined, researchers and practitioners.

Remember some of the high-risk factors that are presently known:

— a past history of depressive episode;
— a family history of depression;
— high levels of life changes;
— high levels of chronic stress;
— substance abuse, including alcohol and tobacco.

People with these and other "real problems" could benefit most from prevention approaches. It is when personal reality is most difficult that attempts at learning the healthy management of reality (see Chapter 24) are most needed.

In our experience, the major obstacle to learning to manage one's own mood is the belief that this is not possible. (This belief may explain both the reluctance of mental health professionals to devote the needed resources to developing ways to prevent depression as well as individuals' reluctance to change their thoughts and behaviors to live a more satisfying life.) Often, this belief is tied to the unexamined assumption that, unless one can control one's mood perfectly, it is not worth the effort to learn to control it in part. But this is precisely what will make practical methods of preventing depression possible: gradual advances in individual lives that reduce the probability that one's mood will become a source of suffering in one's life.

We hope that you will learn to reduce unnecessary suffering in your own life and that you will commit yourself to not inflicting it on others.

Appendix A
Excerpts from the Depression Prevention Course

Ricardo F. Muñoz

Class 1: Introduction

Participants' Handout

The purpose of this course is to teach ways to control one's mood better, to prevent serious depression. *Prevention* in this class means doing things that will make it less likely that one will get seriously depressed. More specifically, we are trying to accomplish three things:

1. to reduce the number of times that one has a serious depression;
2. if one does become depressed, to reduce the duration of the depressive episode; and
3. if one does become depressed, to reduce the intensity of the depressive episode.

How can one deal with depression? There are many ways. The way we will teach in this class is based on *social learning theory.* Social learning theory is a way to think about human behavior. In other words, it is a way of thinking about what "makes people tick," or why people feel the way they do and act the way they do.

Social learning theory says that people *learn* to think, act, and feel in certain ways. These three human abilities influence each other all the time:

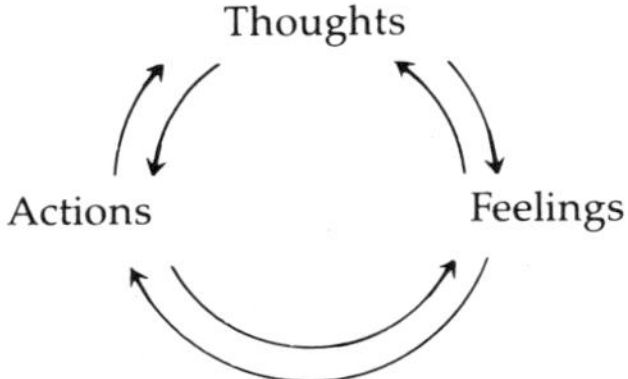

By learning which thoughts and actions influence our feelings, we can learn to get more control over our feelings.

Instructors' Notes

Instructors were reminded of the purpose of the course, assigned to read relevant chapters from *Control Your Depression,* and given suggested ways to present key concepts. A sample presentation of these concepts follows.

The idea of prevention is something that we use a lot, but that we rarely think about. For example, brushing one's teeth is a way to prevent cavities. This doesn't mean that all people who brush their teeth never get cavities. It means that if you compare a group of people who brush their teeth regularly with another group that doesn't, the group that brushes will have fewer cavities and smaller cavities on the average than those who do not brush.

What we are trying to do with this course is to see if those of you who take this course will be less likely to get seriously depressed in the future, and that if any of you do get depressed, the depression won't be as severe or last as long as if you hadn't taken the course.

How Can One Deal with Depression?

There are many ways to deal with depression. The way we will teach in this class is based on a psychological theory known as 'Social Learning Theory.'

A theory is a scientific explanation about how something works. Social Learning Theory tries to explain human behavior in general. Its name includes the words social *and* learning *because this theory states that most of human behavior can be understood in terms of what we learn to do in social situations. By social situations, what is meant is contact with other people. For example, the theory states that most of what we do is the result of what we have learned from our parents, family, friends, acquaintances, and the other role models, that is, other people we have seen in the mass media, at work, school, in our neighborhood and so on.*

What we learn includes our actions, our thoughts, and our feelings. We learn to talk and walk and dress in certain ways, we learn to think along certain lines, and we learn to feel happy in response to certain events. For example, people from different places have different accents; there are people who are good at thinking about numbers, or about food flavors, or about sports; and, depending on where you learned to like them, different songs can bring out many different feelings in different people. These actions, thoughts, and feelings are learned. And that means that one can learn other ways to act, think, and feel.

Most of what we have learned in life has been due to chance; that is, we generally have not decided what we would learn about life. We happened to be born in a certain place, among certain people, and we learned both helpful and harmful things throughout our life. The purpose of this class is to allow each of the students in the class to discover what are the things they learned that contribute to good and bad moods, and then to purposefully, consciously change those things that produce depression and learn ways to achieve a generally good mood.

Of the three things we have been mentioning (that is, actions, thoughts, and feelings), actions and thought are easier to change directly. If one is feeling depressed, just telling oneself to feel better is usually not very helpful. How-

ever, if one is sitting home alone, one could tell oneself to get up and do exercise, turn on the television, pick up a book one has been meaning to read, call up a friend, or go somewhere where there are people one can talk to. Similarly, if one is thinking about all the bad things that have happened in one's life, it is relatively easy to remind oneself of the good things that have happened, or how even the bad things are not as bad as the things that have happened to some other people. Changing thoughts and actions can have an influence on how you feel. Sometimes it makes better sense to work on one's mood indirectly by changing the thoughts and actions that in turn change the mood rather than attempt to change the mood directly.

It is important to remember that thoughts, actions, and feelings affect each other. Therefore, there will be times in which feelings of depression will affect the kinds of thoughts you have or the kinds of things you will do (or not do). It is important at those times to realize that you do not have to be at the mercy of your feelings. Just as the feelings you are experiencing can control your thoughts and actions to some extent, so can you control your feelings by controlling your thoughts and actions.

By learning which thoughts and actions influence our feelings, we can learn to get more control over our feelings.

This course is designed to help you to discover which thoughts and actions are most closely related to your mood. We will be doing this very systematically, that is, step-by-step. Once you learn this, you will be able to have more control over your mood by changing those thoughts and actions.

One of the best ways to learn is by seeing how others do it. This is how we learned to talk, to walk, to dress, to read and write. And we did this little by little, step by step. We were rewarded by our parents for learning to talk, by the way they smiled, or said 'good boy!' or 'good girl!,' by a hug, or by their looking happy when we said something. This step-by-step method made it possible for us to learn a whole language in about three to five years. That's amazing! And if you don't think so, you have never had to learn a new language. It's hard!

In terms of preventing depression, it is important to learn from others by noticing how others handle situations that are difficult for us. For example, how do other people who have the same type of problems that we have face up to them? Of course, we are going to do better than some people, and worse than others. To learn better ways of dealing with difficult situations, it is good to see how people who are doing it well handle them.

Class 2: How Thoughts Influence Mood

Participants' Handout

Thoughts Affect Mood

Specific thoughts make it more or less likely that you will become depressed. By "thoughts" we mean "sentences we tell ourselves."

Working with Thoughts

Good Points. They are always with you. Thoughts are your internal environment. You can work on them anytime, anywhere. They are mainly under your control and no one else's. No one can directly change the way you think.

Bad Points. It is easy to take thoughts for granted—not be aware of them. No one else can see whether you are changing them.

Learning to Recognize Different Types of Thoughts

Constructive versus Destructive Thinking. Constructive thinking "puts you together." (*Example:* "I can learn to control my life to get more of what I want.") Destructive thinking "tears you apart," "destroys you." (*Examples:* "I am no good," "Nothing will ever turn out right for me.")

Necessary versus Unnecessary Thinking. Necessary thinking helps you do what you have to do. (*Example:* "I must remember to put gas in the car.") Unnecessary thinking doesn't change anything (no matter how much you think). (*Example:* "There is going to be an earthquake any day now.")

Positive versus Negative Thinking. Positive thinking helps you feel better. (*Example:* "Things are really rough right now, but at least I am doing something about them.") Negative thinking makes you feel worse. (*Example:* "It's no use.")

Learning to Recognize Typical Thinking Errors We Make When We Are Depressed

Exaggerating. Exaggerating problems and the possible harm they could cause, and underestimating one's ability to deal with them.

Overgeneralizing. Making a broad, general statement that emphasizes the negative, such as "Nobody likes me."

Ignoring the Positive. Being impressed by and remembering only negative events.

Pessimism. Believing that negative things are more likely to happen and that positive things are less likely to happen.

Blaming Oneself. Thinking that negative things that happen are always and entirely one's fault.

Not Giving Oneself Credit. Thinking that positive things that happen are always either just luck or somebody else's doing, and never the result of one's efforts.

These thoughts and other negative thoughts tend to be automatic, and unreasonable, but appear true or plausible when you are depressed. The more uncritically they are accepted, the worse you feel.

Keeping Track of Thoughts

Getting a "baseline," that is, a record of the kind of thoughts you have *now,* before you begin to change them.

Instructors' Notes

Freedom

From the point of view of social learning, freedom is seen as not an absolute, but rather something that one can have more or less of (a continuum). For human beings, the social learning concept of freedom refers to the number of alternatives that a person has in any situation. So, if one person can react to a certain situation by choosing from six alternatives, that person has more freedom than another person who only has two alternatives.

The purpose of this class is to teach ways to come up with many different reactions to real-life situations. We believe that the more choices a person has, the more likely that person is to choose ways to handle life that will not result in serious depression, and that will help him or her to live a more fulfilling, satisfying life. To be more specific, we know that everyone has times that are hard to handle. By learning a number of different ways to cope, we hope to make it possible that more of you will be able to find ways to handle those tough times in a way that produces a reasonably good outcome under the circumstances. We hope to reduce the number of times in which you feel powerless or feel that the situation is totally hopeless, and increase the number of times in which you feel in control, and able to get the most out of life.

Thoughts Affect Mood

Specific thoughts make it more or less likely that you will become depressed. This is a key concept that must be accepted by the participants if they are to consider the rest of the class relevant, and the homework worthwhile. It is best to try to illustrate it with examples. The following section offers suggested ways to present these concepts.

We know that thoughts affect behavior. For example, we keep our doors locked because we think about the fact that there are people who like to steal things, even though that may never have happened to us.

Thoughts also affect our feelings. For example, if I ask you to remember the most embarrassing moment in your life, you might actually feel embarrassed, and some of you might actually get a little red in the face, even though, of course, nothing embarrassing is going on right now. Similarly, if I ask you to think back to a time in which you were really angry, or really sad, you might feel the same emotion again.

Thoughts, then, are very powerful, especially because they are always with you, and so they can continually have an effect on your body and mind. People who are always worrying about their problems never relax. Their bodies are always working: their muscles are tight, their stomach is churning, their eye and neck muscles are straining. It's no wonder, then, that they feel tired, have indigestion, or even ulcers, and get headaches, backaches, and so on. They can also become emotionally exhausted, burned out, or depressed. Once they are depressed, they feel less like doing things, feel more tired, and more pessimistic about whether they can do anything to change things, and so they get into a vicious spiral, in which they worry more, get more depressed, get more tired and less able to carry out their daily activities, and so their problems increase, which gets them more depressed, and so on.

Working with Thoughts

It's amazing to us how little we are taught about how our thoughts affect our lives. Neither at home, nor in school, are we trained to learn to use the power of our thoughts to help us achieve what we want to achieve in life. Of course, people do say things like "That's not a good attitude," or "You are such a negative thinker," but other than comments like that, we do not get real training on exactly which kinds of thinking are good for us, or why.

I would like to begin to talk about thoughts by going over some of the advantages and disadvantages you will find in working with them. The advantages are that thoughts are always with you. You are always thinking about something, and if you pay attention to what you are thinking, you can usually identify what is making you feel the way you are feeling. Even if a particular thought causes you only minor bother, the fact that it is with you constantly can multiply its power, so that soon you are really bothered by what you know should not be a big deal. Similarly, by telling yourself to think in different ways, you can influence your own mood. We will get to some of the things you can say to yourself next week. Today we will be learning to identify different kinds of thoughts, so that you can begin to work with them.

It is helpful to think of your thoughts as your internal environment, that is, a world within yourself in which you live most of the time. Just as we are now concerned with the condition of our physical environment, we should also learn to pay attention to the condition of our mental environment. One can think, for example, of mental "pollution," of thoughts and beliefs that muddy up our mental world, which produce negative emotions, negative mindsets, which in turn make our life miserable. To turn this around, of course, we need to know which of these thoughts and beliefs are producing this negative effect on us, and what kinds of thoughts might help us counteract the negative ones.

We should note at this point that our thoughts are not the only source of negative emotions. There are two types of stress that affect a person: stress from outside, and stress from inside. The stress from outside (external stress) refers to the stress from life in a imperfect world, from lack of money, from illness, from losing loved ones at times, from the conflict and the violence that are real and that are written up in the papers, and talked about in TV and the radio. There are a lot of problems in the world, and it would be unrealistic to try to ignore them. They do affect our mood.

Internal stress is the type of stress that is produced within us as a reaction to the external stress, or the type that we produce ourselves because we have learned unhealthy ways of thinking. This type of stress can include things we say to ourselves, muscular tension, and tension we might produce in our lives with the people with whom we live, for example, taking out our frustrations with our families, friends, or neighbors.

The total amount of stress that affects us can be figured out by adding the stress from the outside and the stress from the inside. Although there are no really precise ways to figure this out in terms of numbers, we can imagine an example that will demonstrate how we can affect this total.

Let's say that two people have the same negative experience happen to them, for example, getting sick with the same illness. Let's say that the kind of illness they both get produces 100 points of stress in terms of pain, discomfort, and so on. These would be the objective, external sources of stress for these two people, and in this case, both would have 100 points worth of external stress.

Now, let's look at how the two people react to the illness. One person (let's call her Linda) realized how much trouble the illness will be, and she decides that she is not going to let the illness get her down anyway. She will do what she needs to do to take care of herself, but she will also take care of other parts of her life so that the illness doesn't become her whole life. Instead of thinking of herself as "a sick person," she decides to think of herself as a person who is good, decent, who has friends, who has plans for her life, and who also happens to have an illness. In reacting to her illness, Linda has produced some internal stress, of course (we can't expect that she will be totally unaffected by having an illness), but it is not very much. Let's say it is 25 points of internal stress.

The other person (let's call him David) reacts very badly to the illness. For him, the illness represents terrible bad luck; he feels that he is being punished for something, or that he doesn't deserve this illness and that it is unfair for him to get sick. He becomes angry at other people who are healthy (as far as he knows, anyway). He stops getting together with friends, becomes sullen and hard to talk to at home, so everyone in the family feels that David is always angry. When they try to cheer him up, he says, "If you were sick, you wouldn't feel like having fun either." Soon he has become a bitter man, whose friends are afraid to talk to him, and who thinks of himself primarily as a "sick man." By his reaction to the illness, David has produced a large amount of internal stress, let's say around 150 points worth of stress.

If we look at Linda's and David's total stress levels, we can see how one's reactions to external stress can create very different levels of total stress. Linda's external stress is 100, and her internal stress is 25, for a total of 125. David's external stress is 100, and his internal stress is 150, for a total of 250. David has twice as much total stress as Linda, even though they both have the same illness. Our purpose in this course is to find out how to reduce total stress by reducing internal stress.

Let's go back to the outline now. We had just been emphasizing the fact that thoughts are always with you. People are always thinking, even though they are often not aware of what they are thinking about. This is not unusual. The best example is that of reading something, getting to the bottom of the page, and then realizing that "your mind was somewhere else." In this case, one is not aware of what one is thinking about until the reading process (in this case, having to turn the page) breaks up your thought so you realize what has happened. Once we get into the habit of doing anything, it is easy to do it without being aware of it (like chewing one's fingernails or playing with one's hair or beard).

Keep in mind, however, that thoughts have meaning, and therefore they affect people's mood. In many ways, your thoughts have an effect on you that is similar to that of people saying things to you. Children learn to do things partly by learning to tell themselves the things that grownups tell them. A small child who is told not to touch a hot stove will often point to the stove and say, "No. Hot!" and maybe shake his head. He or she is learning to control the impulse to touch the stove by telling himself or herself what parents have said. Even adults use this method of "talking to oneself" when we are doing something that is out of the ordinary. For example, when we are going somewhere for the first time, we often carry on a conversation in our head that is like the directions we were given. We might say, "Let's see, go down Potrero Avenue to 23rd Street, find the seven-story gray building, go up the seventh floor, turn right, then left. . . ." There is nothing wrong with talking to yourself like this. We all do it. Once we do it often enough, however, we don't notice it any more. And we don't notice the effect these thoughts have on us.

To learn to use this process to our advantage, we first have to learn to recognize different types of thoughts. For the purpose of this course, by "thoughts" we mean "sentences we tell ourselves."

You should learn to recognize at least three kinds of thoughts. Constructive versus destructive thinking has to do with the effect that these thoughts have on people. If you think of it in terms of how you would feel if people said things to you, this distinction makes a lot of sense. There are people who are good for your morale. They know what to say so that you will feel good about what you are doing. They give "constructive criticism," criticism that helps you "stay together," that "builds up" your self-esteem. Then there are people who say "destructive things," things that help people "fall apart," that "destroy" your self-confidence.

(Encourage participation here. Have the group come up with examples of these types of things people can say, and move to thoughts people can have that have similar constructive or destructive effects.)

Necessary versus unnecessary thinking refers to thoughts that make a difference versus those that don't make a difference. There are thoughts that might be a "pain," but that we need to keep in mind to get through our daily routines, things like "I have to take out the garbage," or "I have to get a shot next week," and so on. Then there are other thoughts that are a "pain" but that are not necessary because it doesn't matter how much you think about them. These kinds of thoughts are thoughts like "There is going to be an earthquake any day now" (especially if you don't do anything about it, like moving out of the area, or getting emergency food and water ready, or other helpful actions). When unnecessary thoughts are endangering your peace of mind, it is time to put a stop to them.

(Encourage participation here. Ask for examples of these kinds of thoughts.)

Then, there are positive versus negative thoughts. These are thoughts that affect your mood for better or for worse. These are possibly the easiest thoughts to learn to recognize, and they are the ones that most has been written about in the past. This is where the "positive thinking" approach comes from, which many people have found useful in bettering their mood.

The "typical thinking errors" are from Beck's work (Beck et al., 1979).

Class 3: Learning to Change Your Thoughts

Participants' Handout

Some ways to change your thoughts:

Priming

This is a way to get yourself to think about your good points. To get a water pump going, you sometimes have to put some water in from the top. When one starts feeling down, sometimes it is hard to begin thinking positive things. Therefore, one can make oneself write down a list of positive things about oneself and one's life, put one such thought on each of a number of 3 × 5 cards, and take one out at certain times during the day, to get used to remembering that one has nice qualities and that there are nice things in life. After a few days, one can start putting in "wild cards," that is, cards without a thought, and you have to come up with a positive thought on the spot. This technique helps to increase the number of positive thoughts you have during your day.

Self-reward ("Self-reinforcement")

One of the nicest things that people can do for us is to compliment us on things we do well. We really like it when someone notices something we have accomplished, and that perhaps took a lot of effort. Hearing such rewarding words can help us feel better.

Since we often do things that no one notices, it can also help us feel better if at least we ourselves notice what we have done, and give ourselves a pat on the back. Many depressed people do not give themselves credit for the things they do. Many don't even notice how much they actually do during their day.

Mental self-rewards can be saying to oneself things like: "Well, that was a tough job, but you did it!" or "You are a good mother, you really care for your children," or "I am learning to get more control over my life."

Thought Interruption

By this, we mean breaking disturbing chains of thought. There are times when we get into a rut with a certain thought, usually a negative one, which keeps on bothering us throughout the day, making us feel bad. It would be good to learn how to stop such thoughts from ruining our mood. There are a number of techniques that have been used: one is to "yell" (in your mind) the word "Stop!" and focus on whatever else it is that you are doing; another is to tell yourself, "This thought is ruining my mood. Let's move on to another"; a third (especially good if it is a "necessary" thought that you have to do something about later) is to write it down to think about later.

Worrying Time

As we said above, there may be thoughts that are necessary and that you cannot ignore altogether. On the other hand, thinking continuously about a problem will generally not take care of the problem, and can use up all of your energy and attention, so that you begin to do badly in other parts of your life. If you have a big problem at work, you might make your family miserable by worrying about it all the time. Instead of having just one big problem, you can turn it into two (or even three, if you start ruining your health).

One way to avoid this is to begin practicing setting up "obsessive time" during which you will do nothing else but devote your entire attention to the problem that is bothering you. Choose a quiet place and a specific amount of time (ten to thirty minutes a day is about the longest one can think of any problem productively) and do nothing else during that time (no talking, reading, eating, sleeping) but consider the problem and try to come up with a solution. At every other time during the day, use "thought interruption" to put off the obsessive thought until you can give it your full attention.

The Blow-up Technique

This technique involves blowing up a worry out of proportion to minimize its impact. For example, if you are worrying about not being a good person, you might imagine being put on the front page of the *Chronicle* with the words "This is a bad person" written next to you. The technique works best if you can exaggerate the worry so much that it becomes ridiculous and funny. If you can chuckle at your mental image, you have been successful at using it. (The point here is that worrying about certain things does nothing to solve them. The best thing to do is to stop worrying about them, and, if something can be done, doing it.)

NOTE: Do not use this technique with worries that could become as bad as you can imagine.

The Worst That Could Happen

This technique does not rely on humor. It involves merely thinking through the worst that will happen if your fears come true. For example, if you are really worried about meeting a certain deadline, and if your fear is getting in the way of your getting it done, perhaps thinking about the fact that the worst that will happen is that someone will be angry at you for some period of time may reduce your fear enough to let you work well.

Time Projection

Sometimes when we get depressed, it seems that things are terrible and that they will always be terrible. There is a feeling that we are stuck behind a thick, heavy curtain, which hides the future, and which we will never go through into a better time than the one we are in. As such, it is helpful to break through that curtain by imagining ourselves moving forward to a time when things will be better. (This is not "just kidding ourselves." We have all had times in our past when we thought we wouldn't be able to make it, that we would never get over some hurt, pain, or suffering, and yet we have all made it, we have all survived those bad times. Even if some pain remains around some memories, the pain tends to lessen with time.)

The Pause: "Time Out"

There are times when the best thing to do is to "hold everything" and let our thoughts and anxieties flow by without our actively engaging them. This is a kind of mini-meditation, in which you let your mind rest even for a few seconds, allow yourself to feel the experience of being relaxed, of being still, at peace, tranquil. This is particularly helpful when you are feeling hurried, having a hectic day, or feeling overwhelmed. Just knowing that you can feel at peace can sometimes give you some energy to face your day again.

Self-instructions

Talking to yourself isn't always crazy. We all do it. It can be like having a coach at your side, giving you directions. You can remind yourself to use these techniques. You can remind yourself of how you want to handle things.

Appendix A

An Argument for Optimism

One of the differences between people who are depressed and those who aren't is that depressed people tend to be less optimistic than nondepressed people. Whether one wants to be an optimist or a pessimist is one's choice, of course, but we would now like to argue why being an optimist might be a better approach to life. An optimist believes that the chances of good things happening are good. *That belief itself can increase the chances that good things actually happen.* There is no magic involved here, just common sense. Let's use an example to explain this.

Two people are looking for work. Joe is a pessimist and Cathy is an optimist. Even if both of them have exactly the same qualifications, Cathy is more likely to get a job. Here's how:

Step 1: "Should I read the Want Ads?"
Joe: *"No use doing it. There probably won't be any jobs for me."*
Cathy: *"Might as well give it a try."*
Result: *If there is a job, of course, Cathy has at least a small chance of finding it. Joe has no chance at all unless he reads the Ads.*

Step 2: "Should I call this number in the Ads?"
Joe: *"The job doesn't quite fit my qualifications."*
Cathy: *"It doesn't fit exactly, but it's close. Let them decide."*
Result: *If there is any chance of getting the job, Cathy's chances are at least greater than zero, if she calls.*

Step 3: "Should I show up for an interview?"
Joe: *"Why be rejected again?"*
Cathy: *"It's a long shot, but at least I'll get practice doing an interview."*
Result: *She will get the practice. If the job doesn't quite fit, they might think of her for another job that fits better; if the job fits, she might get it.*

As you can see, at each step, optimists increase the chances that their goal will in fact be reached. Pessimists continually reduce the chances, maybe even down to zero, by taking away from themselves the motivation to act.

Our recommendation is to notice what you tell yourself about your future. If you have learned to tell yourself negative things, pessimistic things, you may be doing yourself a disservice, you may be adding to your problems. There is something called the "self-fulfilling prophecy," which basically means that if you predict that something bad will happen, you can sometimes contribute (without meaning to) to making it come out badly.

Remember the connection between thoughts, actions, and feelings. Optimism is basically a learned pattern of thinking that good things will happen. That thinking influences what you will do and how you will feel. It is all connected.

Instructors' Notes

The Participants' Handout is very detailed for this session. Some additional suggestions:

The Pause

This is meant to be a very short pause, less than a minute long. Its purpose is to give the user a feeling of control over his or her own thoughts, even for a minute. The technique is ideal for situations that appear overwhelming, in which the person feels as though in the middle of a rushing river of events, with a subjective feeling of being out of control. The pause allows the person to experience the ability to set up a mental "safety zone" within which one can rest briefly, regain some perspective, and allow one's energy to build up enough to tackle the situation. It is also meant to give the user practice in finding that subjective state of being at peace, relaxed, inwardly still, which can serve as a refuge from hectic situations.

An Argument for Optimism

I like to accompany this presentation with a figure (Figure A-1). I begin with the leftmost dot and show that at any instant, one can choose how to think and act, and these choices will have a positive (upward) or negative (downward) effect on one's mood. (The figure represents time from left to right, with each column being "an instant," and mood on the vertical axis, with up being feeling good, down feeling depressed, and the row in the middle being average mood.) The ideal level of mood would be above or at the middle row most of the time. Between columns, I draw arrows as I exemplify a thought or an action one can choose to engage in. Thus, I can show graphically the changes in mood that come about due to specific thoughts and actions.

Figure A.1. Class 3: Figure used with "An argument for optimism"

Class 4: How Activities Affect Mood

Participants' Handout

The fewer pleasant activities people do, the more depressed they feel.

The Big Question. Do you stop doing things because you are depressed? Or: Do you get depressed because you stop doing things?

Thinking about the Answer. It doesn't have to be just one way or the other. Many things in this life influence each other.

The Answer. The concept of the vicious cycle. The less you do, the more depressed you feel, the more depressed you feel, the less you do, which makes you feel even more depressed, and so on.

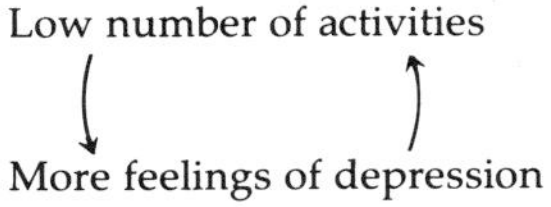

Using this concept to control your mood better. Since it is hard to just tell yourself to "feel better," that is, change your feelings by just telling yourself to do it, you can instead focus on what you do. It is easier to tell yourself to do something pleasant and do it. This should affect your mood. The key here is to use indirect methods (but ones that are easier to control directly) to influence your mood, because it is harder to influence your mood directly.

Instructors' Notes

"The fewer pleasant activities people do, the more depressed they feel." This is a very commonsensical notion, as are most of the techniques we cover in the course. In a way, the more commonsensical the techniques, the more closely they will be connected to everyday issues and the more understandable they will be for most people. One hope is that when we are talking about how human beings tick, the explanations we give will be readily acceptable to human beings, as opposed to being esoteric and distant from everyday experience.

This particular concept can be highlighted in two ways:

First, the usual explanation is that one does fewer things when one feels down. And this explanation is correct, but incomplete. A more complete explanation is that reducing pleasant activities makes you feel worse, and feeling worse reduces your pleasant activity level, which makes you feel even worse, and so on. The concept being addressed here is a key concept for the whole course, and has been addressed before, namely the reciprocal nature of these processes. This concept is what makes it possible to suggest to people that increasing their pleasant activities, even when they feel bad, can elevate their mood.

Second, this approach has been used successfully in the treatment of depression, with people who were feeling low, and not feeling like doing much. As they began to increase their pleasant activities, their mood improved. Then, of course, they felt like doing more pleasant things, and their increased pleasant activity level became more "natural."

The "chicken and egg" question is met here head on. It is best to ask participants to give examples of both kinds of possibilities, that is, times when they felt bad and reduced their activity level, and times when they reduced their activity level, and then began to feel bad.

Here are a couple of examples to sprinkle through the discussion:

Many people find it hard to move from one location to another. One reason this is so is because people, places, and activities they were used to and that were pleasant for them are no longer available to them at the new location. It takes a while to develop new friendships, to find places where one can feel comfortable, and to begin to engage in activities that one enjoys. The point here is that, in addition to missing the people they left behind, their usual level of pleasant activities has gone down a lot, and it has placed an additional burden on their mood. As they find ways to increase their level of pleasant activities, their mood improves, although they usually continue to miss their distant loved ones.

When people have to reduce their usual level of activity because of an illness, the reason many feel low (in addition to their sadness at having the illness, and perhaps having pain or discomfort) is that their usual level of activity is reduced. People who cope well with their illness usually find alternative ways of keeping themselves busy with things they find enjoyable and meaningful, even if this means changing their interests from, say, participating in sports to learning to enjoy being a spectator, or from physical activities to mental or creative activities. In this way, two people with the same disease, and with the same level of pain or discomfort, might feel very different emotionally. The one who has learned to find new ways of enjoying life will feel better than the one whose pleasant activity level dropped and was not replaced with alternative ways to feel good.

Think about the answer to the "chicken and egg" question. The purpose here is to start to sow the seed for the interpersonal skills sessions, and other issues that may come up in the future. Specifically, we want participants to begin to use the reciprocal determinism concept across a number of issues. We have just had a discussion of how mood and activity level affect each other; at this time, other examples can be used. For instance, the way a relationship is formed could be discussed, and how the way we are treated by others can be influenced *to some degree* by the way we treat others.

This is a good place to bring out the probabilistic nature of life in general and of these techniques in particular. We are not saying that the way we treat others determines totally how they will treat us. What we are saying is that it is more likely (or the probability is higher) that we will be treated well if we treat others well. Similarly, we are not saying that if you engage in a lot of pleasant activities you will definitely feel better. What we are saying is that the chances are increased that your mood will improve, or that most of the time, when you increase your activities, your mood will improve. For those times in which it does not, you can try other methods, such as looking at what you are thinking, or your interpersonal relationships, or other areas in your life. This probabilistic concept can be disappointing to some people, but it also has a preventive effect in that, if used properly, it can serve as a buffer against discouragement if the methods they choose to use first do not have an immediate effect.

Let's review the concept of the vicious cycle. In a way, the vicious cycle can be better described as a vicious spiral. The concept of the consequences of engaging in specific thoughts or actions on one's mood is best exemplified with a directional metaphor, that is, the less you do, the lower you move into a depressed mood, the more you do, the higher you move.

Pleasant events are very individualized. We are not trying to get people to engage in activities that others (even most people) consider pleasant. Individuals have their own preferences. Pleasant events should be enjoyable or meaningful to people.

It is also important to point out that pleasant activities need not be expensive or really special. In fact, the more nonspecial they are, the more of them you can build into your everyday life. It is fine, of course, to set up special pleasant events into your life at regular intervals. This can provide you with the pleasant event of thinking about how nice it will be to do your special activity.

This brings up another point: Pleasant activities can be internal or external. Many of our pleasant activities are mental. In fact, to some extent, our mental activities can determine whether something is pleasant or not. If we feel guilty about having fun, for example, this will spoil pleasant events. Not only are pleasant events individually defined, but also the level of pleasant activities is an individual matter. Some people need fewer pleasant activities to feel good.

For example, older people in general engage in fewer numbers of pleasant activities, but their mood is generally not much different from that of younger people. It may be that older people have learned through the years which activities are truly more enjoyable for them, and that they are more efficient at picking things they really find pleasant. Younger people engage in many more activities, but may be less good at knowing which they really like.

Depending on the participants, the following analogy might be useful:

As human beings are learning more and more about the world, they are also learning more and more about what makes us tick. One hopes that as we learn more things, we will be better able to help ourselves live the kinds of lives we want, to be healthy, to feel good.

One of the things we are learning is that we can control our bodies a lot better than we used to think we could. A method called biofeedback *allows people to increase their control over such things as their heartbeat, their skin temperature, and even their brain waves. The way this works is by letting people see exactly how fast their heart beats (by measuring their heartbeat and letting the people know how fast it is beating) and then asking them to try to increase or decrease their heartbeat. If people are told when their heart is changing the speed of beating, they can actually learn to do so on purpose. That's why the method is called* biofeedback, *because people get feedback (that is, they are told how well they are doing) about a biological function.*

We think that getting feedback about how your behavior affects your mood can help you to get better control over your mood. This is a kind of 'behavior feedback'. Specifically, you will learn what level of activities (and exactly which activities) are connected to your mood level.

To come up with an individualized list of activities, we have developed a questionnaire that lists a large number of activities that many people consider pleasant. Out of these activities you will identify 100, which you will then keep track of. Actually, ninety will come from the Pleasant Events Schedule (PES), and ten are self-generated, to allow people to add activities relevant to them that are not in the PES.

NOTE: *The Pleasant Events Schedule is found on pages 76–90 of* Control Your Depression *(Lewinsohn, Muñoz, Youngren & Zeiss, 1986).*

(Help participants to begin completing the Pleasant Events Schedule.)

Class 5: Increasing Pleasant Activities

Participants' Handout

— Planning for pleasant events: why planning is important
— Commitment: choice-making, priorities, perspective
— Balancing what has to be done with what you would like to do
— Anticipation: solving problems that might interfere
— Resisting demands on your time
— Achieving a greater feeling of control

Do the kinds of thoughts you have help to increase your pleasant activities? Which thoughts help you do the things you want? Which thoughts get in the way of doing the things you want?

Consider doing pleasant activities without spending much money. Come up with a set of pleasant activities in San Francisco, for example. Call it "A List of Pleasant Activities One Can Do in San Francisco."

Instructors' Notes

Planning for Pleasant Events

Here is an example of how to discuss ways to increase pleasant activities:

One of the greatest problems that people have with the pleasant events list is that they don't have time to do the pleasant events. Just thinking about that makes some people feel bad! What we have to do, then, is to try to increase the chances that we will do them. Once we are doing them, they will feel good, and we will get used to doing them, and it will get easier and easier. But getting started is hard, even if what we are trying to do is fun.

The best way to get something done is to plan for it in advance.

Once you plan something, you commit yourself to do it, which means that you have made a choice to do it, you have placed doing it high on your priority list, and you have placed it in perspective, that is, you have thought about how it fits into your life.

Another reason for planning ahead of time is to make sure that you are balancing what you have to do with what you want to do. One of the reasons people don't do pleasant things is that they feel they are not finished with all the other things they have to do. By planning ahead, you can make sure you are *done with what is absolutely necessary, and that you build in some recreation time. (*Recreation = re-creation, *that is, creating yourself new again. Every time you take control over a part of your life, even something that seems as unimportant to some people as doing pleasant things, you help to create the person you are going to be in the future.)*

Changing the Future Past

Sometimes people think about how things would have turned out if they had done something or other in the past, say ten years ago. Yet, everyone knows that one cannot change the past. Or can one? See what you think of this idea, which is a way of "changing the past," only in this case it is the "future past."

Consider a person who is thinking like the one above, that things would have been a lot better if she had begun to do this or that ten years ago: "how different things would be now," she thinks. Now use time projection to move forward inside your imagination ten years in time. Now imagine yourself thinking about the past ten years. What kinds of things would you like to have done in that time? What kind of person would you like to have become in that time? Stay ten years ahead in your imagination for a minute more. While still there, think: "It would have been nice to have started doing this or that ten years ago!"

Now, consider the fact that today will be that "ten years ago" when it really is ten years later, way in the future. There in the future, your past, in this case ten years' worth of your past, will no longer be changeable. Your future past will have already happened. But right now, it is still ahead of you, and you can "change it," that is, you can control it, you can make it be more of what you'd like it to be, so that ten years from now it will be the "past" that you have made yourself.

Balancing what has to be done with what you would like to do can be a way of getting more control over your pleasant activities.

Take a piece of paper, draw a line down the middle, and write Have to *on the left side, and* Want to *on the right side. Consider the week ahead, and start writing down the things that you have to do this week. If there are things that you have to do someday, but not necessarily this week, write those in the back of the paper. Don't try to do everything in one week! Now think of the kinds of things that it would be fun to do this week and could be done this week. Again, if there are pleasant things that you have been wanting to do for a long time but that take a lot of time, or a lot of money, or a lot of preparation, write them on the back of the sheet for future reference. Your list for this week should include only things that are reasonable to do in one week.*

Now you can start to plan. The goal of your plan should be to balance the things you have to do with the things you want to do. That does not mean you must do exactly as many "have to's" as "want to's," because some activities take longer than others and are worth more in terms of energy and involvement. The goal is to make sure that you are spending more time than in the past doing things that are pleasant so that you do not feel that you are only doing things that you have to do.

By anticipation, we mean thinking about what might interfere with our plans and solving these possible problems ahead of time. For example, to watch a television program undisturbed, you might have to make arrangements for someone to take care of things during that hour or two, such as answering the phone, taking care of children, or even (if you don't own a television set), arranging to visit someone who does.

Another example might be having two or three alternative places where you could do nothing, such as a park, an indoor shopping mall, and a library. This way, if a park was your first choice and it rains, you could go to the mall instead; and if the mall is closed for some reason, you could go to the library, or even go home and soak in the tub.

Pick a specific special pleasant event now, and see if you think of how to increase the chances that you will do it, by planning ahead.

By resisting demands on your time, we mean being able to negotiate around obstacles that can get in the way of your doing things. If people are likely to ask you to do things for them at times in which you had planned to do a special pleasant event, for example, you simply say that you had another commitment at that time, or simply say you cannot do it (without explaining why—that's okay to do), or offer to help with the particular request at another time, earlier or later.

One of the things depressed people often feel is a lack of control over their own life. By planning for pleasant events, for meaningful events in your everyday life, you will be learning to increase your control over your life, as well as to increase your feeling of control.

Focus on the relationship between thoughts and activities: are there thoughts that will make it more likely that the participants will do the pleasant activities? Are there thoughts that reduce the chances that they will do them? Are there thoughts that help them enjoy the pleasant activities? (e.g., "I work hard, I deserve to have fun," or "The more pleasant activities I do, the better I will feel, and the more energy I'll have to do the things I have to do").

Are there thoughts that make it harder for them to enjoy what they are doing? (e.g., "This is kid's stuff. I am an adult, I shouldn't need to do fun stuff to feel good," or "I haven't done all my chores: I shouldn't relax until I have" (of course, one is never done, so one can never relax)). Continue as follows:

Another big problem that people have regarding increasing their pleasant activities is feeling that pleasant activities cost a lot of money. It is important to remember that there are many things one can do that are free or at least inexpensive.

This is a good chance to exemplify how telling yourself "To do pleasant things you need a lot of money" can work against you, while telling yourself "I want to do more pleasant things that don't cost much. Let's try to think what things I can do that are cheap" will increase your chances of coming up with some good ones, will give you a greater feeling of control, and increase the pleasantness in your life.

Let's help ourselves by coming up with a list of things one can do in San Francisco that are free or don't cost much.

This section is meant to increase chances that people will be successful in achieving the goals we have set for them. The purpose is to deal with doubts or arguments they might use on themselves (not necessarily on purpose) that will be obstacles to their reaching their goals.

This is a time for general discussion regrading the purpose of the course.

Issues regarding gaining greater control over one's mood and over one's life should be covered.

Comments regarding the nature of probabilities in human history and how they apply to individuals might be mentioned, as follows:

Throughout our history, we have attempted to gain greater control over the things that happen to us by chance. Instead of relying on gathering food from plants that grow naturally, for example, we began to choose plants to grow, and to water them, tend them, fertilize them, and even develop new breeds of plants to increase the chances that we would have the food we needed. By now, we have even learned to store food and freeze it, so that we can eat things even out of season. What all these advances do is to increase the chances of positive things happening, in this case, having food to eat. This doesn't mean that people never go hungry. Many still do. But a large percentage of humanity now has enough to eat all the time. Perhaps someday we will be able to say that about all humanity. It's up to all of us to encourage that to happen.

The purpose of this course is to see if we can help people to change the probabilities for living a more fulfilling life, for preventing serious depression, so that positive feelings are more likely to be part of their lives, more of the time, and so that they can have the necessary tools to handle difficulties in the future. How much it's possible to do about this is not known at this time. Research projects such as this one are trying to find out how much we can push back the boundaries of what is now considered ordinary, normal, inescapable, or unavoidable suffering.

There are many examples of ways in which human beings have learned to do things that most people would have said we had no chance of doing. Years ago, human beings would have said it was impossible for people to be underwater for more than four or five minutes, and survive. Now we have scuba gear and submarines. Years ago, it was known that if anyone fell from a great height, he or she would die. Now we have parachutes, hang gliders, even individual flying platforms. Years ago, it was said that if God had meant for humans to fly, God would have given us wings. Now flying is a very ordinary event. When I was born, most intelligent people would have said that the chances of going to the moon were nil. Now we know we can do it.

All of these examples can be seen as instances in which human beings were faced with situations in which the probability of doing what we wanted was considered zero, or near zero. But by thinking carefully about the problem, and by experimenting with ideas that made sense, we were able to change those probabilities, and accomplished things that are positive for us and our descendants.

We hope that as we progress in our work with preventing depression, we will discover ways to reduce the amount of suffering from loss of hope, and make it possible for more people to remain feeling enthusiastic about life, satisfied, and able to share that satisfaction with their loved ones.

You do not have to wait to put these ideas into practice. There is no reason why you can't experiment with your own life, and test these ideas, picking out the ones that work for you, and sharing what you find with your family and friends. You might find that the things that you used to believe were sure to make you depressed can be handled in more constructive ways, so that you do not add the burden of depression to the other burdens that life sometimes places on us.

Class 6: How Contacts with People Affect Mood

Participants' Handout

Some Facts about the Relationship between Depression and Contacts with People

Higher levels of depression are related to:

— less contact with people;
— feeling uncomfortable with people;
— being more quiet, talking less;
— being less assertive, that is, not expressing your likes or dislikes;
— being more sensitive to being ignored, criticized, or rejected.

An important question to consider: Does depression cause people to be less sociable, or does being less sociable cause depression? The answer, once again, is probably both. When we feel down, we are less likely to want to socialize. But not having contact with people takes away from us a good source of happiness, so we become more depressed. When we feel more depressed, we do even fewer things with people, and this continues until we are so depressed that we spend most of our time alone.

Social Support

Psychologists are spending a lot of time these days studying the effect of social support on people's well-being. In general, the stronger your social support system, the better you will be able to face tough situations. By social support system, psychologists mean the people who are near you and with whom you share your life. This includes your family, friends, neighbors, co-workers, and acquaintances.

Two hints for reducing the chances of being seriously depressed follow.

— If your social support system is small, you may want to enlarge it.
— If your social support system is a good size, you may want to appreciate it and keep it strong.

How do you do this? That is what this class and Class 7 are about. We will now go over three ideas:

— how you come across;
— assertion;
— increasing your contacts with people.

The way you feel affects the way you act; the way you act affects the way you feel.

Instructors' Notes

See Chapters 7, 8, and 13 of *Control Your Depression*.

Class 7: Increasing Interpersonal Activities

Participants' Handout

Increasing Pleasant Contacts with People When You Don't Know Many People

One of the easiest ways to meet people without feeling too self-conscious is to do something that you really like doing, in the company of other people. When you are doing something you like, you are more likely to be in a better mood, and therefore, it will be easier to be friendly to others. In addition, even if you don't find anyone in particular whom you would like to get to know better, you will still be doing something pleasant, and you will be less likely to feel that you are wasting your time. Since the main focus is the activity you are doing, and not just meeting others, there will be less pressure on you than there might be in a setting where the whole purpose is to meet people.

Finally, if you do meet people you would like to get to know better, they are likely to be people with whom you share at least the one interest that brought you together.

Examples:

— If you enjoy helping others, you may want to consider joining a group of volunteers who have gotten together to help other people;
— If you enjoy preparing food, you may want to look into groups that get together around pot-luck meals, picnics, and other food-related activities;
— If you enjoy sports, you may want to join a neighborhood team, or a group that goes to sports events together;
— If religion is an important part of your life, you may want to become more active in groups from your church.

Group Exercise. What other suggestions can the group come up with?

The Importance of Planning to Live Your Life the Way You Want to Live It

One of the greatest sources of problems in carrying out some of these ideas is that people often feel that they don't have time to do them. On the other hand, doing these things would probably help them to feel better, so that they could enjoy the things they "have to do" more, and perhaps even learn to do them faster or more effectively.

Part of the problem in doing some of these things is that people often get into ruts, and once they are in them, they no longer consider whether that is the way they want to live. In preparation for our last class, next week, we will begin to think about our lives, and how we would like to live them.

What Are Your Basic Needs?

Abraham Maslow (a psychologist) listed what he thought comprised the "hierarchy" of human needs (i.e., a list that goes in order from the most basic to the most idealistic):

— *Physiological needs:* the needs of the body for survival, such as food, water, and warmth.
— *Safety needs:* the need to guard against danger, to feel physically safe.
— *The need for love and belongingness:* to feel loved and to feel love for others, as well as to feel that you "belong," that you are part of a group of people and have something in common with those people.
— *Self-esteem needs:* a feeling of being worthwhile, of being proud of what you do and what you are.
— *The need for self-actualization:* the need to live up to your highest potential as a human being. (This potential is different for each of us.)

Group Exercise. How does this list sound? Are there things that people would like to add to the list? Any other reactions?

What Are Your Personal Goals?

One of the best ways to "put your life in order" is to become aware of what your goals are. Your goals will probably be influenced by your personal values. Values are general principles or personal guidelines; goals are specific objectives. Are your values and goals compatible?

Values give meaning to goals. When values are in conflict, one has a "dilemma." This means that one has to choose between two equally good or bad alternatives. There is no clear-cut "better" choice. At a time like this, a conscious choice to give precedence to one of your values will make it less likely that you will feel that you are betraying your principles. One way to strengthen your chosen values is to choose a social support system (that is, the people with whom you spend time) that will support the values you want to live by.

There are many types of goals:

— *individual goals:* the goals that have to do primarily with you alone.
— *interpersonal goals:* the goals that have to do with you in relation to others.
— *short-term goals:* the type of goal that can be put on a "to-do" list.
— *long-term goals:* Where would you like to be in regard to your individual and interpersonal goals three, five, ten years from now? In looking at your past three, five, ten years from three, five, ten years in the future, what kinds of memories would you like to have?
— *life goals:* your philosophy of life. If you had to tell someone what life is all about for you, what would you say?
— *destructive goals:*
  - perfectionism (because it is unattainable);
  - considering oneself "a failure" if one isn't "the best"; and
  - setting goals for others and making our happiness dependent on their reaching them.

Note the goals that you have already reached. Note also the goals that require constant progress.

Fill out your list of goals. Describe how you would like to think, behave, and interact with others, in order to prevent serious depression and to live a more pleasant life.

List of Goals

Individual Goals

The Basic Needs (from Maslow)

— Physiological (food, water, warmth, etc.)
— Safety (to feel free of continual danger)
— Love and belongingness
— Self-esteem (feeling pride about what you do or what you are)
— Self-actualization (developing your potential)

Write down the goals that *you* find important. (Consider the goals listed above, as well as how what has been covered in the course could help you reach your goals.)

____

____

____

Other Goals

— Life-style
— Spiritual, religious, philosophical
— Economic
— Educational
— Vocational
— Physical activity level
— Recreational and/or creative

Write down the goals that *you* find important. (Consider the goals listed above, as well as how what has been covered in the course could help you reach your goals.)

____

____

____

Goals That Involve Others

— Family life-style
— Friendships
— Romantic relationships
— Group commitments
— Leadership roles

Write down the goals (which involve others) that *you* find important. (Consider the goals listed above, as well as how what has been covered in the course could help you reach your goals.)

____

____

____

Short-term Goals (things you would like to do within six months)

____

____

____

Long-term Goals (things you would like to do at some point in your life)

____

____

____

Life Goals (philosophies of life: What do you think matters most in life?)

____

____

____

Instructors' Notes

See Chapters 7, 8, and 13 of *Control Your Depression.*

Class 8: Planning for the Future: Preventing Depression

Participants' Handout

Thinking Preventively

Don't wait until things go badly to pay attention to your well-being. Nourish yourself psychologically to attain "positive mental health." Well-adjusted people are good at:

— knowing the consequences of their acts;
— having many alternatives to use in any situation; and
— planning ahead to obtain their goals.

Some people say that one's personality never changes. This is not true. Your "personality" can be defined as:

— the way you react to things;
— the way you see the world; and
— the way you act when you are alone or with others.

Some "personalities" become depressed more easily than others. Try out ways of thinking and behaving that will make it less likely that you will get seriously depressed. You can increase your control over how you feel and how you will react to things.

You can be a scientist with your own life. You can experiment with different ways of doing things. You can evaluate whether you like these new ways and change them again, if you like.

Remember:

— your thoughts affect your mood;
— your behavior affects your mood (especially the number of pleasant activities that you do); and
— your contacts with people affect your mood.

Remember also that although you may not be able to change how you feel directly, you can:

— change your thoughts;
— increase the number of pleasant activities you do; and
— increase the number of pleasant contacts you have with people.

Appendix A

Placing the Course and Techniques in Perspective

Social learning theory is a way to understand how people learn to act, feel, and think in certain ways. It does not tell us what we should strive to experience or do in our lives. As such, it is a tool to be used, not a philosophy to live by. You supply your own philosophy.

The course is targeted specifically at teaching techniques that have been found helpful in the treatment of depression to people who are not presently seriously depressed, with the intention of making these tools available to them so they can gain better control over their mood and prevent serious depression in the future.

The techniques learned in the course can serve as basic skills in the pursuit of one's objectives in life. Those objectives are yours to define, however.

We believe that a positive mood state can make it easier for individuals to decide what values and goals to live for, calmly and constructively, and to pursue these goals effectively.

Where have people sought goals? From

— individual knowledge and experience;
— family and friendship (nurturing and being nurtured by others);
— one's cultural heritage; and
— religion, politics, philosophy, and creativity.

Consider your "assumptive worlds," that is, your basic assumptions about life. What do you think life is all about?

— Do you see existence as friendly, threatening, or indifferent?
— How do you see human beings?
— Do you compare yourself with others? If so, do you compare yourself in a balanced way, that is, with those who are worse off than you, as well as those that are better off?
— Do you enjoy what you have now? *Or,* are you always waiting to achieve the next goals before you can feel satisfied?
— Do you get used to what you have and begin taking it for granted? Or do you remind yourself to enjoy and appreciate it?

The Final Message

Although human freedom is not absolute, humans can increase their freedom by how much they control their lives. This class has tried to teach ways to increase control over your mood by teaching you how your thoughts, behavior, and interactions with others affects your mood. We hope you will be able to use these ideas and methods to have a happier life.

Instructors' Notes

"Promoting positive mental health" is not just trying to get an average level of health but to secure a better-than-average level of health. This way, if crises arise, one has extra resources to use without depleting one's emotional health below the average level. The analogy is to becoming physically fit, so that if an illness or a crisis arises, the body has a lot of extra energy to deal with it.

From a social learning point of view, one's personality is defined by one's behavioral patterns, including the way one thinks, feels, and acts. One's assumptive world (Jerome Frank's term [1973]) is the sum total of one's assumptions about reality. The way to deal with this is to remind participants that our assumptions about reality, or our beliefs, can be considered thoughts, just like any other thoughts, and that we can attempt to identify them, and, if necessary, change them, so that they can help us live life fully, instead of getting in our way.

Appendix B
Measures Used in the Depression Prevention Research Project

Assertion Questionnaire

The following is a list of events. How often have these events happened in your life in the past month? Please answer these questions by rating each item using the following guide:

1 = This has not happened in the past 30 days.
2 = This has happened a few times (1–6 times) in the past 30 days.
3 = This has happened often (7 times or more) in the past 30 days.

Event	Not at All	1–6 Times	7 Times or More
1. Turning down a person's request to borrow my car	1	2	3
2. Asking a favor of someone	1	2	3
3. Resisting sales pressure	1	2	3
4. Admitting fear and requesting consideration	1	2	3
5. Telling a person I am intimately involved with that he/she has said something that bothers me	1	2	3
6. Admitting ignorance in an area being discussed	1	2	3
7. Turning down a friend's request to borrow money	1	2	3
8. Turning off a talkative friend	1	2	3
9. Asking for constructive criticism	1	2	3
10. Asking for clarification when I am confused about what someone has said	1	2	3
11. Asking whether I have offended someone	1	2	3
12. Telling a person of the opposite sex I like him/her	1	2	3
13. Telling a person of the same sex that I like him/her	1	2	3
14. Requesting expected service when it hasn't been offered (e.g., in a restaurant)	1	2	3
15. Discussing openly with a person his/her criticism of my behavior	1	2	3
16. Returning defective items (e.g., at a store or restaurant)	1	2	3
17. Expressing an opinion that differs from that of a person I am talking with	1	2	3

Appendix B

Assertion Questionnaire—*Continued*

Event	Not at All	1–6 Times	7 Times or More
18. Resisting sexual overtures when I am not interested	1	2	3
19. Telling someone how I feel if he/she has done something that is unfair to me	1	2	3
20. Turning down a social invitation from someone I don't particularly like	1	2	3
21. Resisting pressure to drink	1	2	3
22. Resisting an unfair demand from a person who is important to me	1	2	3
23. Requesting the return of borrowed items	1	2	3
24. Telling a friend or co-worker when he/she says or does something that bothers me	1	2	3
25. Asking a person who is annoying me in a public situation to stop (e.g., smoking on a bus)	1	2	3
26. Criticizing a friend	1	2	3
27. Criticizing my spouse	1	2	3
28. Asking someone for help or advice	1	2	3
29. Expressing my love to someone	1	2	3
30. Asking to borrow something	1	2	3
31. Giving my opinion when a group is discussing an important matter	1	2	3
32. Taking a definite stand on a controversial issue	1	2	3
33. When two friends are arguing, supporting the one I agree with	1	2	3
34. Expressing my opinion to someone I don't know very well	1	2	3
35. Interrupting someone to ask him/her to repeat something I didn't hear clearly	1	2	3
36. Contradicting someone when I think I might hurt him/her by doing so	1	2	3
37. Telling someone when I think I might hurt him/her by doing so	1	2	3
38. Asking someone to leave me alone	1	2	3
39. Telling a friend or co-worker that he/she has done a good job	1	2	3
40. Telling someone he/she has made a good point in a discussion	1	2	3
41. Telling someone I have enjoyed talking with him/her	1	2	3
42. Complimenting someone on his/her skill or creativity	1	2	3

Cognitive Events Schedule

The following is a list of thoughts. How often have you had these thoughts in the past month? Please answer these questions by rating each item using the following guide:

1 = This has not happened in the past 30 days.
2 = This has happened a few times (1–6 times) in the past 30 days.
3 = This has happened often (7 times or more) in the past 30 days.

Thought	Not at All	1–6 Times	7 Times or More
1. I'll always be sexually frustrated	1	2	3
2. I am confused	1	2	3
3. It will be fun doing such-and-such this weekend	1	2	3
4. I've gotten more good things in life than the average person	1	2	3
5. Today is the first day of the rest of my life	1	2	3
6. I am wasting my life	1	2	3
7. I'm scared	1	2	3
8. Nobody loves me	1	2	3
9. I'll end up living all alone	1	2	3
10. People don't consider friendship important anymore	1	2	3
11. I don't have any patience	1	2	3
12. Life is interesting	1	2	3
13. It will be fun to see all those new people at the get-together	1	2	3
14. What's the use?	1	2	3
15. I really feel great	1	2	3
16. He's handsome (or she's beautiful)	1	2	3
17. That was a dumb thing for me to do	1	2	3
18. I'll probably have to be placed in a mental institution someday	1	2	3
19. Anybody who thinks I'm nice doesn't know the real me	1	2	3
20. Existence has no meaning (or life has no meaning)	1	2	3
21. This is fun	1	2	3

Appendix B

Cognitive Events Schedule—*Continued*

Thought	Not at All	1–6 Times	7 Times or More
22. I am ugly	1	2	3
23. I can't express my feelings	1	2	3
24. I'll never find what I really want	1	2	3
25. I am not capable of loving	1	2	3
26. I am worthless	1	2	3
27. I have great hopes for the future	1	2	3
28. I have good self-control	1	2	3
29. That's interesting	1	2	3
30. It's all my fault	1	2	3
31. Why do so many bad things happen to me?	1	2	3
32. I can't think of anything that would be fun	1	2	3
33. I don't have what it takes	1	2	3
34. I'm not as prepared as I should be	1	2	3
35. A nice, relaxing evening can sure be enjoyable	1	2	3
36. Bringing kids into the world is cruel because life isn't worth living	1	2	3
37. I'll never get over this depression	1	2	3
38. Things are so messed up that doing anything about them is futile			
39. I don't have enough willpower	1	2	3
40. Why even bother getting up?	1	2	3
41. I wish I were dead	1	2	3
42. I wonder if they are talking about me	1	2	3
43. Things are just going to get worse and	1	2	3
worse	1	2	3
44. I have enough time to accomplish the things I most want to do	1	2	3
45. I have a bad temper	1	2	3
46. No matter how hard one tries, people aren't satisfied	1	2	3
47. Life is unfair	1	2	3
48. I like people	1	2	3
49. I'm a sensitive person	1	2	3
50. I'll never make good friends	1	2	3
51. I don't dare imagine what my life will be like in ten years	1	2	3
52. There is something wrong with me	1	2	3
53. I am selfish	1	2	3
54. I could probably handle a crisis as well as anyone else	1	2	3
55. I'm pretty lucky	1	2	3
56. I'm responsible	1	2	3

Cognitive Events Schedule—*Continued*

Thought	Not at All	1–6 Times	7 Times or More
57. My experiences have prepared me well for the future	1	2	3
58. That's funny (humorous)	1	2	3
59. I'm pretty smart	1	2	3
60. My memory is lousy	1	2	3
61. I'm not as good as so-and-so	1	2	3
62. I don't want to miss that event	1	2	3
63. I get my feelings hurt easily	1	2	3
64. There is no love in the world	1	2	3

Pleasant Activities Schedule

The following is a list of events. How often have these events happened in your life in the past month? Please answer these questions by rating each item using the following guide:

1 = This has not happened in the past 30 days.
2 = This has happened a few times (1–6 times) in the past 30 days.
3 = This has happened often (7 times or more) in the past 30 days.

Event	Not at All	1–6 Times	7 Times or More
1. Laughing	1	2	3
2. Being relaxed	1	2	3
3. Being with happy people	1	2	3
4. Eating good meals	1	2	3
5. Thinking about something good in the future	1	2	3
6. Having people show interest in what you have said	1	2	3
7. Thinking about people I like	1	2	3
8. Seeing beautiful scenery	1	2	3
9. Breathing clean air	1	2	3
10. Being with friends	1	2	3
11. Having peace and quiet	1	2	3
12. Being noticed as sexually attractive	1	2	3
13. Kissing	1	2	3
14. Watching people	1	2	3
15. Having a frank and open conversation	1	2	3
16. Sitting in the sun	1	2	3
17. Wearing clean clothes	1	2	3
18. Having spare time	1	2	3
19. Doing a project in my own way	1	2	3
20. Sleeping soundly at night	1	2	3
21. Listening to music	1	2	3
22. Having sexual relations	1	2	3
23. Smiling at people	1	2	3
24. Being told I am loved	1	2	3
25. Reading stories, novels, poems, or plays	1	2	3
26. Planning or organizing something	1	2	3
27. Going to a restaurant	1	2	3

Pleasant Activities Schedule—*Continued*

Event	Not at All	1–6 Times	7 Times or More
28. Expressing my love to someone	1	2	3
29. Petting, necking	1	2	3
30. Being with someone I love	1	2	3
31. Seeing good things happen to my family or friends	1	2	3
32. Complimenting or praising someone	1	2	3
33. Having coffee, tea, a coke, etc., with friends	1	2	3
34. Meeting someone new of the same sex	1	2	3
35. Driving skillfully	1	2	3
36. Saying something clearly	1	2	3
37. Being with animals	1	2	3
38. Being popular at a gathering	1	2	3
39. Having a lively talk	1	2	3
40. Feeling the presence of the Lord in my life	1	2	3
41. Planning trips or vacations	1	2	3
42. Listening to the radio	1	2	3
43. Learning to do something new	1	2	3
44. Seeing old friends	1	2	3
45. Watching wild animals	1	2	3
46. Doing a job well	1	2	3
47. Being asked for my help or advice	1	2	3
48. Amusing people	1	2	3
49. Being complimented or told I have done well	1	2	3

Social Activities Questionnaire

The following is a list of events. How often have these events happened in your life in the past month? Please answer these questions by rating each item using the following guide:

1 = This has not happened in the past 30 days.
2 = This has happened a few times (1–6 times) in the past 30 days.
3 = This has happened often (7 times or more) in the past 30 days.

Event	Not at All	1–6 Times	7 Times or More
1. Talking with a friend	1	2	3
2. Going on a recreational outing (boating, camping, hiking, etc.)	1	2	3
3. Being in a class, discussion group, or encounter group	1	2	3
4. Going on my first date with someone	1	2	3
5. Receiving a telephone call from a friend	1	2	3
6. Initiating a conversation	1	2	3
7. Talking with my parent(s)	1	2	3
8. Being asked for my help or advice	1	2	3
9. Going to an office party	1	2	3
10. Talking with my child(ren) or grandchild(ren)	1	2	3
11. Visiting friends	1	2	3
12. Doing volunteer work or working on a community service project	1	2	3
13. Accepting a date or social invitation	1	2	3
14. Dancing	1	2	3
15. Being the first to say "hello" when I see someone I know	1	2	3
16. Having lunch or a coffee break with friends	1	2	3
17. Going to a bar or tavern	1	2	3
18. Introducing myself to someone	1	2	3
19. Talking with a stranger of the same sex	1	2	3
20. Introducing people I think would like each other	1	2	3
21. Going to a sports event (football, track meet, etc.)	1	2	3
22. Singing or playing a musical instrument in a group	1	2	3

Social Activities Questionnaire—*Continued*

Event	Not at All	1–6 Times	7 Times or More
23. Talking with my husband or wife	1	2	3
24. Going on a date	1	2	3
25. Being introduced to someone	1	2	3
26. Going to a church function	1	2	3
27. Playing cards or board games (checkers, Monopoly, etc.)	1	2	3
28. Going to a party	1	2	3
29. Inviting a friend or acquaintance to join me for some social activity	1	2	3
30. Walking up and joining a group of people	1	2	3
31. Going to a service, civic, special interest, or social club meeting	1	2	3
32. Going someplace where I know I must be sociable			
33. Talking with someone on the job or in class			
34. Talking with a stranger of the opposite sex	1	2	3
35. Joining a friend or friends for a social	1	2	3
activity	1	2	3
36. Giving a party or get-together	1	2	3
37. Calling a friend on the telephone	1	2	3
38. Having sexual relations	1	2	3
39. Going to a formal social affair	1	2	3
40. Having friends come to visit	1	2	3
41. Being at a party where I hardly know	1	2	3
anyone	1	2	3
42. Going to the movies with someone	1	2	3
43. Playing competitive team sports (softball, basketball, etc.)	1	2	3
44. Going to lectures or hearing speakers	1	2	3
45. Engaging in recreational sports with someone (tennis, bowling, skiing, etc.)	1	2	3
46. Attending a concert, play, opera, or ballet	1	2	3

Subjective Probability Questionnaire

For each item in this questionnaire, indicate what *you* think the chances are that the statement is true or that it will become true.

0 = Absolutely sure the item is not true or never will occur
1 =
2 =
3 =
4 = } Chances are less and less that the item is true or that it will become true.
5 = Chances are fifty-fifty that the item is true or that it will become true.
6 =
7 =
8 =
9 = } Chances are greater and greater than the item is true or that it will occur.
10 = Absolutely sure the item is true or will certainly occur.

Examples

A. "The Republicans will win the next presidential election."
0 1 2 3 4 5 6 7 8 9 10

You would choose:

0 If you are absolutely sure they'll lose.
1 If you are almost absolutely sure they'll lose.
2
3 } If you are more or less sure they will lose.
4 If you think they'll lose, but it will be close.
5 If you think it could go either way.
6 If you think they'll win, but it will be close.
7
8 } If you are more or less sure they will win.
9 If you are almost absolutely sure they'll win.
10 If you are absolutely sure they'll win.

B. "It will rain in San Francisco this winter."
0 1 2 3 4 5 6 7 8 9 (10)
You are absolutely sure it will.

C. "John F. Kennedy was a good president."
0 1 2 3 4 5 6 (7) 8 9 10
You are more or less sure he was.

D. "I have a good singing voice."
0 (1) 2 3 4 5 6 7 8 9 10
You are almost absolutely sure you don't.

---

1. I will accomplish the things that are really important to me in life.
0 1 2 3 4 5 6 7 8 9 10
2. I will commit suicide.
0 1 2 3 4 5 6 7 8 9 10
3. Somebody close to me will become fatally ill in the next five years.
0 1 2 3 4 5 6 7 8 9 10
4. My family and friends would be better off without me.
0 1 2 3 4 5 6 7 8 9 10
5. Life is really full of worthwhile things.
0 1 2 3 4 5 6 7 8 9 10
6. I am more likable than the average person.
0 1 2 3 4 5 6 7 8 9 10
7. I will have periods of great happiness.
0 1 2 3 4 5 6 7 8 9 10
8. I will make good choices during my life.
0 1 2 3 4 5 6 7 8 9 10
9. I can work as productively as the average person.
0 1 2 3 4 5 6 7 8 9 10
10. I am more intelligent than the average person.
0 1 2 3 4 5 6 7 8 9 10
11. My friends and family sincerely care for me.
0 1 2 3 4 5 6 7 8 9 10
12. I will be committed to a mental hospital.
0 1 2 3 4 5 6 7 8 9 10

Subjective Probability Questionnaire—*Continued*

13. I am less capable of loving than the average person.
    0 1 2 3 4 5 6 7 8 9 10
14. I am truly important in someone's life.
    0 1 2 3 4 5 6 7 8 9 10
15. I have less common sense than the average person.
    0 1 2 3 4 5 6 7 8 9 10
16. I have bad judgment about making important purchases.
    0 1 2 3 4 5 6 7 8 9 10
17. I will be able to make friends with the kind of people I really like.
    0 1 2 3 4 5 6 7 8 9 10
18. I am psychologically capable of being happy.
    0 1 2 3 4 5 6 7 8 9 10
19. I will be depressed for most of the next six months.
    0 1 2 3 4 5 6 7 8 9 10
20. I can handle my difficulties better than the average person.
    0 1 2 3 4 5 6 7 8 9 10
21. I am luckier than the average person.
    0 1 2 3 4 5 6 7 8 9 10
22. I will become seriously ill in the next five years.
    0 1 2 3 4 5 6 7 8 9 10
23. I will be selected for an honor.
    0 1 2 3 4 5 6 7 8 9 10
24. An imporant relationship of mine will end with bad feelings.
    0 1 2 3 4 5 6 7 8 9 10
25. I am failing to carry out my major responsibilities properly.
    0 1 2 3 4 5 6 7 8 9 10
26. I will be in good health most of my life.
    0 1 2 3 4 5 6 7 8 9 10
27. I make bad impressions on people.
    0 1 2 3 4 5 6 7 8 9 10

Subjective Probability Questionnaire—*Continued*

28. I will be very important in someone's life in the future.

    0 1 2 3 4 5 6 7 8 9 10

29. People would help me if I were in trouble.

    0 1 2 3 4 5 6 7 8 9 10

30. I am physically predisposed to being depressed.

    0 1 2 3 4 5 6 7 8 9 10

Personal Beliefs Inventory

Please read each of the statements below and indicate the extent of your agreement or disagreement with each item by circling the appropriate number next to each item:

1 = I disagree completely.
2 = I disagree slightly.
3 = I am neutral about this statement.
4 = I agree slightly.
5 = I agree completely.

There are no right or wrong answers. Please respond to each item.

1. Considering the blatant and widespread sexism in our society, it is unlikely that any concerned woman can be truly happy.	1	2	3	4	5
2. Some people could not be happy living in a small town or a large city because some of the things they need are not available there.	1	2	3	4	5
3. There are some people in this world who truly can be described as rotten.	1	2	3	4	5
4. If things are not the way one would like them to be, it is a catastrophe.	1	2	3	4	5
5. Given the kind of home life some people have had, it is almost impossible for them ever to be happy.	1	2	3	4	5
6. What others think of you is most important.	1	2	3	4	5
7. Persons living in slum conditions are almost certain to feel depressed or miserable.	1	2	3	4	5
8. Love and success are two basic human needs.	1	2	3	4	5
9. Avoiding life's difficulties and self-responsibilities is easier than facing them.	1	2	3	4	5
10. The main goal and purpose of life are achievement and success.	1	2	3	4	5
11. Failure at something one really wants to do is terrible.	1	2	3	4	5
12. People really can't help it when they feel angry, depressed, or guilty.	1	2	3	4	5
13. One should blame oneself severely for all mistakes and wrongdoings.	1	2	3	4	5

Symptoms Checklist

Are you *currently* having any of the following complaints of how you are feeling? Please check yes or no.

Complaint	Yes	No	Comments
1. Headaches	______	______	
2. Faintness or dizziness	______	______	
3. Hot or cold spells	______	______	
4. Pain in your neck or upper back	______	______	
5. Trouble getting your breath	______	______	
6. Pains in heart or chest	______	______	
7. Cough with or without phlegm	______	______	
8. Nausea or upset stomach	______	______	
9. Pain in abdomen or stomach	______	______	
10. Trouble swallowing	______	______	
11. Ulcers or sores in mouth	______	______	
12. Constipation	______	______	
13. Diarrhea	______	______	
14. Trouble with urine	______	______	
15. A lump in your throat	______	______	
16. Pains in lower back	______	______	
17. Soreness of your muscles	______	______	
18. Pains in knees, hands, hips, or shoulders	______	______	
19. Heavy feelings in your arms or legs	______	______	
20. Swelling of feet or legs	______	______	
21. Weakness in parts of your body	______	______	
22. Trouble with your speech or understanding other people	______	______	
23. Numbness or tingling in parts of your body	______	______	
24. Skin rashes	______	______	
25. Itching all over	______	______	
26. Fevers	______	______	
27. Tired all the time, no energy	______	______	
28. Pain that doctors couldn't explain	______	______	
29. Heart pounding or racing	______	______	
30. Trouble sleeping at night	______	______	

References

Abramson, L. Y., Seligman, M. E. P., & Teasdale, J. D. (1978). Learned helplessness in humans: Critique and reformulation. *Journal of Abnormal Psychology 87:* 49–74.

Abbey, A. & Andrews, F. M. (1986). Modeling the psychological determinants of life quality. In F. M. Andrews (ed.): *Research on the quality of life* (pp. 85–116). Ann Arbor: University of Michigan Survey Research Center.

Aguilar-Gaxiola, S. A. (1991). A Spanish-language expert system for computer-aided diagnosis of depression. In R. F. Muñoz (chair): *Prevention and treatment of depression in Spanish-speaking populations.* Symposium conducted at the Ninety-ninth Annual Convention of the American Psychological Association, San Francisco, August.

Akiskal, H. (1987). Overview of biobehavioral factors in the prevention of mood disorders. In R. F. Muñoz (ed.): *Depression prevention: Research directions* (pp. 263–280). Washington, D.C.: Hemisphere.

Akiskal, H. S. & McKinney, W. T., Jr. (1973). Depressive disorders: Towards a unified hypothesis. *Science 182:* 20–29.

Albee, G. (1985). The argument for primary prevention. *Journal of Primary Prevention 5:* 213–219.

Albee, G. W. (1982). Preventing psychopathology and promoting human potential. *American Psychologist 37:* 1043–1050.

American Psychiatric Association. (1987). *Diagnostic and statistical manual of mental disorders (DSM-III-R)* (3rd ed. revised). Washington, D.C.: American Psychiatric Association.

Anda, R. F., Williamson, D. F., Escobedo, L. G., Mast, E. E., Giovino, G. A. & Remington, P. L. (1990). Depression and the dynamics of smoking: A national perspective. *Journal of the American Medical Association 264:* 1541–1545.

Andreasen, N. C. (1984). *The broken brain: The biological revolution in psychiatry.* New York: Harper & Row.

Andreasen, N. C. (in press). The genetics of affective disorders: An overview. In B. L. Bloom & K. Schlesinger (eds.): *Boulder symposium on clinical psychology: Depression.* Hillsdale, N.J.: Erlbaum.

Andreasen, N. C., Scheftner, W., Reich, T., Hirschfeld, R. M. A., Endicott, J. & Keller, M. B. (1986). The validation of the concept of endogenous depression: A family study approach. *Archives of General Psychiatry 43:* 246–251.

Andrews, F. M. & McKennell, A. C. (1980). Measures of self-reported well-being: Their affective, cognitive, and other components. *Social Indicators Research 8:* 127–155.

References

Andrews, F. M. & Withey, S. B. (1976). *Social indicators of well-being: Americans' perceptions of life quality.* New York: Plenum Press.

Baldessarini, R. J. (1983). *Biomedical aspects of depression and its treatment.* Washington, D.C.: American Psychiatric Press.

Bandura, A. (1969). *Principles of behavior modification.* New York: Holt, Rinehart & Winston.

Bandura, A. (1977). *Social learning theory.* Englewood Cliffs, N.J.: Prentice-Hall.

Barber, J. G., Bradshaw, R. & Walsh, C. (1989). Reducing alcohol consumption through television advertising. *Journal of Consulting and Clinical Psychology 57:* 613–618.

Barinaga, M. (1989). Manic depression gene put in limbo. *Science 246:* 886–887.

Baron, M., Risch, N., Hamburger, R., Mandel, B., Kushner, S., Newman, M., Drumer, D. & Belmaker, R. H. (1987). Genetic linkage between X-chromosome markers and bipolar affective illness. *Nature 326:* 289–292.

Barrett, J. E., Barrett, J. A., Oxman, T. E. & Gerber, P. D. (1988). The prevalence of psychiatric disorders in a primary care practice. *Archives of General Psychiatry 45:* 1100–1106.

Barsky, A. J. (1981). Hidden reasons some patients visit doctors. *Annals of Internal Medicine 94:* 492.

Batki, S. L., Sorensen, J. L., Gibson, D. R. & Maude-Griffin, P. (1988). HIV-infected drug users in methadone treatment: Outcome and psychological correlates—A preliminary report. In L. S. Harris (ed.): *Problems of drug dependence 1989: Proceedings of the Fifty-first annual scientific meeting of the committee on the problems of drug dependence: NIDA research monograph series 95* (pp. 405–406). Washington, D.C.: U.S. Government Printing Office.

Batki, S. L., Sorensen, J. L., Faltz, G. & Madover, S. (1989). Psychiatric aspects of treatment of IV drug abusers with AIDS. *Hospital and Community Psychiatry 39:* 439–441.

Beardslee, W. P. (1990). Development of a clinician-based preventive intervention for families with affective disorders. *Journal of Preventive Psychiatry and Allied Disciplines 4:* 39–61.

Beck, A. T. (1967). *Depression: Causes and treatment.* Philadelphia: University of Pennsylvania Press.

Beck, A. T., Rush, A. J., Shaw, B. F. & Emery, G. (1979). *Cognitive therapy of depression.* New York: Guilford.

Beck, A. T., Steer, R. A. & Garbin, M. G. (1988). Psychometric properties of the Beck Depression Inventory: Twenty-five years of evaluation. *Clinical Psychology Review 8:* 77–100.

Beck, A. T., Ward, C. H., Mendelsohn, M., Mock, J. & Erbaugh, J. (1961). An inventory for measuring depression. *Archives of General Psychiatry 4:* 561–571.

Bellack, A. S., Hersen, M. & Himmelhoch, J. (1981). Social skills training compared with pharmacotherapy and psychotherapy in the treatment of unipolar depression. *American Journal of Psychiatry 138:* 1562–1567.

Bergland, R. (1985). *The fabric of mind.* New York: Viking Penguin.

Berrettini, W. H., Goldin, L. R., Gelernter, J., Gejman, P. V., Gershon, E. S. & Detera-Wadleigh, S. (1990). X-chromosome markers and manic-depressive illness. *Archives of General Psychiatry 47:* 366–373.

Bloom, B. L. (1977). *Community mental health: A general introduction.* Monterey, Calif.: Brooks/Cole.

Bloom, B. L. (1985). Stressful life event theory and research: Implications for primary prevention (DHHS Publication No. ADM 85-1385). Washington, D.C.: U.S. Government Printing Office.

Bloom, B. L., Hodges, W. F. & Caldwell, R. A. (1982). A preventive intervention program for the newly separated: Initial evaluation. *American Journal of Community Psychology 10:* 251–264.

Bond, L. A. & Joffe, J. M. (1982). *Facilitating infant and early childhood development.* Hanover, N.H.: University Press of New England.

Boulette, T. R. (1980). Priority issues for mental health promotion among low-income Chicanos/Mexicanos. In R. Valle & W. Vega (eds.): *Hispanic natural support systems: Mental health promotion perspectives* (pp. 15–23). State of California, Department of Mental Health, Office of Prevention.

Bower, G. (1981). Mood and memory. *American Psychologist 36:* 129–148.

Boyd, J. H. & Weissman, M. M. (1982). Epidemiology. In E. S. Paykel (ed.): *Handbook of affective disorders* (pp. 109–125). New York: Guilford.

Bradburn, N. (1969). *The structure of psychological well-being.* Chicago: Aldine.

Bradburn, N. & Caplovitz, D. (1965). *Reports on happiness: A pilot study of behavior related to mental health.* Chicago: Aldine.

Breckenridge, J. N. (1987). Structural equation models for depression prevention research. In R. F. Muñoz (ed.): *Depression prevention: Research directions* (pp. 235–262). Washington, D.C.: Hemisphere.

Brown, G. W. & Harris, T. (1978). *Social origins of depression.* London: Tavistock Publications.

Brown, J. H., Henteleff, P. & Barakat, S. (1986). Is it normal for terminally ill patients to desire death? *American Journal of Psychiatry 143:* 208–211.

Brown, R. & Lewinsohn, P. M. (1984). A psychoeducational approach to the treatment of depression: Comparison of group, individual, and minimal contact procedures. *Journal of Consulting and Clinical Psychology 52:* 774–783.

Bruce, M. L., Takeuchi, D. T. & Leaf, P. J. (1991). Poverty and psychiatric status: Longitudinal evidence from the New Haven Epidemiologic Catchment Area Study. *Archives of General Psychiatry 48:* 470–474.

Buckner, J. C., Trickett, E. J. & Corse, S. J. (1985). *Primary prevention in mental health: An annotated bibliography* (DHHS Publication No. ADM 85-1405). Washington, D.C.: U.S. Government Printing Office.

Burling, T. A., Marotta, J., González, R., Moltzen, J. O., Eng, A. M., Schmidt, G. A., Welch, R. L., Ziff, D. C. & Reilly, P. M. (1989). Computerized smoking cessation program for the worksite: Treatment outcome and feasibility. *Journal of Consulting and Clinical Psychology 57:* 619–622.

Burnam, M. A., Hough, R. L., Escobar, J. I., Karno, M., Timers, D. M., Telles, C. A. & Locke, B. Z. (1987). Six-month prevalence of specific psychiatric disorders among Mexican American and non-Hispanic whites in Los Angeles. *Archives of General Psychiatry 44:* 687–694.

Burnam, M. A., Wells, K. B., Leake, B. & Landsverk, J. (1988). Development of a brief screening instrument for detecting depressive disorders. *Medical Care 26:* 775–789.

Burns, D. (1980). *Feeling good: The new mood therapy.* New York: William Morrow.

Cadoret, R. J. & Widmer, R. B. (1980). Somatic complaints—harbinger of depression in primary care. *Journal of Affective Disorders 2:* 61–70.

Campbell, A., Converse, R. E. & Rodgers, W. L. (1976). *The quality of American life.* New York: Russell Sage.

Campbell, D. T. & Stanley, J. C. (1963). *Experimental and quasi-experimental designs for research.* Chicago: Rand McNally.

Canino, G. J., Bird, H. R., Shrout, P. E., Rubio-Stipec, M., Bravo, M., Martinez, R., Sesman, M. & Guevara, L. M. (1987). The prevalence of specific psychiatric disorders in Puerto Rico. *Archives of General Psychiatry 44:* 727–735.

Caplan, G. & Grunebaum, H. (1972). Perspectives on primary prevention: A review. In H. Gottesfeld (ed.): *The critical issues of community mental health.* New York: Behavioral Press.

Caplan, R. D., Cobb, S., French, J. R. P., Van Hamson, R. & Pinneau, S. R. (1975). *Job demands and worker health: Main effects and occupational difference.* Washington, D.C.: National Institute of Occupational Safety and Health Research Report, DHEW Publication No. NIOSH 75-160.

Caplan, R. D., Vinokur, A. D., Price, R. H. & van Ryn, M. (1989). Job seeking, reemployment, and mental health: A randomized field experiment coping with job loss. *Journal of Applied Psychology 74:* 759–769.

Centers for Disease Control. (1987). Premature mortality due to suicide and homicide—United States, 1984. *Morbidity Mortalilty Weekly Report 36:* 531–534.

Chiang, C. L. (1968). *An introduction to stochastic processes and their applications.* Huntington, N.Y.: Robert E. Krieger Publishing Company.

Christensen, A., Miller, W. R. & Muñoz, R. F. (1978). Paraprofessionals, partners, peers, paraphernalia, and print: Expanding mental health service delivery. *Professional Psychology 9:* 249–270.

Ciaranello, R. D. & Ciaranello, A. L. (1991). Genetics of major psychiatric disorders. *Annual Review of Medicine 42:* 151–158.

Clarke, G. N. (1990). *Health class curriculum for the primary prevention of affective symptoms and disorder in high school adolescents.* Unpublished manuscript, Oregon Health Sciences University.

Clayton, P. J. (1987). Preventing depression: The symptoms, the syndrome, or the disorder? In R. F. Muñoz (ed.): *Depression prevention: Research directions* (pp. 31–43). Washington, D.C.: Hemisphere.

Coffman, J. A. (1989). Computed tomography. In N. C. Andreasen (ed.): *Brain imaging: Applications in psychiatry* (pp. 1–65). Washington, D.C.: American Psychiatric Press.

Coulehan, J. L., Schulberg, H. C. & Block, M. R. (1989). The efficiency of depression questionnaires for case finding in primary medical care. *Journal of General Internal Medicine 4:* 541–547.

Coyne, J. C. & Gotlib, I. H. (1983). The role of cognition in depression: A critical appraisal. *Psychological Bulletin 94:* 472–505.

Crowne, D. & Marlowe, D. (1960). A new scale of social desirability independent of psychopathology. *Journal of Consulting Psychology 24:* 349–354.

Crowne, D. & Marlowe, D. (1964). *The approval motive.* New York: Wiley.

DeGowin, E. L. & DeGowin, R. L. (1976). *Bedside diagnostic examination.* New York: Macmillan.

Depue, R. A. & Iacono, W. G. (1989). Neurobehavioral aspects of affective disorders. *Annual Review of Psychology 40:* 457–492.

Detera-Wadleigh, S. D., Berrettini, W. H., Goldin, L. R., Boorman, D., Anderson, S. & Gershon, E. S. (1987). Close linkage of c-Harvey-*ras*-1 and the insulin gene to affective disorder is ruled out in three North American pedigrees. *Nature 325:* 806–807.

DiMascio, A., Weissman, M. M., Prusoff, B. A., Neu, C., Zwilling, M. & Klerman, G. L. (1979). Differential symptom reduction by drugs and psychotherapy in acute depression. *Archives of General Psychiatry 36:* 1450–1456.

Dorr, D. (1977). Intervention and prevention: I. Preventive intervention. In I. Iscoe, B. L. Bloom & C. D. Spielberger (eds.): *Community psychology in transition* (pp. 87–93). Washington, D.C.: Hemisphere.

Dubos, R. (1959). *Mirage of health: Utopias, progress, and biological change.* Garden City, N.Y.: Doubleday.

Eaton, W. W. & Kessler, L. G. (eds.). (1985). *Epidemiologic field methods in psychiatry: The NIMH epidemiologic catchment area program.* Orlando, Fla.: Academic Press.

Eaton, W. W., Kramer, M., Anthony, J. C., Dryman, A., Shapiro, S. & Locke, B. Z. (1989). The incidence of specific DIS/DSM-III mental disorders: Data from the NIMH Epidemiologic Catchment Area Program. *Acta Psychiatrica Scandinavica 79:* 163–178.

Egeland, J. A., Gerhard, D. S., Pauls, D. L., Sussex, J. N., Kidd, K. K., Allen, C. R., Hostetter, A. M. & Housman, D. E. (1987). Bipolar affective disorders linked to DNA markers on chromosome 11. *Nature 325:* 783–787.

Ehlers, C. L., Frank, E. & Kupfer, D. J. (1988). Social zeitgebers and biological rhythms: A unified approach to understanding the etiology of depression. *Archives of General Psychiatry 45:* 948–952.

Eisenberg, L. (1986). Primary prevention and child development. In J. T. Barter & S. W. Talbott (eds.): *Primary prevention in psychiatry* (pp. 71–84). Washington, D.C.: American Psychiatric Press, Inc.

Elkin, I., Shea, T., Watkins, J. T., Imber, S. D., Sotsky, S. M., Collins, J. F., Glass, D. R., Pilkonis, P. A., Leber, W. R., Docherty, J. P., Fiester, S. J. & Parloff, M. B. (1989). National Institute of Mental Health Treatment of Depression Collaborative Research Program: General effectiveness of treatments. *Archives of General Psychiatry 46:* 971–982.

Ellis, A. (1962). *Reason and emotion in psychotherapy.* New York: Stewart.

Ellis, A. & Harper, R. A. (1961). *A guide to rational living.* Hollywood: Wilshire.

Ellis, A. & Harper, R. A. (1975). *New guide to rational living.* Englewood Cliffs, N.J.: Prentice-Hall.

Escobar, J. I., Golding, J. M., Hough, R. L., Karno, M., Burnam, M. A. & Wells, K. B. (1987). Somatization in the community: Relationship of disability and use of services. *American Journal of Public Health 77:* 837–840.

Escobar, J. I., Rubio-Stipec, M., Canino, G. & Karno, M. (1989). Somatic Symptoms Index (SSI): A new abridged somatization construct. *Journal of Nervous and Mental Disease 177:* 140–146.

Field, T., Healy, B., Goldstein, S., Perry, S. & Bendell, D. (1988). Infants of depressed mothers show "depressed" behavior even with nondepressed adults. *Child Development 59:* 1569–1579.

Flanagan, J. C. (1978). A research approach to improving our quality of life. *American Psychologist 33:* 138–147.

Flanagan, J. C. (1979). *Identifying opportunities for improving the quality of life of older age groups.* Palo Alto: American Institute for Research.

Fletcher, R. H., Fletcher, S. W. & Wagner, E. H. (1988). *Clinical epidemiology: The essentials* (2nd ed.). Baltimore: Williams & Wilkins.

Follette, W. & Cummings, N. A. (1967). Psychiatric services and medical utilization in a prepaid health plan setting. *Medical Care 5:* 25–35.

Fox, J. P., Hall, C. E. & Elveback, L. R. (1970). *Epidemiology: Man and disease.* London: Macmillan.

Frances, A. J., Widiger, T. A. & Pincus, H. A. (1989). The development of DSM-IV. *Archives of General Psychiatry 46:* 373–375.

Frank, J. D. (1973). *Persuasion and healing: A comparative study of psychotherapy* (2nd ed.). Baltimore: Johns Hopkins University Press.

Frank, J. D. & Frank, J. B. (1991). *Persuasion and healing: A comparative study of psychotherapy* (3rd ed.). Baltimore: Johns Hopkins University Press.

Frankl, V. (1955). *The doctor and the soul: An introduction to logotherapy.* New York: Alfred A. Knopf.

Freymann, J. G. (1975). Medicine's great schism: Prevention vs. cure: An historical interpretation. *Medical Care 13:* 539–552.

Gambrill, E. D. & Richey, C. A. (1975). An assertion inventory for use in assessment and research. *Behavior Therapy 6:* 550–561.

German, P. S., Shapiro, S., Skinner, E. A. et al. (1987). Detection and management of mental health problems of older patients by primary care providers. *Journal of the American Medical Association 257:* 489–493.

Gershon, E. S. (1983). The genetics of affective disorders. In L. Grinspoon (ed.): *Psychiatry update* (vol. 2, pp. 434–457). Washington, D.C.: American Psychiatric Press.

Gershon, E. S., Hamovit, J. Guroff, J. J., Dibble, E., Leckman, J. F., Sceery, W., Targum, S., Nurnberger, J. I., Goldin, L. R. & Bunney, W. E. (1982). A family study of schizoaffective, bipolar I, bipolar II, unipolar, and normal control probands. *Archives of General Psychiatry 39:* 1157–1167.

Glassman, A. H., Helzer, J. E., Covey, L. S., Cottler, L. B., Stetner, F., Tipp, J. E. & Johnson, J. (1990). Smoking, smoking cessation, and major depression. *Journal of the American Medical Association 264:* 1546–1549.

Glassman, A. H., Stetner, F., Walsh, B. T., Raizman, P. S., Fleiss, J. L., Cooper, T. B. & Covey, L. S. (1988). Heavy smokers, smoking cessation and clonidine: Results of a double-blind, randomized trial. *Journal of the American Medical Association 259:* 2863–2866.

Glidewell, J. C. (1983). Afterword: Prevention—The threat and the promise. In R. D. Felner, L. A. Jason, J. N. Moritsugu & S. S. Farber (eds.): *Preventive psychology: Theory, research, and practice* (pp. 310–312). New York: Pergamon Press.

Gold, P. W., Goodwin, F. K. & Chrousos, G. P. (1988). Clinical and biochemical manifestations of depression: Relation to the neurobiology of stress. *New England Journal of Medicine 319:* 348–353; 413–420.

Gold, M. S., Pottash, L. C. & Extein, I. (1981). Hypothyroidism and depression. *Journal of the American Medical Association 245:* 1919–1922.

Goldin, L. R. & Gershon, E. S. (1988). The genetic epidemiology of major depressive illness. In A. J. Frances & R. E. Hales (eds.): *Review of psychiatry* (vol. 7, pp. 149–168). Washington, D.C.: American Psychiatric Press.

Goldston, S. E. (1977). Defining primary prevention. In G. W. Albee & J. M. Joffe (eds.): *Primary prevention of psychopathology* (vol. 1, pp. 18–23). Hanover, N.H.: University Press of New England.

González, G. M., Muñoz, R. F., Pérez-Arce, P. & Batki, S. (in press). Depression and HIV disease in injection drug users: A Spanish-language feasibility study. *Psychology of Addictive Behaviors.*

González, G. M., Muñoz, R. F. & Starkweather, J. (1991). Automated screening for depression using computerized speech recognition. In R. F. Muñoz (Chair), *Prevention and treatment of depression in Spanish-speaking populations.* Symposium conducted at the 99th Annual Convention of the American Psychological Association, San Francisco, August.

Goodman, J. (1990). The laugh resort. *Sesame Street Magazine: Parents' Guide,* November, pp. 40–43.

Gruenberg, E. M. (1981). Risk factor research methods. In D. A. Regier & G. Allen (eds.): *Risk factor research in the major mental disorders* (DHHS Publication No. ADM 81-1086, pp. 8–19). Washington, D.C.: U.S. Government Printing Office.

Halbreich, U. (1987). Hormones and depression—conceptual transitions. In U. Halbreich (ed.): *Hormones and depression* (pp. 1–20). New York: Raven Press.

Hall, S. M., Muñoz, R. F. & Reus, V. (1991). Depression and smoking treatment: A clinical trial of an affect regulation treatment. In *Problems of Drug Dependence 1991: Proceedings of the 53rd Annual Scientific Meeting, The Committee on Problems of Drug Dependence, Inc.* Rockville, Md.: NIDA. Abstract.

Hammen, C. (in press). Psychological vulnerability to depression: A cognitive-environmental perspective. In B. L. Bloom & K. Schlesinger (eds.): *Boulder symposium on clinical psychology: Depression.* Hillsdale, N.J.: Erlbaum.

Hankin, J., Steinwachs, D., Regier, D., Burns, B., Goldberg, I. & Hoeper, E. (1982). Use of general medical care services by persons with mental disorders. *Archives of General Psychiatry 39:* 225–231.

Harding, S. D. (1982). Psychological well-being in Great Britain: An evaluation of the Bradburn Affect-Balance Scale. *Personality and Individual Differences 3:* 167–175.

Harrington, R., Fudge, H., Rutter, M., Pickles, A. & Hill, J. (1990). Adult outcomes of childhood and adolescent depression: I. Psychiatric status. *Archives of General Psychiatry 47:* 465–473.

Hartman, B. J. (1968). Sixty revealing questions for twenty minutes. *Rational Living 3:* 7–8.

Hodgkinson, S., Sherrington, R., Gurling, H., Marchbanks, R., Reeders, S., Mallet, J., McInnis, M., Petursson, H. & Brynjolfsson, J. (1987). Molecular genetic evidence for heterogeneity in manic depression. *Nature 325:* 805–806.

Hoeper, E. W., Nycz, G. R., Cleary, P. D., Regier, D. A. & Goldberg, I. D. (1979). Estimated prevalence of RDC mental disorder in primary medical care. *International Journal of Mental Health 8:* 6–15.

Hoeper, E., Nycz, G., Regier, D., Goldberg, I., Jacobson, A. & Hankin, J. (1980). Diagnosis of mental disorder in adults and increased use of health services in four outpatient settings. *American Journal of Psychiatry 137:* 207–210.

Hollon, S. D. & Najavits, L. (1988). Review of empirical studies on cognitive therapy. In A. J. Frances & R. E. Hales (eds.): *Review of psychiatry,* (vol. 7, pp. 643–666). Washington, D.C.: American Psychiatry Press.

Hollon, S. D., Shelton, R. C. & Loosen, P. T. (1991). Cognitive therapy and pharmacotherapy for depression. *Journal of Consulting and Clinical Psychology 59:* 88–99.

Holmes, T. H. & Rahe, R. H. (1967). The social adjustment rating scale. *Journal of Psychosomatic Research 11:* 213–218.

Hough, R. L., Gongla, P. A., Brown, V. B. & Goldston, S. E. (eds.). (1986). *Psychiatric epidemiology and prevention: The possibilities.* Los Angeles: University of California, Neuropsychiatric Institute.

Hough, R. L., Landsverk, J. A., Karno, M., Burnam, M. A., Timbers, D. M., Escobar, J. I. & Regier, D. A. (1987). Utilization of health and mental health services by Los Angeles Mexican Americans and non-Hispanic whites. *Archives of General Psychiatry 44:* 702–709.

Hulley, S. B. & Cummings, S. R. (eds.). (1988). *Designing clinical research: An epidemiologic approach.* Baltimore: Williams & Wilkins.

Imber, S. D., Pilkonis, P. A., Sotsky, S. M., Elkin, I., Watkins, J. T., Collins, J. F., Shea, M. T., Leber, W. R. & Glass, D. R. (1990). Mode-specific effects among three treatments for depression. *Journal of Consulting and Clinical Psychology 58:* 352–359.

Iscoe, I. (1977). Introduction. In I. Iscoe, B. L. Bloom & C. D. Spielberger (eds.): *Community psychology in transition* (pp. 68–70). Washington, D.C.: Hemisphere.

Iscoe, I. & Spielberger, C. D. (1977). Community psychology: The historical context. In I. Iscoe, B. L. Bloom & C. D. Spielberger (eds.): *Community psychology in transition* (pp. 3–16). Washington, D.C.: Hemisphere.

Joffe, J. M. & Albee, G. W. (eds.). (1981). *Prevention through political action and social change.* Hanover, N.H.: University Press of New England.

Jones, L. R., Badger, L. W., Ficken, R. P., Leeper, J. D. & Anderson, R. L. (1987). Inside the hidden mental health network: Examining mental health care delivery of primary care physicians. *General Hospital Psychiatry 9:* 287–293.

Joyce, P. R. & Paykel, E. S. (1989). Predictors of drug response in depression. *Archives of General Psychiatry 46:* 89–99.

Kandel, D. B. & Davies, M. (1986). Adult sequelae of adolescent depressive symptoms. *Archives of General Psychiatry 43:* 255–262.

Kaplan, R. M. (1985). Behavioral epidemiology: Health promotion and health services. *Medical Care 23:* 564–583.

Kaplan, G. A., Roberts, R. E., Camacho, T. & Coyne, J. C. (1987). Psychosocial predictors of depression. *American Journal of Epidemiology 125:* 206–220.

Karno, M., Burnam, M. A., Escobar, J. I., Hough, R. L. & Eaton, W. W. (1983). Development of the Spanish-language version of the National Institute of Mental Health Diagnostic Interview Schedule. *Archives of General Psychiatry 40:* 1183–1188.

Katon, W. (1987). The epidemiology of depression in medical care. *International Journal of Psychiatry and Medicine 17:* 93–112.

Katon, W., Berg, A. O., Robins, A. J. & Risse, S. (1986). Depression—Medical utilization and somatization. *Western Journal of Medicine 144:* 564–568.

Katz, M. M., Secunda, S. K., Hirschfeld, R. M. A. & Koslow, S. H. (1979). NIMH clinical research branch collaborative program on the psychobiology of depression. *Archives of General Psychiatry 36:* 765–771.

Kellam, S. G. & Werthamer-Larsson, L. (1986). Developmental epidemiology: A basis for prevention. In M. Kessler & S. E. Goldston (eds.): *A decade of progress in primary prevention.* Hanover, N.H.: University Press of New England.

Kelly, G. A. (1955). *The psychology of personal constructs.* New York: Norton.

Kelly, J. G., Dassoff, N., Levin, I., Schreckengost, J., Stelzner, S. P. & Altman, B. E. (1988). *A guide to conducting prevention research in the community: First steps.* New York: Haworth.

Kelly, J. G., Snowden, L. R. & Muñoz, R. F. (1977). Social and community interventions. *Annual Review of Psychology, 28:* 323–361.

Kelsoe, J. R., Ginns, E. I., Egeland, J. A., Gerhard, D. S., Goldstein, A. M., Bale, S. J., Pauls, D. L., Long, R. T., Kidd, K. K., Conte, G., Housman, D. E. & Paul, S. M. (1989). Re-evaluation of the linkage relationship between chromosome 11p loci and the gene for bipolar affective disorder in the Old Order Amish. *Nature 342:* 238–243.

Kennedy, J. F. (1963). *Message from the President of the United States relative to mental illness and mental retardation* (88th Congress, First Session, U.S. House of Representatives Document No. 58). Washington, D.C.: U.S. Government Printing Office.

Kessler, M. & Goldston, S. E. (eds.). (1986). *A decade of progress in primary prevention.* Hanover, N.H.: University Press of New England.

Kuo, W. (1984). Prevalence of depression among Asian-Americans. *Journal of Nervous and Mental Disease 172:* 449–457.

Kupfer, D. J., Frank, E. & Perel, J. M. (1989). The advantage of early treatment intervention in recurrent depression. *Archives of General Psychiatry 46:* 771–775.

Lang, J. G., Muñoz, R. F., Bernal, G. & Sorensen, J. L. (1982). Quality of life and psychological well-being in a bicultural Latino community. *Hispanic Journal of Behavioral Sciences 4:* 433–450.

Lamb, H. R. (1985). The argument against primary prevention. *Journal of Primary Prevention 5:* 220–224.

Laycock, S. R. (1966). Promoting mental health in the school. In H. P. David (ed.): *International trends in mental health*. New York: McGraw-Hill.

Leighton, A. (1990). Community mental health and information underload. *Community Mental Health Journal 26:* 49–67.

Lewinsohn, P. M. (1975). The behavioral study and treatment of depression. In M. Hersen, R. M. Eisler & P. M. Miller (eds.): *Progress in behavior modification* (vol. 1, pp. 19–64). New York: Academic Press.

Lewinsohn, P. M. (1987). The coping-with-depression course. In R. F. Muñoz (ed.): *Depression prevention: Research directions* (pp. 159–170). Washington, D.C.: Hemisphere.

Lewinsohn, P. M., Antonuccio, D. O., Steinmetz, J. & Teri, L. (1984). *The coping with depression course: A psychoeducational intervention for unipolar depression*. Eugene, Oreg.: Castalia Press.

Lewinsohn, P. M., Biglan, A. & Zeiss, A. M. (1976). Behavioral treatment of depression. In P. O. Davidson (ed.): *The behavioral management of anxiety, depression and pain* (pp. 91–146). New York: Brunner/Mazel.

Lewinsohn, P. M. & Graf, M. (1973). Pleasant activities and depression. *Journal of Consulting and Clinical Psychology 41:* 261–268.

Lewinsohn, P. M., Hoberman, H. M. & Clarke, G. N. (1989). The coping with depression course: Review and future directions. *Canadian Journal of Behavioral Science 21:* 471–493.

Lewinsohn, P. M., Hoberman, H. M. & Rosenbaum, M. (1988). A prospective study of risk factors for unipolar depression. *Journal of Abnormal Psychology 97:* 251–264.

Lewinsohn, P. M., Hoberman, H., Teri, L. & Hautzinger, M. (1985). An integrative theory of depression. In S. Reiss & R. Bootzin (eds.): *Theoretical issues in behavior therapy* (pp. 331–359). New York: Academic Press.

Lewinsohn, P. M., Hops, H., Roberts, R. E. & Seeley, J. R. (1988). *The prevalence of affective and other disorders among older adolescents*. Paper presented at the annual meeting of the American Public Health Association, Boston, Mass., November.

Lewinsohn, P. M. & Libet, J. (1972). Pleasant events, activity schedules and depression. *Journal of Abnormal Psychology 79:* 291–295.

Lewinsohn, P. M. & MacPhillamy, D. J. (1974). The relationship between age and engagement in pleasant activities. *Journal of Gerontology 29:* 290–294.

Lewinsohn, P. M., Muñoz, R. F., Youngren, M. A. & Zeiss, A. M. (1978). *Control your depression*. New York: Prentice Hall.

Lewinsohn, P. M., Muñoz, R. F., Youngren, M. A. & Zeiss, A. M. (1986). *Control your depression* (rev. ed.). New York: Prentice Hall.

Lewinsohn, P. M., Steinmetz, J. L., Larson, D. W. & Franklin, J. (1981). Depression-related cognitions: Antecedent or consequence? *Journal of Abnormal Psychology 90:* 213–219.

Lieberman, A. F., Weston, D. R. & Pawl, J. H. (1991). Preventive intervention and outcome with anxiously attached dyads. *Child Development 62:* 199–209.

Lieberman, M. A. & Borman, L. D. (1981). The impact of self-help groups on widows' mental health. The National Research and Information Center's *National Reporter 4:* 2–6.

Linehan, M. M., Goldfried, M. R. & Goldfried, A. P. (1979). Assertion therapy: Skill training or cognitive restructuring. *Behavior Therapy 10:* 372–388.

Link, B. & Dohrenwend, B. (1980). Formulation of hypotheses about the true prevalence of demoralization in the United States. In B. P. Dohrenwend, B. S. Dohrenwend, M. S. Gould, B. Lind, R. Neugebauer & R. Wunsch-Hitzig (eds.): *Mental illness in the United States: Epidemiological estimates.* New York: Praeger.

Lipman, R. S., Covi, L. & Shapiro, A. K. (1979). The Hopkins Symptom Checklist. *Journal of Affective Disorders 1:* 9–24.

Linn, L. S. & Yager, J. (1980). The effect of screening, sensitization, and feedback on notation of depression. *Journal of Medical Education 55:* 942–949.

Linn, L. S. & Yager, J. (1984). Recognition of depression and anxiety by primary physicians. *Psychosomatics 25:* 593–600.

Lobel, B. & Hirschfeld, R. M. A. (1984). *Depression: What we know* (DHHS Publication No. ADM 85-1318). Washington, D.C.: U.S. Government Printing Office.

Louks, J., Hayne, C. & Smith, J. (1989). Replicated factor structure of the Beck Depression Inventory. *Journal of Nervous and Mental Disease 177:* 473–479.

Lowry, M. R. (1984). *Major depression: Prevention and treatment.* St. Louis: W. H. Green.

Maccoby, N. & Alexander, J. (1979). Reducing heart disease risk using the mass media: Comparing the effects on three communities. In R. F. Muñoz, L. R. Snowden & J. G. Kelly (eds.): *Social and psychological research in community settings* (pp. 69–100). San Francisco: Jossey-Bass.

MacPhillamy, D. J. & Lewinsohn, P. M. (1971). The Pleasant Events Schedule. Mimeograph, University of Oregon.

MacPhillamy, D. J. & Lewinsohn, P. M. (1974). Depression as a function of levels of desired and obtained pleasure. *Journal of Abnormal Psychology 83:* 651–657.

Mahoney, M. J. & Thoresen, C. E. (1974). *Self-control: Power to the person.* Monterey, Calif.: Brooks/Cole.

Marsella, A. J., Hirschfeld, R. M. A. & Katz, M. M. (1987). *The measurement of depression.* New York: Guilford.

Martinsen, E. W., Medhus, A. & Sandvik, L. (1985). Effects of aerobic exercise on depression: a controlled study. *British Medical Journal 291:* 109.

McGuffin, P. & Katz, R. (1986a). Genetics and psychopathology: Prospects for prevention. In M. Kessler & S. E. Goldston (eds.): *A decade of progress in primary prevention* (pp. 49–86). Hanover, N.H.: University Press of New England.

McGuffin, P. & Katz, R. (1986b). Nature, nurture and affective disorder. In J. F. W. Deakin (ed.): *The biology of depression: Proceedings of a meeting of the Biological Group of the Royal College of Psychiatrists held at Manchester University, 1985* (pp. 26–52). U.K.: Gaskell.

McKennell, A. C. (1978). Cognition and affect in the perception of well-being. *Social Indicators Research 5:* 389–426.
McKennell, A. C. & Andrews, F. M. (1980). Models for cognition and affect in the perception of well-being. *Social Indicators Research 8:* 257–298.
McReynolds, P. (1989). Diagnosis and clinical assessment: Current status and major issues. *Annual Review of Psychology 40:* 83–108.
Mechanic, D. (1972). Social and psychological factors affecting the presentation of bodily complaints. *New England Journal of Medicine 286:* 1132–1139.
Mechanic, D., Cleary, P. D. & Greenley, J. R. (1982). Distress syndrome, illness behavior, access to care, and medical utilization in a defined population. *Medical Care 20:* 361–372.
Meichenbaum, D. (1975). A self-instructional approach to stress management: A proposal for stress inoculation training. In I. Sarason & C. P. Spielberger (eds.): *Stress and anxiety* (pp. 213–247). New York: Wiley.
Mendlewicz, J. (1988). Genetics of depression and mania. In A. Georgotas & R. Cancro (eds.): *Depression and mania* (pp. 196–212). New York: Elsevier.
Metalsky, G. I., Abramson, L. Y., Seligman, M. E. P., Semmel, A. & Peterson, C. (1982). Attributional styles and life events in the classroom: Vulnerability and invulnerability to depressive mood reactions. *Journal of Personality and Social Psychology 43:* 612–617.
Miller, W. R. & Muñoz, R. F. (1982). *How to control your drinking* (rev. ed.). Albuquerque, N.M.: University of New Mexico Press.
Millon, T. & Klerman, G. L. (eds.). (1986). *Contemporary directions in psychopathology: Toward the DSM-IV.* New York: Guilford.
Miranda, J., Muñoz, R. F. & Shumway, M. (1990). Depression prevention research: The need for screening scales that truly predict. In C. C. Attkisson & J. M. Zich (eds.): *Depression in primary care: Screening and detection* (pp. 232–250). New York: Routledge.
Miranda, J., Pérez-Stable, E. J., Muñoz, R. F., Hargreaves, W. & Henke, C. J. (1991). Somatization, psychiatric disorder, and stress in utilization of ambulatory medical services. *Health Psychology 10:* 46–51.
Miranda, J. & Persons, J. B. (1988). Dysfunctional attitudes are mood-state dependent. *Journal of Abnormal Psychology 97:* 76–79.
Moore, J. T., Silimperi, D. R. & Bobula, J. A. (1978). Recognition of depression by family medicine residents: The impact of screening. *Journal of Family Practice 7:* 509–513.
Moscicki, E. K., Rae, D. S., Regier, D. A. & Locke, B. Z. (1987). The Hispanic health and nutrition examination survey: Depression among Mexican Americans, Cuban Americans, and Puerto Ricans. In M. Gaviria & J. D. Arana (eds.): *Health and behavior: Research agenda for Hispanics* (pp. 145–159). Chicago: University of Illinois.
Mumford, E., Schlesinger, H. & Glass, G. (1981). Reducing medical costs through mental health treatment. In A. Broskowski, E. Marks & S. Budman (eds.): *Linking Health and Mental Health* (pp. 257–273). Beverly Hills: Sage Publications.
Muñoz, R. F. (1977). A cognitive approach to the assessment and treatment of depression. *Dissertation Abstracts International 38:* 2873B.

Muñoz, R. F. (1983). A family history of psychological disorders questionnaire. Unpublished instrument.

Muñoz, R. F. (1984). The depression prevention course. Unpublished protocol. University of California, San Francisco.

Muñoz, R. F. (ed.). (1987). *Depression prevention: Research directions.* Washington, D.C.: Hemisphere.

Muñoz, R. F. (1990). *The prevention of depression: The state of research and practice in 1990.* Paper presented at the National Conference on Prevention Research, Bethesda, Md. Rockville, Md.: National Institute of Mental Health.

Muñoz, R. F. (in press). Prevention of depression: Training issues for research and practice. In B. L. Bloom & K. Schlesinger (eds.): *Boulder Symposium on Clinical Psychology: Depression.* Hillsdale, N.J.: Erlbaum.

Muñoz, R. F. (1976). The primary prevention of psychological problems: A review of the literature. *Community Mental Health Review 1:* 1–15.

Muñoz, R. F. (1982). The Spanish-speaking consumer and the community mental health center. In E. E. Jones & S. J. Korchin (eds.): *Minority Mental Health* (pp. 362–398). New York: Praeger.

Muñoz, R. F. (1980). A strategy for the prevention of psychological problems in Latinos: Emphasizing accessibility and effectiveness. In R. Valle & W. Vega (eds.): *Hispanic natural support systems* (pp. 85–96). Sacramento, Calif.: California Department of Mental Health.

Muñoz, R. F. (1991a). The San Francisco General Hospital Public Service and Minority Training Cluster of the University of California, San Francisco. In H. F. Myers, P. Wohlford, L. P. Guzman & R. J. Echemendia (eds.): *Ethnic minority perspectives on clinical training and services in psychology* (pp. 137–142). Washington, D.C.: American Psychological Association.

Muñoz, R. F. (1991b). *Should we begin to focus on the prevention of major depression?* Paper presented at the Annual Convention of the National Alliance for the Mentally Ill, San Francisco, July.

Muñoz, R. F., Glish, M., Soo-Hoo, T. & Robertson, J. L. (1982). The San Francisco mood survey project: Preliminary work toward the prevention of depression. *American Journal of Community Psychology 10:* 317–329.

Muñoz, R. F., González, G. M. & Pérez-Arce, P. (1991). *Curso para Mantener un Estado de Animo Saludable.* San Francisco: Universidad de California, Departamento de Psiquiatría.

Muñoz, R. F. & Kelly, J. G. (1975). *The prevention of mental disorders.* Homewood, Ill.: Richard D. Irwin.

Muñoz, R. F., Snowden, L. R. & Kelly, J. G. (eds.). (1979). *Social and psychological research in community settings.* San Francisco: Jossey-Bass.

Murphy, G. E. (1975). The physician's responsibility for suicide. I. An error of commission. II. Errors of omission. *Annals of Internal Medicine 82:* 301–309.

Murphy, G. E., Simons, A. D., Wetzel, R. D. & Lustman, P. J. (1984). Cognitive therapy and pharmacotherapy: Singly and together in the treatment of depression. *Archives of General Psychiatry 41:* 33–41.

Myers, J. K. & Weissman, M. M. (1980a). Psychiatric disorders and their treatment. *Medical Care 18:* 117–123.

Myers, J. K. & Weissman, M. M. (1980b). Use of a self-report symptom scale to detect depression in a community sample. *American Journal of Psychiatry 137:* 1081–1084.

National Science Foundation. (1988). *Profiles—psychology: Human resources and funding* (NSF 88-325). Washington, D.C.

Neiswanger, K. et al. (1990). Evidence against close linkage of unipolar affective illness to human chromosome 11p markers HRAS1 and INS and chromosome Xq marker DXS52. *Biological Psychiatry 28:* 63–72.

Nielsen, A. C. & Williams, T. A. (1980). Depression in ambulatory medical patients. *Archives of General Psychiatry 37:* 999–1004.

O'Connor, J. (1984). Patient characteristics at the San Francisco General Hospital Family Practice Clinic. Personal Communication.

Okin, R. L. (1977). Primary prevention of psychopathology from the perspective of a state mental health program director. In G. W. Albee & J. M. Joffe (eds.): *Primary prevention of psychopathology: The issues* (vol. 1, pp. 289–296). Hanover, N.H.: University Press of New England.

Oliver, J. M. & Simmons, M. E. (1984). Depression as measured by the DSM-III and the Beck Depression Inventory in an unselected adult population. *Journal of Consulting and Clinical Psychology 52:* 892–898.

Organista, K., Muñoz, R. F. & González, G. (1991). Cognitive-behavioral therapy with low-income medical patients: Utilization and outcome. In R. F. Muñoz (Chair), *Prevention and treatment of depression in Spanish-speaking populations.* Symposium conducted at the 99th Annual Convention of the American Psychological Association, San Francisco, August.

Osmond, H., Mullaly, R. & Bisbee, C. (1984). The pain of depression compared with physical pain. *Practitioner 228:* 849–853.

Pagels, H. R. (1988). *The dreams of reason: The computer and the rise of the sciences of complexity.* New York: Simon & Schuster.

Peale, N. V. (1952). *The power of positive thinking.* Englewood Cliffs, N.J.: Prentice-Hall.

Pérez-Stable, E. J. (1991). Demographic characteristics of UCSF Internal Medicine Clinic, 1988. Personal communication, June 6, 1991.

Pérez-Stable, E. J., Marín, G., Marín, B. V. & Katz, M. H. (1990). Depressive symptoms and cigarette smoking among Latinos in San Francisco. *American Journal of Public Health 80:* 1500–1502.

Pérez-Stable, E. J., Miranda, J., Muñoz, R. F. & Ying, Y. W. (1990). Depression in medical outpatients: Underrecognition and misdiagnosis. *Archives of Internal Medicine 150:* 1083–1088.

Peterson, C. & Seligman, M. E. P. (1984). Causal explanations as a risk factor for depression: Theory and evidence. *Psychological Review 91:* 347–374.

Peterson, C., Seligman, M. E. P. & Vaillant, G. E. (1988). Pessimistic explanatory style is a risk factor for physical illness: A thirty-five-year longitudinal study. *Journal of Personality and Social Psychology 55:* 23–27.

Post, R. M., Rubinow, D. R. & Ballenger, J. C. (1984). Conditioning, sensitization, and kindling: Implications for the course of affective illness. In R. M. Post & J. C. Ballenger (eds.): *Neurobiology of mood disorders* (pp. 432–466). Baltimore: Williams & Wilkins.

Price, R. H. & Smith, S. S. (1985). *A guide to evaluating prevention programs in mental health* (DHHS Publication No. ADM 85-1365). Washington, D.C.: U.S. Government Printing Office.

Puig-Antich, J. (1986). Possible prevention strategies for depression in children and adolescents. In J. T. Barter & S. W. Talbott (eds.): *Primary prevention in psychiatry* (pp. 71–84). Washington, D.C.: American Psychiatric Press, Inc.

Radloff, L. S. (1977). The CES-D scale: A self-report depression scale for research in the general population. *Applied Psychological Measurement 1:* 385–401.

Raphael, B. (1977). Preventive intervention with the recently bereaved. *Archives of General Psychiatry 34:* 1450–1454.

Rappaport, J. (1977). *Community psychology: Values, research, and action.* New York: Holt, Rinehart & Winston.

Rappaport, J. (1981). In praise of paradox: A social policy of empowerment over prevention. *American Journal of Community Psychology 9:* 1–25.

Rappaport, J., Seidman, E. & Davidson II, W. S. (1979). Demonstration research and manifest versus true adoption: The natural history of a research project to divert adolescents from the legal system. In R. F. Muñoz, L. R. Snowden & J. G. Kelly (eds.): *Social and psychological research in community settings* (pp. 101–144). San Francisco: Jossey-Bass.

Regier, D. A., Boyd, J. H., Burke, J. D., Rae, D. S., Myers, J. K., Kramer, M., Robins, L. N., George, L. K., Karno, M. & Locke, B. Z. (1988). One-month prevalence of mental disorders in the United States. *Archives of General Psychiatry 45:* 977–986.

Rehm, L. P. (1977). A self-control model of depression. *Behavior Therapy 8:* 787–804.

Rehm, L. P. (1987). Approaches to the prevention of depression with children: A self-management perspective. In R. F. Muñoz (ed.): *Depression prevention: Research directions* (pp. 79–91). Washington, D.C.: Hemisphere.

Rehm, L. P. (in press). Psychotherapies for depression. In B. L. Bloom & K. Schlesinger (eds.): *Boulder Symposium on Clinical Psychology: Depression.* Hillsdale, N.J.: Erlbaum.

Rehm, L. P., Kaslow, N. J. & Rabin, A. S. (1987). Cognitive and behavioral targets in a self-control therapy program for depression. *Journal of Consulting and Clinical Psychology 55:* 60–67.

Reus, V. I. (1987). Behavioral implications of hypothalamic-pituitary-adrenal dysfunction. In U. Halbreich (ed.): *Hormones and depression* (pp. 385–401). New York: Raven Press.

Riessman, F. (1986). Support groups as preventive intervention. In M. Kessler & S. E. Goldston (eds.): *A decade of progress in primary prevention* (pp. 275–288). Hanover, N.H.: University Press of New England.

Roberts, L. (1990). CF screening delayed for a while, perhaps forever. *Science 247:* 1296–1297.

Roberts, L. (1991). A call to action on a human brain project. *Science 252:* 1794.

Roberts, R. (1987). Epidemiological issues in measuring preventive effects. In R. F. Muñoz (ed.): *Depression prevention: Research directions.* Washington, D.C.: Hemisphere.

Roberts, R. E. (1980). Reliability of the CES-D in different ethnic contexts. *Psychological Research 2:* 125–134.

Roberts, R. E. (1981). Prevalence of depressive symptoms among Mexican Americans. *Journal of Nervous and Mental Disease 169:* 213–219.

Roberts, R. E. & Vernon, S. W. (1983). The Center for Epidemiological Studies—Depression Scale: Its use in a community sample. *American Journal of Psychiatry 140:* 41–46.

Roberts, R. E. & Vernon, S. W. (1981). Usefulness of the PERI Demoralization Scale to screen for psychiatric disorder in a community sample. *Psychiatric Research 5:* 183–193.

Roberts, R. E., Vernon, S. W. & Rhoades, H. M. (1989). Effects of language and ethnic status on reliability and validity of the Center of Epidemiological Studies—Depression Scale with psychiatric patients. *Journal of Nervous and Mental Disease, 177:* 581–592.

Robins, L. N., Helzer, J. E., Croughan, J. & Ratcliff, K. S. (1981). National Institute of Mental Health Diagnostic Interview Schedule: Its history, characteristics and validity. *Archives of General Psychiatry 38:* 381–389.

Robins, L. N., Helzer, J. E., Weissman, M. M., Orvaschel, H., Gruenberg, E., Burke, J. D. & Regier, D. A. (1984). Lifetime prevalence of specific psychiatric disorders in three sites. *Archives of General Psychiatry 41:* 949–958.

Robins, L. N. & Regier, D. A. (eds.). (1991). *Psychiatric disorders in America: The Epidemiological Catchment Area Study.* New York: Free Press.

Rosenthal, M. P., Goldfarb, N. I., Carlson, B. L., Sagi, P. C. & Balaban, D. J. (1987). Assessment of depression in a family practice center. *Journal of Family Practice 25:* 143–149.

Rucker, L., Frye, E. B. & Cygan, R. W. (1986). Feasibility and usefulness of depression screening in medical outpatients. *Archives of Internal Medicine 146:* 729–731.

Rush, A. J., Beck, A. T., Kovacs, M. & Hollon, S. (1977). Comparative efficacy of cognitive therapy and pharmacotherapy in the treatment of depressed outpatients. *Cognitive Therapy and Research 1:* 17–37.

Russell, L. B. (1986). *Is prevention better than cure?* Washington, D.C.: Brookings Institution.

Rutter, M. (1989). Psychiatric disorder in parents as a risk factor for children. In Shaffer, D., Philips, I. & Enzer, N. B. (eds.): *Prevention of mental disorders, alcohol and other drug use in children and adolescents* (DHHS Publication No. ADM 89-1646). Washington, D.C.: U.S. Government Printing Office.

Sachar, E. J. (1982). Endocrine abnormalities in depression. In E. S. Paykel (ed.): *Handbook of affective disorders* (pp. 191–201). New York: Guilford.

Sarason, I., Johnson, J. & Siegel, J. (1978). Assessing the impact of life change: Development of the life experiences survey. *Journal of Consulting and Clinical Psychology 46:* 932–946.

Sayetta, R. B. & Johnson, D. P. (1980). *Basic data on depressive symptomatology: United States, 1974–1975. Vital and Health Statistics.* Series 11, Number 216. (DHEW Publication No. PHS 80-1666). Hyattsville, Md.: National Center for Health Statistics.

Scarr, S. & McCartney, K. (1983). How people make their own environments: A theory of genotype-environment effects. *Child Development 54:* 424–435.

Schleifer, S. J., Macari-Hinson, M. M., Coyle, D. A., Slater, W. R., Kahn, M., Gorlin, R. & Zucker, H. D. (1989). The nature and course of depression following myocardial infarction. *Archives of Internal Medicine 149:* 1785–1789.

Schulberg, H. C., McClelland, M. & Gooding, W. (1987). Six-month outcomes for medical patients with major depressive disorders. *Journal of General Internal Medicine 2:* 312–317.

Schulberg, H. C., Saul, M., McClelland, M., Ganguli, M., Christy, W. & Frank, R. (1985). Assessing depression in primary medical and psychiatric practices. *Archives of General Psychiatry 42:* 1164–1170.

Scogin, F., Jamison, C. & Davis, N. (1990). Two-year follow-up of bibliotherapy for depression in older adults. *Journal of Consulting and Clinical Psychology 58:* 665–667.

Scogin, F., Jamison, C. & Gochneaur, K. (1989). Comparative efficacy of cognitive and behavioral bibliotherapy for mildly and moderately depressed older adults. *Journal of Consulting and Clinical Psychology 57:* 403–407.

Seligman, M. E. P., Peterson, C., Kaslow, N. J., Tanenbaum, R. L., Alloy, L. B. & Abramson, L. Y. (1984). Attributional style and depressive symptoms among children. *Journal of Abnormal Psychology 93:* 235–238.

Selmi, P. M., Klein, M. H., Greist, J. H., Sorrell, S. P. & Erdman, H. P. (1990). Computer-administered cognitive-behavioral therapy for depression. *American Journal of Psychiatry 147:* 51–56.

Shaffer, D., Philips, I. & Enzer, N. B. (1989). *OSAP prevention monograph-2: Prevention of mental disorders, alcohol and other drug use in children and adolescents* (DHHS Publication No. ADM 89-1646). Washington, D.C.: U.S. Government Printing Office.

Shapiro, S., Skinner, E. A., Kessler, L. G., Von Korff, M., German, P. S., Tischler, G. L., Leaf, P. J., Benham, L., Cottler, L. & Regier, D. A. (1984). Utilization of health and mental health services: Three epidemiological catchment area sites. *Archives of General Psychiatry 41:* 971–978.

Silverman, P. R. & Murrow, H. G. (1976). Mutual help during critical role transitions. *Journal of Applied Behavioral Sciences 12:* 410–418.

Simons, A. D., Levine, J. L., Lustman, P. J. & Murphy, E. E. (1984). Patient attrition in a comparative outcome study of depression: A follow-up report. *Journal of Affective Disorders 6:* 163–173.

Simons, A. D., Murphy, G. E., Levine, J. L. & Wetzel, R. D. (1986). Cognitive therapy and pharmacotherapy for depression: Sustained improvement over one year. *Archives of General Psychiatry 43:* 43–48.

Starkweather, J. A. & Muñoz, R. F. (1989). *Identification of clinical depression among foreign speakers.* Paper presented at the meeting of the American Association for Medical Systems and Informatics, San Francisco, Calif., May.

Steinmetz, J. L., Lewinsohn, P. M. & Antonuccio, D. O. (1983). Prediction of individual outcome in a group intervention for depression. *Journal of Consulting and Clinical Psychology 51:* 331–337.

Steinmetz-Breckenridge, J., Zeiss, A. M. & Thompson, L. W. (1987). The Life

Satisfaction Course: An intervention for the elderly. In R. F. Muñoz (ed.): *Depression prevention: Research directions* (pp. 185–196). Washington, D.C.: Hemisphere.

Stoeckle, J. D., Zola, J. K. & Davidson, G. E. (1964). The quantity and significance of psychological distress in medical patients. *Journal of Chronic Disease 17:* 959–970.

Stoudemire, A., Frank, R., Kamlet, M. & Hedemark, N. (1987). Depression. In R. W. Amler & H. B. Dull (eds.): *Closing the gap: The burden of unnecessary illness* (pp. 65–71). New York: Oxford.

Tableman, B. (1987). Stress management training: An approach to the prevention of depression in low-income populations. In R. F. Muñoz (ed.): *Depression prevention: Research directions* (pp. 171–184). Washington, D.C.: Hemisphere.

Teuting, P., Koslow, S. H. & Hirschfeld, R. M. A. (1981). *Special report on depression research* (DHHS Publication No. ADM 81-1085). Washington, D.C.: U.S. Government Printing Office.

Thompson II, T. L., Stoudemire, A., Mitchell, W. D. & Grant, R. L. (1983). Underrecognition of patient's psychosocial distress in a university hospital medical clinic. *American Journal of Psychiatry 140:* 158–161.

Thoresen, C. E. & Mahoney, M. J. (1974). *Behavioral self-control.* New York: Holt, Rinehart & Winston.

Time. (1990). Asia: Discarding daughters (Fall, p. 40).

Tønnesen, P., Nørregaard, J., Simonsen, K. & Säwe, U. (1991). A double-blind trial of a 16-hour transdermal nicotine patch in smoking cessation. *New England Journal of Medicine 325:* 311–315.

U.S. Bureau of the Census. (1991). *The Hispanic population in the United States: March 1991* (Current Population Reports, Series P-20, No. 455). Washington, D.C.: U.S. Government Printing Office.

U.S. Bureau of the Census. (1991). *Statistical abstracts of the United States* (111th ed.). Washington, D.C.: U.S. Government Printing Office.

U.S. Preventive Services Task Force. (1989). *Guide to clinical preventive services: An assessment of the effectiveness of 169 interventions* (chap. 44). Baltimore: Williams & Wilkins.

Vachon, M. L. S., Lyall, W. A. L., Rogers, J., Freedman-Letofsky, K. & Freeman, S. J. J. (1980). A controlled study of self-help intervention for widows. *American Journal of Psychiatry 137:* 1380–1384.

Valle, R. (1990). Panel on Prevention [Update on Hispanic social network prevention intervention study]. Paper presented at the NIMH Workshop on Mental Disorders in the Hispanic Population. Washington, D.C., April.

Van der Gaag, J. & Van de Ven, W. (1978). The demand for primary health care. *Medical Care 16:* 299.

Vega, W. A. (1980). Defining Hispanic high risk groups: Targeting populations for health promotion. In R. Valle & W. Vega (eds.): *Hispanic natural support systems: Mental health promotion perspectives.* Sacramento, Calif.: State of California Department of Mental Health.

Vega, W. A., Valle, R., Kolody, B. & Hough, R. (1987). The Hispanic social network prevention intervention study: A community-based randomized trial. In R. F. Muñoz (ed.): *Depression prevention: Research directions* (pp. 217–231). Washington, D.C.: Hemisphere.

Vinokur, A. D., Price, R. H. & Caplan, R. D. (1991). From field experiments to program implementation: Assessing the potential outcomes of an experimental intervention program for unemployed persons. *American Journal of Community Psychology 19:* 543–562.

Von Korff, M., Shapiro, S., Burke, J. D., Teitlebaum, M., Skinner, E. A., German, P., Turner, R. W., Klein, L. & Burns, B. (1987). Anxiety and depression in a primary care clinic: Comparison of diagnostic interview schedule, general health questionnaire, and practitioner assessments. *Archives of General Psychiatry 44:* 152–156.

Watson, D. & Friend, R. (1969). Measurement of social-evaluative anxiety. *Journal of Consulting and Clinical Psychology 33:* 448–457.

Watson, J. D., Tooze, J. & Kurtz, D. T. (1983). *Recombinant DNA: A short course.* New York: W. H. Freeman.

Weissman, M. M. (1987). Advances in psychiatric epidemiology: Rates and risks for major depression. *American Journal of Public Health 77:* 445–451.

Weissman, M. M., Jarrett, R. B. & Rush, J. A. (1987). Psychotherapy and its relevance to the pharmacotherapy of major depression: A decade later (1976–1985). In H. Y. Meltzer (ed.): *Psychopharmacology: The third generation of progress* (pp. 1059–1069). New York: Raven Press.

Weissman, M., Myers, J. & Thompson, W. (1981). Depression and its treatment in a United States urban community, 1975–1976. *Archives of General Psychiatry 38:* 417–421.

Wells, K. B., Hays, R. D., Burnam, A. M., Rogers, W., Greenfield, S. & Ware, J. E., Jr. (1989). Detection of depressive disorder for patients receiving prepaid or fee-for-service care: Results from the medical outcomes study. *Journal of the American Medical Association 262:* 3298–3302.

Wells, K. B., Stewart, A., Hays, R. D., Burnam, M. A., Rogers, W., Daniels, M., Berry, S., Greenfield, S. & Ware, J. (1989). The functioning and well-being of depressed patients: Results from the Medical Outcomes Study. *Journal of the American Medical Association 262:* 914–919.

Wender, P. H. & Klein, D. F. (1981). *Mind, mood, and medicine.* New York: Farrar, Straus, Giroux.

Whitaker, A., Johnson, J., Shaffer, D., Rapoport, J. L., Kalikow, K., Walsh, B. T., Davies, M., Braiman, S. & Dolinsky, A. (1990). Uncommon troubles in young people: Prevalence estimates of selected psychiatric disorders in a nonreferred adolescent population. *Archives of General Psychiatry 47:* 487–496.

Whybrow, P. C., Akiskal, H. S. & McKinney, W. T. (1984). *Mood disorders: Toward a new psychobiology.* New York: Plenum Press.

Williams, J. B. W. & Spitzer, R. L. (eds.). (1984). *Psychotherapy research: Where are we and where should we go?* New York: Guilford.

Wise, S. P. (1989). Cortical consolidation [Review of *Neurobiology of neocortex*]. *Science 243:* 1617.

Ying, Y. (1988). Depressive symptomatology among Chinese-Americans as measured by the CES-D. *Journal of Clinical Psychology 44:* 739–746.

Youngren, M. A. (1978). The functional relationship of depression and problematic interpersonal behavior. Doctoral dissertation. University of Oregon.

Youngren, M. A., Zeiss, A. M. & Lewinsohn, P. M. (1975). The interpersonal events schedule. Mimeograph, University of Oregon.

Zeiss, A. M., Lewinsohn, P. M. & Muñoz, R. F. (1979). Non-specific improvement effects in depression using interpersonal skills training, pleasant activities schedules, or cognitive training. *Journal of Consulting and Clinical Psychology 47:* 427–439.

Zonderman, A. B., Costa, P. T. & McCrae, R. R. (1989). Depression as a risk for cancer morbidity and mortality in a nationally representative sample. *Journal of the American Medical Association 262:* 1191–1195.

Zung, W. W. K., Magill, M., Moore, J. T. & George, D. T. (1983). Recognition and treatment of depression in a family medicine practice. *Journal of Clinical Psychiatry 44:* 3–6.

Zuravin, S. J. (1989). Severity of maternal depression and three types of mother-to-child aggression. *American Journal of Orthopsychiatry 59:* 377–389.

Index

Index

Index

Index